The Seven Eyes

of Grace

EMPOWERED TO LIVE

By
Ted J. Hanson

House of Bread Publishing
Bellingham, Washington

The Seven Eyes of Grace

EMPOWERED TO LIVE

© 2006 Ted J. Hanson

Non-Published Printing 2007
Revised Published Printing 2013
Revised 2nd Printing 2022

House of Bread Publishing
3210 Meridian St., Bellingham, WA. 98225

Library of Congress Catalog Number 2013943797
ISBN 978-0-9968053-7-7

Cover By Ted J. Hanson
House of Bread Publishing
3210 Meridian St.
Bellingham, WA 98225

Printed in the United States of America

About the Author

Ted J. Hanson has been a born-again believer in Christ since May 12, 1973. He has served as a worship leader, youth leader, administrator, associate pastor, senior pastor, and is presently an apostolic minister to the Body of Christ throughout the world. He and his wife, Bonnie, reside in Bellingham, Washington.

Ted is an apostolic leader with a prophetic mantle. He is a dynamic preacher/teacher who has a heart to share, uncompromisingly, the Word of God and the Lordship of Jesus Christ. He holds a Bachelor's of Theology and a Master's of Biblical Studies through Christian International Ministries Network and is ordained through Abundant Life Ministry and House of Bread Ministry.

God has given Ted a vision for the liberty of the Spirit of God within the Church. Like Joshua, his vision is to see the Church come into the abundance of the inheritance of God. His heart is to equip God's people for the work of Christ life ministry and see all come into the reality of the abundant life that Jesus came to give. He presently serves as an equipping and resource ministry to the body of Christ globally. He has developed and led School of Eagles Ministry Academy for training, equipping, and activating ministry in God's people. This is now known as Christ Life Training, an in class and online training school (*www.christlifetraining.org*).

Ted travels to various places throughout the U.S. as well as other countries. He not only ministers the Word of God and operates in the prophetic, he also activates others in prophetic ministry. He has served to plant and establish many ministries. He is a resource to a network of ministries through House of Bread Ministry (*www.houseofbreadministry.org* and *www.houseofbreadnetwork.com*) He provides apostolic training, direction, and counsel to many churches and ministries at home and abroad in this network of ministries.

Ted has written several books, including *Spiritual Man, The New Testament Prophet, Properly Judging Prophetic Ministry, Prophetic Ministry – A Ministry of Life, The Redeemed Earth – Healing the Curse of the Fall, The Seven Eyes of Grace, Generational Leadership, Understanding Authority, For His Glory – You Have Been Left Behind, Christ Unveiled – A Revelation of Jesus Christ, The NOW Covenant – Christ In You the Hope of Glory, Worship and Praise - A Revelation of Love,* and *Grafted Into Love – Parenting, Family and the Destiny of Life.* He also writes weekly blogs at *www.ted4you.com* and *www.ted4leaders.com*.

Contents

Preface:

God has placed it within the heart of every man or woman to know there is a God. No person is with excuse to a basic awareness of God. God placed that inner knowing in the heart of mankind in His original creation of Adam. However, an inner knowing that there is a God is not enough to cause men to know who He truly is. Information about God alone is not enough to cause us to experience the fullness of who God is. God wants each of us to know who He is. He wants each of us to know who He is as a being. To make my point more clearly, God wants each of us to know Him as a "person". The most important thing to Him is "relationship". For this reason God has given to us the power of His amazing grace!

The objective of the material in this book is to give the reader an experience with God in the increasing fullness of His grace! I am not merely interested in presenting information whereby the reader can simply understand truth. My objective is to present this truth in a way that the reader can practically apply and experience the grace described within the pages of this book. My desire is that the material presented in this book will activate the reader to a fuller experience of relationship with God in his or her life.

After the fall of man in the Garden of Eden, mankind was left with a government based upon being informed of good and evil. Another way of saying good and evil is "right and wrong". The fall of Adam cost him the intimate trust relationship that God desired for him to have. He not only lost that intimacy for himself, he lost it for all of his generations. As it went with Adam, so it goes with all of his descendants. Adam's life, and each descendent who would follow, was bound to a governing administration of the knowledge of good and evil. God had placed it within the heart of Adam, and all of his descendants, to know that there is a God. When we read the Scriptures we find that very quickly man's consciences became seared to the knowledge of God and wickedness ruled on the earth. Only the family of Noah was found

1

righteous in his generations. His awareness of God caused God to preserve him and his family from the flood of destruction sent to the earth by God to wash the earth of the wickedness of men. Under an administration of conscience, eight souls were preserved in an ark.

Man continued to live under the administration of conscience after the flood. It wasn't long before mankind attempted to ascend to heaven in their earthly efforts to become like God. God confused their languages and scattered them across the face of the earth to assure that man would continue on a path toward discovering the intimate relationship He desired with mankind. From among the scattered nations of the world, God chose one man, Abram, who became a father of the seed of God's inheritance and the patriarch of a holy nation set apart to God, Israel. That nation was given the Law to give them perfect "information" of all that is good under an administration of the knowledge of good and evil. That information of good was nothing less than perfect information as to who God is as a being. That information served as a tutor to cause the nation of Israel to be perfectly aware of who God is. Under the administration of Law, one nation knew perfectly well there was a God and He was greater than all!

Jesus Christ came to put the information of the Law into use. He didn't come to inform the world by merely the inner knowing that there is a God. He didn't come to clarify the greatness of God to men by the information of God's character, nature, way, power, and authority (Law). He came to empower mankind to be able to enter into an intimate relationship with Him in Spirit and Truth. He came to reconcile the people of the world to a personal relationship with God in the Body of Christ, the dwelling place of God in His presence. This is made possible by the gift of the Holy Spirit in and upon the Body of Christ. He has come to confirm and transform the house of God's presence in the earth. He has come to submerge the nations of the world into the power of God's amazing grace. His grace is His transformation power to cause the world to be saved in Christ.

The Holy Spirit is a sevenfold Spirit. He is God among us and He has come to cause the evidence of what Jesus has done as the Last Adam to overtake the evidence of what first Adam did in his fall. Holy Spirit has come to put the life of God to use in the lives of redeemed humanity. The material presented in this book is meant to activate the reader to seek the fullness of the transforming sevenfold Spirit of grace and to experience God's plan for the maturation of the Body of Christ. May all who read this book be inspired to find the fullness of God's amazing grace at work in their lives.

Suggested
Study
Structure:

The purpose of the material presented in this book is to inspire the reader to experience the fullness of God's sevenfold grace of life. Since the truths of this book pertain to the sevenfold Spirit of God and the Body of Christ, it is suggested that this book be read with group participation. The chapters of this book are presented in such a way that they can be used for daily contemplation and weekly group discussion. Sometimes when we discuss our discoveries with others, we inspire one another to a fuller understanding of truth. An individual can read this book, but it is especially structured for group participation.

There are seven graces presented in this book. Each of these graces is presented in a five-day or a six-day reading structure. The reader should read one section of each of the seven subject chapters each day. Don't just read the material to understand what is written. Take the time to allow the Holy Spirit to speak to you in regard to the material given for each day of your study. I suggest you read the chapter at the beginning of your day and then allow the Holy Spirit to minister to you throughout the day through your meditation and contemplation of the material presented.

If you can be a part of a group doing this study, it will be very beneficial. To get your group off to a good start, have an informal fellowship night to introduce the material and explain how the group and its members will do the study. Meet two weeks before your first group discussion night. At your introduction meeting, be sure to have books available for each of the group participants. Assign them to read the book through the Introduction during the

3

first week and then to read the Chapter 1 sections the second week. The group study and discussion can be accomplished by simply doing the following:

Pick a time each week to come together as a group and discuss your discoveries while studying the material as individuals. I have given a suggested outline for discussion at the end of each completed chapter. A completed chapter is all of the chapter sections given for each week. An example might be to have each individual of the group begin by reading Chapter 1.1 on Tuesday. Each reader meditates on and contemplates the material presented in Chapter 1.1 all day Tuesday. On Wednesday, each participant reads Chapter 1.2 and allows the Holy Spirit to minister to them in regard to the material presented. On Thursday each member reads Chapter 1.3, on Friday Chapter 1.4, and on Saturday they each read Chapter 1.5. Since Chapter 1 inclueds a 1.6 section, each member of the group would read Chapter 1.6 on Sunday. The following Monday, the group comes together and discusses what the Holy Spirit has done in their lives during their personal study. The group can discuss some or all of the suggested thoughts for discussion given in the book following Chapter 1.6.

May God bless you richly in your study and your time of experiencing His amazing grace in your life!

Introduction

In this book, I am going to present a basic truth that is both simple and complex. It involves the amazing grace of God. Many people confuse mercy and grace. Mercy is given to us based upon God's ability to give what He has to give. He is rich in mercy and His mercy is new every morning (Eph. 2:4; Lam. 3:22, 23). Grace is a substance given to us by God. Grace is based upon God's own ability to empower us to become all that He is in His character, nature, way, power, and authority. It has to do with God's ability to complete the work that He has begun in us (Phil. 1:6). It was an act of God's mercy that enabled us to be justified to live. It is the grace of God that empowers us to live. It is the power of God's grace that gives us His amazing salvation! Salvation is not just a ticket to heaven. Salvation is the empowerment of God's life-giving transformation in our lives. It includes the fullness of our resurrection from the dead and eternal life in Christ!

Rom. 5:6 For when we were still without strength, in due time Christ died for the ungodly. 7 For scarcely for a righteous man will one die; yet perhaps for a good man someone would even dare to die. 8 But God demonstrates His own love toward us, in that while we were still sinners, Christ died for us 9 Much more then, having now been justified by His blood, we shall be saved from wrath through Him. 10 For if when we were enemies we were reconciled to God through the death of His Son, much more, having been reconciled, we shall be saved by His life.

Rom. 5:17 For if by the one man's offense death reigned through the one, much more those who receive abundance of grace and of the gift of righteousness will reign in life through the One, Jesus Christ.

Rom. 5:21 so that as sin reigned in death, even so grace might reign through righteousness to eternal life through Jesus Christ our Lord.

The Seven Eyes of Grace

Many have defined God's grace as being, "the unmerited favor of God" in our lives. This is true, but I don't think we really understand the word "favor". We often see favor as merely the approval, friendship, or supportive attitude of another. Favor includes that, but it is much more! It is a substance. If a rich man shows us favor, it is going to be good news for us! God is the richest individual we will ever know. If He shows us favor, it is good news on our behalf! God's mercy kept us from having to suffer the consequence of sin. God's grace empowers us to experience the full inheritance of God's house! It includes receiving His character, nature, way, power, and authority in our lives!

Mercy and grace are often spoken of in synonymous ways. In the Dutch culture the word for mercy and grace is the same word. This can create a problem in the thinking of a society. We have the same problem in English for the word love. We have one word for what can be known in many different understandings. This can cause a dilemma in understanding what true love is. We are all challenged by this thing we call communication. So, let me clarify what I believe God views as mercy and grace.

The most common word for grace in the New Testament is the Greek word χάρις (charis, khar´-ece). This word implies the power of God's divine influence upon our lives. The most common word for mercy is the Greek word ἔλεος (eleos, el´-eh-os). It implies an action of compassion and love for the sake of another. These two words are inherently connected to one another, but they are two distinctly different words.

I believe grace is God's divine influence upon our lives. It is His ability to transform our lives by the power of His love. It is the grace of God that causes us to become the weight of the Father's influence and the substance of His person (Heb. 1:3). Mercy is an act of compassion on God's part that gives us a pardon from our failure and an invitation to the power of God's grace. Mercy invites us into God's house and grace is the testimony of God in our house.

If our view of grace is the same as our view of mercy, we will come short in God's power to change our lives. God's mercy says we can be changed, but God's grace actually changes us. Let's look at a couple of verses in Scripture and clarify this subject a bit more.

Hebrews 4:15 For we do not have a High Priest who cannot sympathize with our weaknesses, but was in all points tempted as we are, yet without sin. 16 Let us therefore come boldly to the throne of grace,

6

that we may obtain mercy and find grace to help in time of need.

In this Scripture we see that God is well aware of our weaknesses. He can empathize with us in our weaknesses since Jesus became a man of flesh and experienced the same temptations that we do. He came in our lives so we could find our lives in Him. Think of mercy as the end of a very bad day so we can finally find a really good never-ending day in Christ. Mercy was a testimony to the setting of the sun on our never-ending, never-arriving, never-accomplishing days of yesterday. Grace is the empowerment of the rising of the sun to a new forever reigning, always arriving, always fulfilling purpose in a very good day in Christ. We can boldly come before the throne of God's influence that forever and increasingly enables us to live and find an end to what is not life and an empowerment to what is life in our every time of need.

Let me present an example that I believe will help us understand the power of God's grace. God created us that He might love us. The testimony of God's love for each of us is found in the celebration of life in Him. We were born to live and not die! Our problem was that we were looking for love in all the wrong places. We were searching for life in the bars and the taverns of the world. We visited the establishments of life-less pleasures to drink the drink of stupidity. In America we have a law concerning drinking. We are not allowed to drink and drive. If our blood alcohol level proves that we are under the influence of intoxicating drink, we will receive a ticket for driving under the influence (known as a D.U.I.). The drink of earthly bars and taverns can impair our judgment and make us stupid and dangerous unto death. We can cause harm to others. We can be financially penalized, lose our privileges, or even be imprisoned for such actions. People in those earthly taverns are not looking for death. They are looking to fulfill a real need placed within the heart of every man. They are looking for life!

Jesus didn't come to condemn the bars and taverns of this world. He came to restore heaven's bar in every place of man's attempt to find the true meaning and celebration of life. Heaven's bar is a place where real life is found in Christ. It is found in every place where man is reconnected to God in Christ. The problem for man was that they didn't have access to heaven's bar. They had to make feeble attempts in finding life in the bars and taverns of this world. Jesus came to give us back the key to heaven's bar. Jesus walked through the taverns and bars of earthly sin that He might empathize with us in every way. He came to end the futile efforts of man's attempt to find life in the wrong places and to give us back the true place of life and the drink of life only found

7

in Christ in the place of heaven's grace. He didn't come to condemn the bars of men nor the drinks of earthly places. He came to bring the life of heaven's bar in the formerly dead places of this world.

So let me define mercy and grace. It was the mercy of God that gave you and I the privilege of exiting the lifeless places of sin and finding ourselves entering the door of heaven's bar. Mercy says we can come in the door. But in the bar, they are serving drinks. Those drinks are not like the drinks that lead to stupidity and actions that cause harm to self and men. Those drinks lead to sharpness of mind, the testimony of life, and an empowerment to bring life to this world. Those drinks are more powerful than the drinks of the earthly taverns and bars of men. Those drinks can lead to LIVING UNDER THE INFLUENCE (known as an L.U.I.). Human beings were meant to live their lives under the influence of God's grace. Grace is the substance of the drink you drink in heaven's bar! So, mercy got us out of the bars of the past and in through the door of heaven's bar. It was mercy that granted us the right to boldly come to the throne of grace.

God is serving drinks on the throne of grace! Drink those drinks and you can be marked with an 'L.U.I.'. LIVING UNDER THE INFLUENCE (L.U.I.) will change your life forever! God has given mercy to all men in that He has reconciled all men to God in the true bar of life. We must first recognize that He has done it all in the power of His mercy that we might all come to this bar of grace. We must then boldly enter and drink the drink of grace. Without drinking the potent life of God's amazing grace, we will never understand the full reason for the restored place. It is not enough to know the pardon of our past. It is not enough to know the invitation to our present. We must drink the drinks of grace that we might become empowered to live life to the fullest measure from the place of heaven's grace. It would be stupid to enter the bar of life, but never drink the drink that gives us life.

We must boldly come to the throne of God's divine influence upon our lives, that we may obtain compassion and find God's divine empowerment to help us in our time of need.

God's grace is His power to change our lives! Grace is a tangible substance, and it empowers us to live in the reality of God's kingdom of life. The old administration of the earth was a government of the knowledge of good and evil, or right and wrong. That administration was the consequence of Adam's decision of choosing the tree of the knowledge of good and evil

8

above a relationship of trust in and love for God and obedience to His words of life. This resulted in man losing access to the Tree of Life (Gen. 3:22-24). The new administration is a government of the Tree of Life and the reality of the love of God's Son (Col. 1:13). When Jesus came to the earth, He came as a man. He came to fulfill the requirements of the old administration and to introduce the empowerment of a new administration. The wage of the old administration was death (Rom. 6:23). Eating of the tree of the knowledge of good and evil carried with it the consequence of death for mankind (Gen. 2:17). Jesus came to show us mercy and to give us grace. He showed us mercy by completing once for all the old administration's consequence of death (Rom. 6:10; Heb. 7:27; Heb. 10:10). He showed us grace by giving us eternal life (Jn. 3:16, 17). Mercy was the conclusion of the law and the introduction to grace. Grace is the introduction to life. It is the increasing influence of God upon our lives to know God the Father and Jesus the Son whom He has sent. In knowing them, we are continually changed to become like them in our nature, character, way, power and authority.

History of the Revelation:

Many years ago I began a journey of learning to understand the message and power of God's grace for His Church. In the 1970's and 80's, I was involved in the construction trade. By 1981, I had become a general contractor. I was a worship leader in the church during that time, but most of my hours were occupied with building projects and the construction trade. I always felt a call from God upon my life, but I felt that calling was about kingdom business and supplying financial resources to the church. Something in me desired to know revelation truth from God, but most of the time God spoke to me about building things and supervising construction crews. God spoke to me often in practical ways. He would tell me how to accomplish a construction project. He would give me instruction pertaining to leading people in my overseeing responsibilities of accomplishing work projects. One day I had a very unique experience with God. On that particular day, I sat down to eat my lunch while overseeing a construction project. In a somewhat frustrated state, I asked God why He spoke to me about practical things but never gave me any spiritual revelation. He told me to take out my Bible and look up the beatitudes. As I was reading the account in Matthew, He directed my attention to the phrase, "Blessed are the poor in spirit". Upon reading that phrase, the Holy Spirit instructed me to look up that same phrase in the book of Luke. In Luke's account, I discovered that it read,

"Blessed are the poor". God then questioned me, "Which is it? Is the news of the kingdom a blessing for the poor in spirit or for the poor?" God then told me to look up the story of the Centurion in the book of Matthew and compare it to the account in Luke. Upon reading Matthew's account, I was directed to notice that the Scripture revealed that the Centurion came to Jesus on behalf of his servant. In Luke's account, I found that the Centurion never came to Jesus. He sent the elders and servants on his behalf for the request of his servant's healing. God confronted me, "Who is telling the truth? Did the Centurion come to Jesus? Why is Luke's account different than Matthew's?" As I contemplated these questions, I heard God speak to me clearly. A summary of His conversation with me went something like this:

"It's not an accident that Matthew was a tax collector. He was a man who understood government. He would never say 'blessed are the poor' if the root of poverty was the spirit. If Matthew came to collect your taxes he would never say he had come to collect your taxes. He would come in the name of the government. Matthew would not see it necessary to mention the elders and servants in the story of the Centurion. He would see their coming as the coming of the Centurion. Matthew didn't become a tax collector so that he would think like a government man. He was fashioned and formed by Me to be a governmental thinker; therefore, he became a tax collector by trade. His gospel is filled with terms of the 'kingdom of God'. He was a government man. It was not an accident that Luke was a physician. He was a people man. He didn't become a physician so that he would care about people. He cared about people; thus, he became a physician. He would never say the poor in spirit are blessed if in fact poor people are also blessed. He would never say the Centurion came to Jesus, if in fact there were other people involved as well. He would make a point of all involved. Whereas Matthew would say a person was healed, Luke will give you the name of the person who was healed."

Then God spoke the nugget of revelation that I needed. He said, "It's not an accident that you are a builder. I made you a builder, now build." I understood immediately that the season I was in would prove to be foundational to the seasons of my future.

It is in light of that revelation that I believe God has spoken to me so clearly in regard to His sevenfold grace. I believe God's grace is the key to the building of His Church in the earth! It is the power of His kingdom coming and His will being done in the earth as it is in heaven. I have spent more than thirty-five years laboring in the building of God's Church as a fivefold minister of God's grace.

I believe a revelation of the sevenfold grace of God is both the power and the key to the building of His Church in the earth!

Now let me give a brief introduction to God's grace as a sevenfold reality of the power of His light. In 1988, God began to speak to me about the rainbow. The Scripture says that all that can be known of the Godhead is concealed in nature (Rom. 1:20). God is Light. The world we live in is made visible by white light. White light is made up of seven color spectrums of light frequency. Those seven spectrums are refracted in the rainbow. This rainbow was set in the earth as a testimony of the covenant promise of God to Noah after God had washed the earth with the great flood.

Gen. 9:13 "I set My rainbow in the cloud, and it shall be for the sign of the covenant between Me and the earth. 14 It shall be, when I bring a cloud over the earth, that the rainbow shall be seen in the cloud; 15 and I will remember My covenant which is between Me and you and every living creature of all flesh; the waters shall never again become a flood to destroy all flesh. 16 The rainbow shall be in the cloud, and I will look on it to remember the everlasting covenant between God and every living creature of all flesh that is on the earth." 17 And God said to Noah, "This is the sign of the covenant which I have established between Me and all flesh that is on the earth."

The rainbow was a sign of God's covenant to never again destroy all the flesh of the earth by a flood. God plans to transform the earth by the power of His light. The flood was the result of man's darkness. The rainbow was a sign to man of God's coming light to men (Jn. 1:4). He wants to cover the earth with the knowledge of His glory as the waters presently cover the sea (Isa. 11:9; Hab. 2:14). The waters that cover the sea are the result of the great flood sent by God to destroy all flesh in the earth, except the eight souls of Noah's house. The waters of the sea are the result of Man's choice of a government of the knowledge of good and evil. The rainbow was a sign of the coming administration of grace that would not again destroy flesh but would instead transform it to the express image of the Father and the likeness of His glory (Heb. 1:3). The glory of God is man fully alive! Man being made alive was made possible by the one true eternal living one, Jesus Christ. He was the firstborn of the generation of the living!

The earthly rainbow is merely a sign of a spiritual reality found in heaven. That truth is found in the manifest presence of the Lamb of God in heaven.

The Seven Eyes of Grace

He is the resurrected man to bring God's grace to a redeemed human race. The apostle John was given a vision of this heavenly reality found in Christ.

> *Rev. 4:1 After these things I looked, and behold, a door standing open in heaven. And the first voice which I heard was like a trumpet speaking with me, saying, "Come up here, and I will show you things which must take place after this." 2 Immediately I was in the Spirit; and behold, a throne set in heaven, and One sat on the throne. 3 And He who sat there was like a jasper and a sardius stone in appearance; and there was a rainbow around the throne, in appearance like an emerald.*

Around the throne of God there is a rainbow. The rainbow is significant of the sevenfold Spirit of God. Seven is a Biblical number symbolic of perfection. It is a testimony to God's ability to perfect our lives in His presence. I believe the rainbow is a signification of the Holy Spirit. The Holy Spirit is the one who perfects our lives. He is God with us and in us. He reveals to us the reality of being seated with Christ in heavenly places (Eph. 1:20; 2:6). He is the one who began a good work in us, and He is the one who is faithful to complete it (Phil 1:6). The Holy Spirit has come as the Light of Christ into our lives. He has come with the testimony of Christ. He is the One who will make the realities of heaven seen in the earth. He is the One who changes us from within.

The Holy Spirit is one Spirit, but He is the power and presence of the sevenfold grace of God at work in our lives. He is the sevenfold Spirit of God.

> *Isa. 11:1 There shall come forth a Rod from the stem of Jesse, and a Branch shall grow out of his roots. 2 The Spirit of the LORD shall rest upon Him, the Spirit of wisdom and understanding, the Spirit of counsel and might, the Spirit of knowledge and of the fear of the LORD.*

The Holy Spirit is the Spirit that rests upon Jesus, the Rod, and the Body of Christ, the Branch. Jesus came as both the Son of God and the Son of Man to redeem the human race and reconcile them to their Father in Heaven. The Spirit of God anointed Him in both His calling and His purpose. These verses in the book of Isaiah reveal the seven attributes of the Holy Spirit of God. He is:

1. The Spirit of the Lord
2. The Spirit of Wisdom
3. The Spirit of Understanding

4. The Spirit of Counsel
5. The Spirit of Might
6. The Spirit of Knowledge (Knowing)
7. The Spirit of the Fear of the Lord

These are His attributes, and He is God's grace given to our lives. He is the One who has come to transform our lives. He has come to perfect us into the image of Christ (Rom. 8:29; 1 Cor. 15:49; Col. 3:10, 11). These seven attributes of the Spirit of God are also known in Scripture as *The Seven Eyes of Grace*. We can find the truth of these *Seven Eyes* in the book of Zechariah.

*Zech. 3:8 'Hear, O Joshua, the high priest, you and your companions who sit before you, for they are a wondrous sign; for behold, I am bringing forth My Servant the BRANCH. 9 For behold, the stone that I have laid before Joshua: **upon the stone are seven eyes**. Behold, I will engrave its inscription,' says the LORD of hosts, 'and I will remove the iniquity of that land in one day.'*

Just as the prophet Isaiah revealed that the sevenfold Spirit of God would rest upon the Rod and Branch of Christ (Isa. 11:1, 2), the prophet Zechariah reveals that there would come a Servant known as the BRANCH that would find its foundation in the stone laid before Joshua. Upon that stone there would be seven eyes, just as Isaiah had said there would be seven Spirits upon the Branch. We have no problem recognizing that this Branch is Christ, but we easily forget that the Branch includes all that is the Body of Christ. We are members of His Body joined to His headship in the Spirit (Eph. 1:22, 23). We are part of the Branch in heaven and earth. Jesus said He was the vine, but we are the "branches" (Jn. 15:5). Jesus (Joshua) is the foundation stone of the Church (1 Cor. 3:10, 11; Eph. 2:20; Dan. 2:35). It is the sevenfold Spirit of Grace in that foundation stone that empowers the Church to be built upon that stone. That sevenfold Spirit is the overcoming grace of life! It is the transforming power of God! These *Seven Eyes of Grace* are the key to intimacy with the Father in Heaven. These are the true eyes of faith (2 Cor. 5:7). These are the eyes of the Spirit, and they lead to heavenly sight. These Seven Eyes are the Seven Spirits of God (Rev. 5:6). They are the Holy Spirit's power for bringing Christ's perfection in the life of the Church! He is one Spirit, but He reveals Himself in seven ways. He reveals Himself in the power of perfection (as the number 7 is a symbol of perfection).

Zech. 4:6 So he answered and said to me: "This is the word of the

The Seven Eyes of Grace

LORD to Zerubbabel: 'Not by might nor by power, but by My Spirit,' says the LORD of hosts. 7 'Who are you, O great mountain? Before Zerubbabel you shall become a plain! And he shall bring forth the capstone with shouts of "Grace, grace to it!"' 8 Moreover the word of the LORD came to me, saying: 9 "The hands of Zerubbabel have laid the foundation of this temple; his hands shall also finish it. Then you will know that the LORD of hosts has sent Me to you. 10 For who has despised the day of small things? For these seven rejoice to see the plumb line in the hand of Zerubbabel. They are the eyes of the LORD, which scan to and fro throughout the whole earth."

The name "Zerubbabel" means, "seed in Babel". That is literally, "seed in confusion". The nations without God are the testimony of "Babel". Without God we are all bound to confusion. Zerubbabel was the "son of Shealtiel" (Hag 1:1, 12, 14). The name "Shealtiel" means, "asked-of", or "I have asked God". Jesus taught us that the asked-of seed of the Father is the Holy Spirit. He said that we can ask our Father in Heaven for the gift of the Holy Spirit, and we can expect to receive the seed of His kingdom life within our hearts (Lk. 11:11-13). The Holy Spirit comes into the midst of our confusion and begins to transform our lives by the testimony of Jesus Christ. This Scripture in Zechariah is testifying of the grace of God that would come to our lives by the testimony of the Holy Spirit within and upon our lives. Just as the cornerstone of Christ had been set by the power of the Holy Spirit (Acts 4:11; Eph. 2:20; 1 Pet. 2:6), so the capstone will be set on the fullness of the restored house of God in the earth! The work of God was established by a man of grace and truth. That work will also be finished in the lives of humanity as a testimony of grace and truth.

The seven that rejoice to see the plum line in the hand of Zerubbabel are the graces of the Spirit of the Lord, Wisdom, Understanding, Counsel, Might, Knowing, and the Fear of the Lord (Isa. 11:2). The plumb line is the Holy Spirit's means of building the true Church of Christ. It is true to the foundation of Christ. It is true to the material of the Stone with seven eyes. *The Seven Eyes of Grace* are in the hand of the Holy Spirit to complete the work of Christ with shouts of, "Grace, grace to it!" God's grace will establish the spiritual house of God in heaven and earth (1 Pet. 2:5).

We can pursue this pattern of God's grace throughout the Scriptures. There are seven foundations of Christianity presented in Heb. 6:1, 2. To understand these two verses, we must first understand that the writer was addressing the

14

fact that the principles of God should be in use and not just in belief (Heb. 5:14). The writer of Hebrews was challenging the Hebrew people to move from mere instruction to the reality of empowerment. What had been the teaching of principles in times past was now being presented as a source of empowerment unto perfection. It is no longer a time for a discussion of what we believe about God. It is time to be empowered by the grace of God. This is what will make us teachers of nations. This is what will empower us to finally transform the world and reveal the likeness and image of the Father in heaven to the world. The words of Hebrews, Chapter 6 verses 1 and 2 carry a strong wording of empowerment, not merely leaving the principles behind. The word leaving in the Greek implies an empowerment to move forward. In light of this, we could understand verse 1 of Chapter 6 to read:

> *Therefore, being sent forth by the principality of the logos (word) of Christ, let us bear and carry the substance unto perfection and completion.*
> *Or...*
> *A Man (the Word made flesh), having become the express image of the Father and the likeness of His image in the earth, has been exalted above all men in order to empower us all to finally become what we were destined to be – the glory of God in the earth!*

Now let's consider the result of this empowerment by God's grace. Let's consider verse one that says, *"Therefore, leaving the discussion of the elementary principles (principality) of Christ"*... Let me state it as, *Having finally been empowered to be sent forth, let us go on to:*
 7) *perfection, not laying again the foundation of*
 1) *repentance from dead works* and of
 2) *faith toward God* ...... of
 3) *the doctrine of baptisms*, of
 4) *laying on of hands*, of
 5) *resurrection of the dead*, and of
 6) *eternal judgment.*

I believe these seven foundational and progressive truths testify of the sevenfold power of God's grace at work in building a spiritual house for His habitation. What is the place of God's habitation? God was not looking for a house of stone. He was looking for a house of flesh empowered by the life of His Spirit! God's sevenfold Spirit came to establish the Body of Christ as a place for His habitation.

The Seven Eyes of Grace

*Heb. 10:5 Therefore, when He came into the world, He said: "Sacrifice
and offerings You did not desire, but a body You have prepared for
Me 6 In burnt offerings and sacrifices for sin You had no pleasure.
7 Then I said, 'Behold, I have come—In the volume of the book it is
written of Me—To do Your will, O God' "*

If God did not desire "sacrifice and offerings", why did He require them?
He didn't desire them, but He is the one who commanded them. I believe we
have to look at the sacrifices and offerings in a different light. If God didn't
desire them, they must be a type and shadow of a greater truth that He did
desire. If what He desired was a Body, they must have something to do with
His "Body". The sevenfold grace of God can be seen as seven levels of
relationship in the Body of Christ. These seven levels of relationship relate
directly to seven offerings that God instructed the children of Israel to bring
to the place that God chose for His name to abide for them.

*Deut. 12:5 "But you shall seek the place where the LORD your God
chooses, out of all your tribes, to put His name for His habitation; and
there you shall go. 6 There you shall take your*
1) *burnt offerings, your*
2) *sacrifices, your*
3) *tithes, the*
4) *heave offerings of your hand, your*
5) *vowed offerings, your*
6) *freewill offerings, and the*
7) *firstlings of your herds and flocks."*

I will be applying these seven levels of relationship to each grace
presented in this book. For now, it is sufficient to simply mention that these
seven offerings are part of a Scriptural pattern revealing the power of the
sevenfold grace of God at work in the Church.

The sevenfold grace of God can be seen in seven actions of the New
Testament Church. I will also be applying this in each of the seven topics of
God's grace presented in this book. For now, I want to point out the pattern
of their existence as presented in the second chapter of the book of Acts.

Acts 2:38 Then Peter said to them,
1) *"Repent, and let every one of you*
2) *be baptized in the name of Jesus Christ for the remission of sins;*

16

and you shall
3) receive the gift of the Holy Spirit."
      Acts 2:42 = And
4) they continued steadfastly in the apostles' doctrine
      (instruction taught them by the apostles) and
5) they continued steadfastly in fellowship, and
6) they continued steadfastly in breaking of bread, and
7) they continued steadfastly in prayers.

Acts 2:43 Then fear came upon every soul, and many wonders and signs were done through the apostles.

Acts 2:47 ...And the Lord added to the church daily those who were being saved.

The pattern of the sevenfold grace of God can be found throughout Scripture. I doubt that I have found all of the places that they can be clearly seen, although I have found numerous places they can be seen. I want to present a few of the places of the pattern, simply to reveal that there is a pattern to confirm the reality of the sevenfold grace of God.

There are seven stars or seven angels (messengers) to the Church. I believe these are the Seven Spirits of God, also known as the sevenfold Spirit of God sent to perfect the Church. God's sevenfold Spirit is the fullness of His grace to cause God's Church to manifest His life to the world.

Rev. 1:20 "The mystery of the seven stars, which you saw in My right hand, and the seven golden lampstands: The seven stars are the angels of the seven churches, and the seven lampstands which you saw are the seven churches."

There are seven lamps before the throne of God. I believe these "lamps" represent the Holy Spirit's anointing and authority to reveal the power of God's REIGNING GRACE in His Church.

Rev. 4:5 And from the throne proceeded lightnings, thunderings, and voices. And there were seven lamps of fire burning before the throne, which are the seven Spirits of God.

These lamps are associated with lightnings, thunderings, and voices.

The Seven Eyes of Grace

Lightning represents REVELATION. Lightning is the revelation of the life-changing power and light of God in our lives. When lightning strikes, thunder follows. Thunder is the TESTIMONY of that Revelation revealed in our lives. When lightning strikes and thunder rolls, it produces an effect in the earth. Voices represent CHANGED LIVES by the testimony of the Revelation. We can see that in this verse of Scripture, the sevenfold Spirit of God is connected to God's ability to bring the power of heaven to the earth in which we live.

Another pattern can be seen in the letters to the churches of the book of Revelation. There are seven letters of Revelation with seven overcoming promises (Rev. 2 & 3). These overcoming promises can easily be associated to the foundation principles of Christ (Heb. 6:1, 2). They relate directly to the antidotes of the curses of the fall. I have addressed those antidotes in my book, _The Redeemed Earth - Healing the Curse of the Fall_. The focus of the first letter is a return to our first love. It involves a renewed relationship with God through the power of the Spirit of the Lord. It is the grace of repentance from dead works. The second letter involves the ability to have faith toward God. It involves the grace of the Spirit of Wisdom that overcomes the temptation of the fear of death. God's wisdom promises victory over the power of death. The third letter relates to a personal testimony in God through the grace of the Spirit of Understanding. The Holy Spirit is revealed as the true teacher of our lives with the power of His transformation. He is the One who gives a personal testimony in Christ and a changed life. We are submerged in Him to receive His testimony of a changed life. The fourth letter relates to the ability to bring God's light to the darkness of the world. The grace of the Spirit of Counsel enables us to lay the hands of Christ upon the world. We can keep in submission to His sent will and we can become the Body of Christ that reveals His light to the darkness of the world. Through His Spirit of Counsel we can change the world in which we live. The fifth letter relates to the grace of the Spirit of Might. In Christ, we find the works that have been prepared for us to walk in. We can be clothed in Christ and the power of His resurrection. We are confessed before the Father and before His angels as His sent ones clothed in His Resurrection Might. We are commissioned to forever know His eternal resurrection life. The sixth letter is directly linked to the grace of the Spirit of Knowing and the true testimony of communion with His Body and Spirit. In Christ we have the testimony of His eternal judgment of love. We judge no one according to the flesh, but commune with God and one another through the intimacy of His Spirit of Love. We are a part of the New Jerusalem and the testimony of the Bread of Life. The seventh letter of Revelation corresponds to the grace of the Spirit of the Fear of the Lord. It testifies of the Spirit's ability

18

to ignite a zeal for God and His manifest glory in our lives. It is through the power of a face-to-face relationship with God that we will know the power of prayer and His perfected work in the earth. We can rule and reign with Him throughout the generations to come in increasing and maturing measures.

Another pattern for the sevenfold grace of God can be seen in the "seven thunders" of God. These are mentioned in the Book of Revelation and defined in Psalms, Chapter 29.

Rev. 10:4 Now when the seven thunders uttered their voices, I was about to write; but I heard a voice from heaven saying to me, "Seal up the things which the seven thunders uttered, and do not write them."
...11 And he said to me, "You must prophesy again about many peoples, nations, tongues, and kings."

Ps. 29:1 Give unto the LORD, O you mighty ones, Give unto the LORD glory and strength. 2 Give unto the LORD the glory due to His name; Worship the LORD in the beauty of holiness. 3 The voice of the LORD is over the waters; The God of glory thunders; The LORD is over many waters.

Ps. 29:4 The voice of the LORD is powerful; The voice of the LORD is full of majesty.

I believe this verse four reveals the power of the grace of the Spirit of the Lord. He returns us to the wonder of His majesty and a testimony of our first love.

Ps. 29:5 The voice of the LORD breaks the cedars, Yes, the LORD splinters the cedars of Lebanon.

In the Scripture, trees represent men and the generations of men. It is the grace of the Spirit of Wisdom that causes the generations and the experiences of men to give way to the wisdom and inheritance of God. The fear of death is broken when the strength of men dies and we find our future and hope in His Spirit of Wisdom. There is no more fear of death and we can do works that demonstrate our faith toward God by the power of His Spirit of Wisdom.

Ps. 29:6 He makes them also skip like a calf, Lebanon (the heart) and Sirion (God has prevailed) like a young wild ox.

The Holy Spirit brings the testimony of life and freedom. The grace of the Spirit of Understanding gives us a personal testimony in Christ. There is a spillover from our hearts of the testimony of Christ's prevailing power within us.

> *Ps. 29:7 The voice of the LORD divides the flames of fire.*

The grace of the Spirit of Counsel gives us the power of God's light to the darkness of the world. We are given the power of the morning star in Christ. We are anointed as His ministers of light to the darkness of the world. He makes His ministers as flames of fire (Ps. 104:4).

> *Ps. 29:8 The voice of the LORD shakes the wilderness; The LORD shakes the Wilderness of Kadesh (holiness).*

Jesus is the Resurrection. The Spirit of Might causes our wilderness to make way for the holiness of the Lord. We can be found clothed in Him by the power of His Resurrection Might.

> *Ps. 29:9 The voice of the LORD makes the deer give birth, and strips the forests bare; And in His temple everyone says, "Glory!"*

In the knowing of Him, the life of men expires, and the Life of God begins. The Eternal Judgment of life forevermore in Christ is made known by the grace of the Spirit of Knowing. The New Jerusalem is made known to men. Our places of hiding are removed, and we are finally able to show up for our lives in Christ! The old hiding places are removed, and the sure-footedness of trust and love is birthed in our lives.

> *Ps. 29:10 The LORD sat enthroned at the Flood, And the LORD sits as King forever. 11 The LORD will give strength to His people; The LORD will bless His people with peace.*

Jesus is the key to the change, the rule, and reign of our world. The grace of the Spirit of the Fear of the Lord gives us the true awe of His presence. It is through a face-to-face relationship with Him that all things become dedicated to Him. We will experience the power of His perfections in the earth!

The seven aspects of grace are also revealed as the testimony of the one Body of Christ and the life given by one Spirit in that Body (Eph. 4:4-6). It reveals that in one Body and by one Spirit we increasingly come to know: 1) One Lord; 2) One Faith; 3) One Baptism (Submersion); 4) One God and

Father of all; 5) One God above all; 6) One God through all; and 7) One God in all. These seven things are also revealed as: 1) A belt of truth - (one Lord, one desire of our hearts that reveals our destiny as new creations in God); 2) A breastplate of righteousness - (actions of faith toward God from our hearts through a right relationship with God); 3) Feet shod with the readiness of the gospel of peace (the evidence of our submersion in God's heavenly testimony that brings a heavenly testimony to the places we walk); 4) The shield of faith (a testimony of submission one to another in the testimony of one Father of all); 5) The helmet of salvation (the revealing of one God above all); 6) The sword of the Spirit (the *rhema* word of God - the testimony of One God through us all); 7) Prayer in the Spirit (the testimony of one God in us all) - Eph. 6:14-18.

In the following chapters, we will look at each of the seven graces of God as revealed by His sevenfold Spirit. *The Seven Eyes of Grace* are nothing less than the power of God's Spirit to perfect us as His Church in the earth. Each grace is presented in five or six chapters. These chapters are presented in a way they can easily be a part of your individual study or a group study on this topic of God's sevenfold grace. I suggest that you read and meditate a chapter each day and allow the Holy Spirit to give you an understanding of His amazing grace.

God's GRACE is the power of Jubilee. Jubilee is a testimony of debts forgiven and inheritance restored. It is by God's grace that these things can be increasingly true in our lives. In this study, you will find that the Spirit of the Lord relates to *Repentance From Dead Works*. It is a level of relationship with God that was foreshadowed in the Burnt Offering of the Old Testament. I will present how the Spirit of Wisdom relates to *Faith Toward God* and the actions that speak of our faith toward Him. Just as Water Baptism is an act of faith, there is a level of relationship in the Body of Christ that was foreshadowed in an offering known as the Sacrifice. You will discover how the grace of the Spirit of Understanding relates to the *Doctrine of Baptisms*, the transforming teaching power of the Holy Spirit in your life. This is a level of relationship that was foreshadowed in the Tithe, a spillover to God. You will see that the grace of the Spirit of Counsel relates to the *Laying on of Hands* of the Body of Christ. It is directly linked to your ability to submit to apostolic instruction – the sent word of God for your connection to the corporate purpose of the Body of Christ. This is a level of relationship that was foreshadowed in the Heave Offering - a submission one to another in the Body of Christ. In like manner you will be inspired to know how the grace of the Spirit of Might relates to the *Resurrection of the Dead*. It is the testimony of your fellowship in the Body of Christ by the Spirit and your ability to bring your individual contribution to His testimony of Christ's resurrection to the world in which you live. This is a level of relationship foreshadowed in the Vowed Offering. That vow is the testimony of who God declares you to be in Christ. You will see how the grace of the Spirit of Knowing relates to *Eternal Judgment*. All men have been pronounced guilty of God's mercy and are now eligible for His Eternal Life. By the power of this grace, legitimate doors open and illegitimate doors close. It is possible to have Love for God and Love for one another through true Communion – the breaking of living bread and the drinking of the living cup. This is a level of relationship that was foreshadowed in the Freewill Offering. Finally, you will see how the Spirit of The Fear of The Lord relates to *Perfections*. This grace will reveal the testimony of a face-to-face relationship with God and the power of prayer. You will see how devoted things to God release inheritance and destiny. The grace of the Spirit of the Fear of the Lord releases generational longevity and the ability to appropriate the rule and reign of Christ. This grace pertains to the glory of God. It is a level of relationship that was foreshadowed in the offering of the Firstlings of herds and flocks.

Chapter 1.1

The First Eye of Grace
- The Spirit of The Lord

Let's begin by looking at the first of *Seven Eyes of Grace*. The first grace is the Spirit of the Lord. It is a grace of the Holy Spirit at work in our lives allowing us to be born again believers in Christ. It is important for each Christian to become a part of the Body of Christ. It is not about what we can do for God. It is about being in a relationship with Him. God gives us grace so that we can be valid and active members of His family, also known as the Body of Christ. God wants us to become something, not merely do something for Him. God never wanted sacrifices and offerings. He wanted a place to live, a place where He has a relationship with us and we with Him.

> *Heb. 10:5 Therefore, when He came into the world, He said: "Sacrifice and offering You did not desire, but a body You have prepared for Me. 6 In burnt offerings and sacrifices for sin you had no pleasure. 7 Then I said, 'Behold, I have come—in the volume of the book it is written of Me—to do Your will, O God.'"*

We must keep this in mind when we read the Old Testament Scriptures. If God never desired sacrifices and offerings, why did He require them? We must look at the sacrifices and offerings in the Old Testament from a different perspective. The context in this Scripture in Hebrews is that sacrifice and offerings are compared to a Body, the Body of Christ. Jesus is the one who finally came as a real human being destined to glorify His Father in heaven. He was the brightness of His glory and the express image of His person (Heb. 1:3). He was the living will of God sent to do the will of God in the earth. He was the very habitation of life (Jn. 1:4).

The Old Testament was a shadow of that which is made real in Christ.

23

The Seven Eyes of Grace

It was a shadow of things yet to come. That shadow was merely an imprint of information concerning the real image in heaven. The light of God shown through the image of life and cast an exact imprint called the shadow of the truth of Christ. If we look directly at the shadow of a person on the ground, we look at the exact information about a real person. It reveals to us there is a person, but it doesn't allow us to personally meet that person or get to know him or her. A shadow is like a diagram or a picture of something that is real. The Old Testament is full of ceremonies and requirements that are like a diagram or a picture that speak of something that God wants to be alive, practical, and real in the life of every human being. They are informational truths of transformational realities only found in heaven or in Christ's heavenly Body upon the earth. Since the writer of Hebrews equated sacrifices and offerings to a comparison of the Body of Christ, we must look at sacrifice and offerings in the light of a living relationship of a living organism. We can no longer view sacrifices and offerings as merely an order of service or ceremony. They must apply to the power of transformation to Christ's image and not information about His image. They can be understood as expressions of relationship to God from the heart of the Body. The sacrifices and offerings were merely shadows cast by the truth of a heartfelt relationship with God in Christ.

> _Deut. 12:5 "But you shall seek the place where the LORD your God chooses, out of all your tribes, to put His name for His habitation; and there you shall go. 6 There you shall take your ¹⁾burnt offerings, your ²⁾sacrifices, your ³⁾tithes, the ⁴⁾heave offerings of your hand, your ⁵⁾vowed offerings, your ⁶⁾freewill offerings, and the ⁷⁾firstlings of your herds and flocks. 7 And there you shall eat before the LORD your God, and you shall rejoice in all to which you have put your hand, you and your households, in which the LORD your God has blessed you."_

In this Scripture we see the type and shadow of something that is very real in the New Covenant. The children of Israel were told to seek the place where the LORD their God chose, out of all their tribes, to put His name for His habitation, and to go there. In order for us to find the place that God desires for His habitation in our lives, we must also seek the place from among our tribes (spiritual family members) that God chooses for us to relate. We must seek a legitimate expression of local church that God desires to be our spiritual family. The full dynamic of God's house can only happen in a corporate expression of His house. We have a responsibility before God to find that place. That place is not a place that we choose; it is the place that God chooses for His name to abide for us. In this modern world of commerce, we are taught to shop for

24

the best deals. We are taught to shop by convenience, not by conviction. This same weakness has entered into our view of finding the right church. Many people have the idea that the place of God's choosing is the place of natural convenience, natural likes, or natural benefits. Rather than seeking the place of God's choosing for the divine relationships of our lives, many people seek the place of their choosing. They join their lives to what they think is the right program, the right preaching, or what they perceive to be the right environment. They don't understand that true life comes from right relationships. God wants us to find the place of right relationships. In the Old Covenant it was your family tribe; in the New Covenant it is your divine connection in the family of God. They are the relationships that will make us truly come alive!

When we find the divine place of God's choosing, we are to experience the full dynamic of seven offerings. These offerings were shadows cast into the past by the greater truth of relationship in the Body of Christ. Each of these offerings speaks of a level of relationship in the House of God – the Body of Christ. Each offering represents a level of relationship granted to us as an expression of relationship to God and our life-giving function as members of His House – His Body – His Family. I will begin by addressing the "burnt offering" and how it relates to *the Seven Eyes of Grace*. Before we can begin with the Old Testament shadow, we must look at the New Testament account of when the Body of Christ became anointed and real. It is at that moment that the sacrifices and offerings mentioned in Deuteronomy, Chapter 12, became real expressions of relationship to God in the Body of Christ.

When the day of Pentecost had fully come, God poured out His Spirit upon all flesh (Acts 2). I believe His Spirit is the full expression of Christ's sevenfold grace in our lives. These are the graces of the foundation of the Church. These graces are a part of the Spirit of 'Pentecost'. 'Pentecost' means "fifty". In the Scripture, a Jubilee feast was supposed to be celebrated every 50th year as a year of release from oppression and bondage (Lev. 25:10-13). Jubilee is significant of a time when all debts are forgiven and inheritances are restored. This sevenfold grace of God is nothing less than the jubilee realities of God in Christ. They are the evidence of the year of the Lord's favor in our lives (Isa. 61:2). God's graces are a testimony of "promised land destiny" and not "wilderness wanderings". Each grace is a grace of "Pentecost" (the spirit of jubilee) as the foundation of the house. Each grace is an expression of God's Spirit that empowers us to experience increasing measures of our inheritance in Christ. These graces found in the Holy Spirit of God activate and empower us to come fully alive in Christ. They confirm that we are the

Body of Christ. They confirm that we are the Body that Jesus came looking for. He desired a place to rest His head, and the Holy Spirit has confirmed that habitation with His abiding presence (Lk. 9:57, 58). This is the sevenfold grace found in the sevenfold Spirit of Christ (Isa. 11:2).

The first evidence of this sevenfold grace is found in Acts 2:38. When the crowd saw and heard the evidence of Christ's Spirit upon the 120, they asked Peter what they must do to be saved. Peter said they must first "repent".

Acts 2:38 Then Peter said to them, "Repent"…

What does it mean to "repent"? Is there a difference between the repentance required by John the Baptist and the repentance required by Jesus Christ? What is it that we must repent from? How do we repent? How does the repentance of the Old Covenant burnt offering relate to the repentance grace of the New Covenant in Christ?

If true repentance were merely an action to change our lives from evil to good, the repentance of John the Baptist would have been enough. John preached repentance from evil (Mt. 3 & Lk. 3). His message was one of preparation for the kingdom to come. He was a prophet under the administration of the knowledge of good and evil. He was the best of that old system of government. The Scripture says that of those born of women there is no one greater than John (Mt. 11:11). It also says that even the least in the kingdom of heaven is greater than him. When Jesus came, He brought a new administration (Eph. 1:10). He brought us an administration of grace. John's message of repentance concerned the requirements of the Law. Jesus commands repentance in accordance with the power of His grace! Under a government of the knowledge of good and evil, the best that one can hope for is the perfect knowledge of good. The Law (the Torah) was the fullness of the information of "good". Israel was fully "informed" as to the requirements of God. They were fully "informed", but they could never be fully "transformed" under the government (administration) of the knowledge of good and evil. When John the Baptist came on the scene, the system of the world had gotten as good and as bad as it could get without the power of God's transforming grace. Rome was as sinful as sin can get. John's message was as good as it could get. Under a government of the knowledge of good and evil, there was a full testimony of "good" in the "Law" and the "Prophets". John was the best of the human expression of God in the message that he proclaimed. Under that old administration, there was also a full expression of that which was evil in the nation of Rome. This was the culmination of the four kingdoms of darkness revealed through the prophet Daniel (Dan. 2:36-45). With the culmination of the knowledge of good and evil, the fullness of the time had come, and Jesus came to bring the government of grace. He was a man who was full of grace and truth (Jn. 1:14). He came to bring the administration of grace to humankind (Jn. 1:17). It was an administration of transformation whereby we can know God as our Father (Gal. 4:4-7). It was an administration that is suitable for the summing up of all things in Christ (Eph. 1:10). Even the least in this kingdom of grace was greater than the best of the kingdom of Law. Even the least in the kingdom of transformation was greater than the best of the kingdom of "information". John's repentance was a repentance based upon the knowledge of right and wrong. The repentance required by God in Christ is one of transformation. His repentance grants us changed hearts and minds. John's repentance was one of changed actions while the repentance granted in Christ is one of changed ways.

NOTE: Stop here and consider the subject material of this chapter. Allow the Holy Spirit to speak to your heart as you meditate this subject of repentance from dead works.

Chapter 1.2

The First Eye of Grace

In our various paths of life, we have all experienced the influence of the old government of the knowledge of good and evil. We have all experienced the feeling that we were born to be "right". We knew it was true the first time we felt bad for being "wrong". We knew it was true the moment we judged others for being wrong. In any case, it left us feeling dead inside our hearts.

God did not create us to be "right". God created human beings to be loved. It was Adam's choosing of the tree of the knowledge of good and evil that left mankind with the looming shadow of having to be "right". God intended for human beings to be loved by Him. He in turn would guide us into all truth. Human beings were created to be loved by God. Having been loved by God, we would then be activated in our hearts to love Him and to love others as we love ourselves. It is the mystery of God's grace. Jesus came to give us the administration of His grace. The first step to tasting of that grace is to return to our first love. We have to come to the place where we know we were born to be loved by God. We then experience the power of a new birth to love God and to love others as we love ourselves. We eat of the Tree of Life (Rev. 2:7), because we experience the power of true life in Christ. It is a restoration of knowing God in our hearts. It is truly paradise restored in our lives! When we experience the paradise of being loved by God, we experience the empowerment of loving God! It is the beginning of the power of His administration of grace.

Under the administration of grace, the first power of transformation is the grace of repentance from dead works. It is the grace of the Spirit of the Lord. To understand this repentance, we must look at the Scripture concerning Christ's repentance.

Heb. 6:1 Therefore, leaving the discussion of the elementary principles (principality) of Christ, let us go on to perfection, <u>not laying again the foundation of repentance from dead works</u> …

The first expression of the grace of God in our lives is not repentance from being evil. It is more powerful than that. It is repentance from dead works. Our real problem was not that we were evil. Our real problem is that without the grace of God we are dead. Because we are dead, we become a habitation for deceiving, devouring, and conflicting spirits. We are a place for the Devil to influence, since God has bound him to the dry places of the earth (Gen. 3:14, 15). Repentance from dead works is really repentance from being dead! It is impossible to do any living work if we in fact are dead. If we are dead, every work we do is a dead work. It doesn't matter how good that work might appear. It is merely a lifeless shadow of something that is real. Repentance from dead works is the first step toward entering the kingdom of God and it is a continual process in the house of God, the Body of Christ.

Before I knew Christ, I can remember trying to do good things. Those good things never really left me feeling good for long. There was still an empty hole in my heart. My good efforts were simply surface attempts at satisfying a need in my heart. They were efforts from the outside in and never proved to have any lasting effect of life. I wanted to be good but ended up needing to find life! My search led me down a path of seeking to find things that satisfied the passions of my heart. It left me in bondage to drugs, alcohol, and loose living. I was really a bad person, but I really thought of myself as a "good" person for some time. I made a few attempts at doing good things, but my lifestyle was filled with the evidence of "evil". I could never really change. I was bound to a lifestyle of dead works. I was unable to repent from my way of life. I merely adjusted my activities in an attempt to produce different results. It was a vain effort in every case!

The word "repentance" is defined in the Greek words *matenoeo* and *matanaia*. It means, "to have another mind, a change of mind, after consideration and regret". It is not just a change of thoughts. It is to have a change in the source of our thoughts. It includes a change in the desires of our hearts. It is the ability to come alive in Christ and to be empowered by His grace to have a changed attitude, a changed thought, and a changed action. True repentance exhibits the evidence of changed actions that are the fruit of a changed heart.

Mt. 21:28 "But what do you think about this? A man with two sons told the older boy, 'Son, go out and work in the vineyard today.' 29 The son answered, 'No, I won't go,' but later he changed his mind and went anyway. 30 Then the father told the other son, 'You go,' and he said, 'Yes, sir, I will.' But he didn't go. 31 Which of the two was obeying his father?" They replied, "The first, of course." Then Jesus explained his meaning: "I assure you, corrupt tax collectors and prostitutes will get into the Kingdom of God before you do." (NLT)

Repentance is not merely a confession made with the words of our mouths. True repentance is evidenced by the change of our actions. Words are the true expressions of our hearts. Words are not merely the verbal articulations of our lips. What we do speaks louder than what we merely say. If we say we love someone, but then we beat them with a brick, which speaks louder? Is it the words of our mouths or the actions of our lives that really confess what we believe? The truth is, we always do what we want to do. Even when it comes to doing what we didn't want to do in the first place, we must decide to want to do it. The real key to repentance is the desire of our hearts. It is not the confession of our lips. For this reason, the first step toward repentance is to experience a piercing of our hearts. Repentance cuts the heart.

Acts 2:37 Now when they heard this, they were cut to the heart, and said to Peter and the rest of the apostles, "Men and brethren, what shall we do?" 38 Then Peter said to them, "Repent"…

I remember when I first experienced the grace of repentance from dead works. It was May 11, 1973. I had been in bondage to a loose lifestyle for some time. I drank alcohol extensively, I used drugs daily, and I pursued a lifestyle of sin continuously. I wasn't just evil. I was dead. I wasn't trying to do evil things. I was trying to find life, but I was looking for life in all the wrong places. I was looking for life in things. My life was a dry place susceptible to the deceptions, devouring, and conflict of the Devil. In the fall of 1972, a group of girls that I called "Jesus freaks" heard a word from God. God said, "Pray for Ted Hanson, he'll be a fire for Me." They began to pray that God would make me so miserable I couldn't stand myself until I came to Him. I immediately began to pursue my sinful lifestyle in an even more fervent manner. I was miserable, but I was looking for life! I still thought that life could be found in the things I did. In March of 1973, God spoke this same thing again to this group of Christian believers. Again, they prayed that God would make me miserable until I came to Him. I began to feel very bad about my life. I contemplated the ending of my life. I began to take steps of improving my life. I was selling drugs and using them. I quit selling drugs in an attempt to "do good", but I still used drugs as a life source to my inner needs. I began to attend church on Sundays. I would go to the service drunk or stoned. I would hear the word of God being read and I would begin to cry, only to quickly retreat beneath a pretend veneer of life. I was involved in music and was a part of a rock band. On May 11, 1973, I decided to play music at a church event. I thought it would perhaps help me to be "good" and maybe that would give me life. When I arrived at the church, I went to open the case containing my guitar. I had forgotten my key to the case, so I had to drive back home to get the key. When I got back with the key, I opened the case only to find that my guitar was warped and ruined. I had played at a party in the rain during a drunken binge the previous week. The locked case and ruined guitar were really the story of my life. My world was confronting me in the face. That night, a man I had known previously shared how he had asked Jesus into his heart. He testified as to how his experience had totally changed his life. I knew this man. I could see that he was different than he was before. I could see God on his face. I was pierced in my heart, and I began to cry. On my way home that night, I pulled my car to a secluded place alongside the road and confessed all the sins I had ever done to God. I asked Him to forgive me and to come into my life. I went home exhausted and broken. I woke up on May 12, 1973, a totally changed person. A new desire had come into my heart! I had a tremendous love for God! I had been born again. I was no longer dead. I had been brought to life by the Spirit of the Lord! I had experienced my first measure of "repentance from dead works". I had not merely repented from being evil. I had been given a gift! It was a grace to be alive and no longer bound to dead works! I was, for the very first time, able to present my life to God as a living sacrifice!

The apostle Paul had something to say about that. He wrote:

Rom. 12:1 I beseech you therefore, brethren, by the mercies of God, that you present your bodies a living sacrifice, holy, acceptable to God, which is your reasonable service.

I had come to know the mercy of God and I was able to present my body as a living sacrifice to Him. I was acceptable to Him! It was my reasonable service to commit my life fully to Him. This is the level of relationship that was shadowed as a "burnt offering" in the Old Testament. In the Old Testament the burnt offering was a blood sacrifice for sin. Jesus Christ was that blood sacrifice for the sins of us all (Rom. 6:10; 2 Cor. 5:14; Heb. 10:10). He drank the cup of the life of the flesh so that we could come and freely drink the cup of the Spirit (Mt. 26:29).

NOTE: It is recommended that you stop and meditate upon these thoughts today. Let the Holy Spirit speak to you today. Allow Him to influence you by the power of His grace - the grace of the Spirit of the Lord.

31

Chapter 1.3

The First Eye of Grace

The grace of the Spirit of the Lord and the testimony of repentance from dead works is nothing short of a miracle of God. It is the power of transformation that comes to our hearts from the love of God in heaven. It is not something we earn. It is a free gift of life from the one who gives all life. Repentance is not an act of the human will. It is the empowerment of God's grace within the human heart. It is not merely the change of our actions. It is a change of our hearts. It is a change in the source of our thoughts. This change in the source of our hearts then propagates a passionate change in our actions. Our lifestyles change by a change of our hearts. We have to position ourselves to believe it is true, but God has already positioned Himself to make it true!

Jesus didn't come to merely destroy evil. We will one day see all evil destroyed, but Jesus came to reconcile us to the Father (Rom. 5:10; 2 Cor. 5:18; Col. 1:21). He came to destroy the resting place of demons (Mt. 12:43; Lk. 11:24). He came to change the dry places of the earth to pools of refreshing living water (Isa. 41:18). He came to destroy the habitation of evil ways (Isa. 35:7). He came to cause rivers of living water to flow from our hearts (Jn. 7:37-39). Jesus was the Word made flesh so that our flesh could receive the everlasting, ever increasing, engrafted word of life for the salvation of our souls (Jam. 1:21). Repentance from dead works is not the repentance from evil. It is the repentance of the resting place of evil. It is repentance from the works of the dead. To the extent we are made alive to God in our hearts is the degree we can experience the testimony of true life.

When Jesus came into my heart, a love for God erupted from within me. He didn't just love me. He gave me love! I know He gave me love, because I had love in my heart for Him and all that He had done for me. It was the substance of faith (Heb. 11:1). That faith motivated me to tell everyone I knew about the amazing grace of God's love that had entered my heart. I began to tell others

32

about the love of Christ immediately. My heart was motivated to tell them! It wasn't an act of obligation. It was an expression of the freedom I had found in the power of God's grace. The repentance of dead works wasn't a doctrine that I had learned. It was a reality that had taken place in my heart. I was dead, but now I was alive in Christ. My heart had changed! I positioned my mind to believe everything of Him. I grew daily in my experience. I remember a specific incident that happened one week after I was saved. I had smoked two packs of cigarettes every day for several years. I had tried to quit smoking at times, only to start again. I was actually good at quitting smoking. The problem was, I was also good at starting! One week after my conversion, I had a supernatural experience from God in regard to my issue of smoking. I was sitting in my car, smoking a cigarette. The Holy Spirit asked me a question. He spoke as the voice of Jesus to my heart. He said, "Do you love Me?" I immediately responded in my heart with a tear of joy to say I loved Him. He then said to me, "If you love Me, quit smoking". Without hesitation I threw my cigarettes away. It was absolutely miraculous! I went a week without any desire of smoking! It felt so abnormal to me. I decided to light up a cigarette one week later, just to see what would happen. It was amazing! I became sick in my heart and physically nauseated. My heart had changed! There was no desire to smoke! I had been completely delivered from my addiction. It wasn't merely an act on my part to change my action. It was an act on God's part to change my desires. I was alive to God in the area that I had been in bondage to cigarettes!

Repentance doesn't always work that quickly, but it is always an act of grace on God's part. It is a decision of mind on our part, but it is a decision of grace on God's part. God literally changes the desire of our hearts! Repentance is a substance of life that comes from the Spirit of the Lord and the Tree of Life!

I believe repentance is one of the most misunderstood subjects in the Church. We confess that we repent of this, and we repent of that. We repent for the dog, the cat, grandma, and cousin Jim! I don't believe it is possible to repent for someone else. We can intercede and ask forgiveness. We can ask God that He would grant us repentance from the consequence of generational iniquity. We can ask Him to grant a changed heart to a people or even a nation, but I don't believe it is humanly possible to repent without the empowerment of the grace of God. Repentance is not merely a confession of our mouths; it is an act of grace on God's part in changing the desires of our hearts. It is the grace of the Spirit of the Lord at work in our lives!

I believe repentance is a heavenly empowered act of grace on God's part.

33

The Seven Eyes of Grace

It is a change of government. The government of the knowledge of good and evil could not produce true repentance. Repentance is a changed thinker, not merely adjusted thoughts. Repentance is a changed thought source. It is a changed heart. It is not something that is possible by mere knowledge of good and evil. It is a transformation of the dead heart to come alive in Christ! True repentance is the ability to present our bodies a living sacrifice to God (Rom. 12:1). We tried to do works for God, but we ourselves were dead! God has made a way through the Man, Christ Jesus, to empower us to be born-again. We can be born alive to God again. We can receive the Spirit of the Lord and freely offer our bodies as living sacrifices to God.

How does the burnt offering relate to the grace of the Spirit of the Lord and the repentance from dead works? Before we can understand how the two correlate to one another, we must understand how the type and shadow related to humanity under the government of the knowledge of good and evil. In the Old Covenant, the burnt offering was an offering for sin. If someone committed the sin of transgression, that is they unintentionally sinned against God, they would go to the priest with an offering whereby the priest could make atonement for their sins (Num. 15:22-29). There was another law for the person who knew something was wrong and did it anyway. This was the law of the sin of presumption. If a person committed a sin presumptuously, or in defiance of the Law, he would be cut off from God's people forever (Num. 15:30, 31). The information was clear, and the consequences were plain to see. Jesus did an amazing thing upon His death upon our cross. Though the executing crowd knew what they were doing, He said some powerful eternal words. He said, "Father, forgive them, for they do not know what they do" (Lk. 23:34). In these amazing words, Jesus released every person on planet earth to the sin of transgression. If we are truly honest, we will have to admit that our rejection of Christ was also knowingly. We knew the truth within us, but it wasn't until we accepted that truth that we found the free forgiveness that is in Christ. We were all really guilty of the sin of presumption, but Christ released us to the sin of transgression. All we have to do is acknowledge our sin when the Holy Spirit convicts our hearts and simply receive the forgiveness of our sins through the gift of God's mercy in Christ.

Without the shedding of blood there can be no remission of our sins (Heb. 9:22; 10:16-18). Jesus shed His blood to remove the condemnation of our lives. Through His shed blood, our sins were remitted before God (Mt. 26:28). His sacrifice was not so we could be forgiven of our evil. It was so we could gain victory over our dead condition! Jesus was the burnt offering

34

for our sins, that we might be granted repentance from dead works. Our lives that we now live, we live by faith in Christ (Gal. 2:20). We are justified by faith and not by works that we have done (Rom. 1:17; Gal. 3:11; Heb. 10:38). It was the death of Jesus Christ that justified us to live, but the key word is "live" (Rom. 5:8-10).

When someone's life truly changes in Christ, it is not due to right information. It is the power of Christ's transformation! It has more to do with life in Christ than it does with death to our old life. It is about putting on Christ, not merely putting off the old man. To find our lives, we have to lose our lives (Mt. 10:39; 16:25; Mk. 8:35; Lk. 9:24; 17:33). The secret is, however, we find our lives! In order to live, we have to die, but the secret is that we live! Dead religion will put us into the bondage of condemnation and control. Life in Christ will liberate us into the freedom of the Spirit of the Lord (2 Cor. 3:17, 18). The Spirit of Life in Christ Jesus puts the deeds of the flesh to death. It is not by the decision of the human will that our hearts can change! It's not about death; it's about life!

Rom. 8:13 For if you live according to the flesh you will die; but if by the Spirit you put to death the deeds of the body, you will live.

Too many sermons have been preached concerning killing the things of the flesh. Jesus brought us the good news of the change that comes by His Spirit of Life. He is the One who writes a letter upon our hearts and changes the desires of our ways (2 Cor. 3:3). Repentance is not merely a change of our actions. It is a change of character, nature, and way. Repentance bears the fruit of life. John the Baptist preached the need for true repentance, but only Jesus was able to "grant" repentance to us.

(NKJ) Mt. 3:8 "Therefore bear fruits worthy of repentance"...
(NLT) "Prove by the way you live that you have really turned from your sins and turned to God."

Repentance is commanded, but it is not a command to merely change our behavior (Acts 17:26-31). It is a command to receive God's grace of the Spirit of the Lord to come to life in Christ. We can only present our bodies as living sacrifices to God if we ourselves are alive in Him! It is an act of grace on God's part that initiates a true action of life on our part.

One day I was driving my truck down the road and God spoke to me. He said, "Grace is the evidence that I live in your house, and peace is the evidence that you live in Mine." No wonder Paul continued to pray that grace and peace would be multiplied to the Church! Grace is not a cover-up for our sins or an excuse for our carnal behavior. It is a government grant from the government of life. The knowledge of good and evil was a government of death. It was an administration of works, and those works were the fruit of a dead administration. They were dead works! Jesus came to give us a new government. He came to give us an administration of grace (Gal. 4:4-7; Eph. 1:10). It is the empowerment of the Spirit of Christ within and upon our lives to grant us the character, nature, way, power, and authority of Christ! The more that God reveals Himself in our lives, the more grace we know! His grace is fully real for everyone, but it is only fully experienced by those who receive His government "grants" of grace.

NOTE: Stop and allow the Holy Spirit to minister to you in regard to the subject of this chapter reading.

Chapter 1.4

The First Eye of Grace

Grace is a power from heaven. Grace is not a cover-up for our weaknesses. It is the power of God's strength made known to our weaknesses. This is true for the issue of repentance. God determined that in Christ we would be delivered from the bondage of death into the liberty of His life! Evil and wicked ways are merely the fruit of dead lives. The strongholds of the enemy inhabit the dry places of our lives. Those are the dead places within our hearts. It is the Spirit of the Lord that grants us repentance from those dead places in our hearts. The Spirit of the Lord is a grace from heaven sent to deliver us from the root cause of the dead works of our lives.

The grace of the Spirit of the Lord is granted to those who call upon the Lordship of Christ. We do not need a word from heaven pertaining to what we must do in life. The Law was sufficient in telling us what to do. It was sufficient in knowledge, but it lacked the ability to give us intimacy with God. It was perfect information, but it lacked the ability to bring God's transformation to our lives. It told us the "what to do", but it failed to give us the "want to do". It is the Spirit of the Lord that grants us a changed heart. The Spirit of the Lord is one of *Seven Eyes of Grace* brought to our lives by the presence of the Holy Spirit (Isa. 11:2).

Let me relate to you another story in my life pertaining to the grace of the Spirit of the Lord and repentance from dead works. As a young Christian, I was filled with a passion for Christ. I loved God to the best of my ability, yet there was an area in my life that I wrestled with immensely. It involved an action that I regretted often. I repeatedly tried to change my behavior in a certain area. I repeatedly fell to my old behavior of sin. I read the Scriptures and knew that what I was doing was wrong. I was convicted by the Holy Spirit to know clearly that my actions were opposed to the will of God. I would cry and beg for God's forgiveness. I would discipline myself to change in my actions, only to find that after a period of time I would again fail in my actions. I would cry and say I was sorry. One day, I heard a story from a pastor who was a mentor and spiritual father in my life. He related a story that happened in his life as a young preacher. He had smoked cigars for many years. He liked smoking cigars! God had spoken to him in regard to his habit. The Holy Spirit had convicted his heart that as a young preacher he shouldn't be in bondage to smoking cigars. He tried to discipline his lifestyle, only to find that he repeatedly failed in his actions. He would smoke a cigar and then he would cry and confess repentance to God. He would beg for forgiveness and confess that he was sorry. This went on for a long time. One day, after falling to the temptation of smoking cigars, he approached God with his typical prayer of repentance. He told God he was sorry for smoking the cigar. He confessed to God that he didn't want to smoke cigars anymore. God confronted him in his confession. God said, "You liar! You love cigars!" He had to admit it was true. He told God, "You are right! I love cigars! I'd make sandwiches out of them if I could, but I know You don't want me to smoke them anymore. God, would You change my want to? God, would You change my heart?" God changed his heart, and he found the victory over his addiction! That story changed my life! I grabbed hold of the principle immediately. I told God that I loved my problem. My problem wasn't a "what to do", it was a "want to do". I asked Jesus to be the Lord of my want to. He granted me a gift. It was the power of the grace of the Spirit of the Lord. It was a grant of repentance from dead works. My heart was dead to God in an area; therefore, my legitimate need was being met in an illegitimate way. I had a false lord in my life. An area of wickedness was residing in the dead area of my heart. God changed the desire of my heart. I was instantly delivered from that area of warfare in my life. I was delivered from the temptation of that false life source in my life. The Spirit of the Lord motivated my heart to the overcoming grace of passionate love for God. I was released from my addictive problem by a grace of returning to my first love in that area of my heart that had been bound to the life-taking distraction. The grace of the Spirit of the Lord had changed my heart. I had come alive to God and was no longer bound to the dead work of sin in that area of my life.

I have since told God that I don't want Him to merely tell me what to do in life. I want Him to go deeper than that. I want Him to be the Lord of my "want to". I want Him to be the Lord of my heart! I want Him to literally give me the desires of my heart. I am not talking about what I want, but what He wants in my life. My problem was not one of smoking, like the preacher had shared. My problem was totally different, but the Holy Spirit revealed to me that my problem was the same in its root. My problem was a wrong desire in my heart. There was an area of my heart that was dead to God and alive to my problem of carnality. We cannot overcome the strongholds of the flesh by resisting the power of the flesh. We have to become empowered to walk in the Spirit! This will cause a true change of our hearts!

Gal. 5:16 I say then: Walk in the Spirit, and you shall not fulfill the lust of the flesh.

Dead works are obvious (Gal. 5:19-21). They produce death! They are things like adultery, fornication, pornography, or some other form of sexual perversion. We may have been sexually abused as a child and an area of our heart has become dead to healthy relationships. Our perverted thoughts may be the result of a generational iniquity inherited through our parents. Dead works include the idolization of worldly things, addiction to ministry, vanity, or addiction to demonic influences. It may be that in our search to satisfy the emptiness within our hearts we ended up in bondage to some cult or occult. Dead works are works of the flesh like hatred, contentions, jealousies, outbursts of wrath, or selfish ambitions. They are often implanted and inspired by unjust things that have happened to us in our lives. We may have been abused, so we entertain hatred in our hearts. We may have been overlooked as a child, so we wrestle with the envy of others. We may have experienced physical abuse, so we think thoughts of murder in our heart. The pressures of life or the realities of an imperfect world may inspire us to live a lifestyle of drunkenness, drug addiction, or some other form of loose living. We may have been wounded by an authority figure, so we do things that cause division in churches, in our marriages, in our families, or in the places we work. It is not that we set out to be wicked or evil. Things happen to us that make us cold in our hearts, bitter in our attitudes, and restrained in our hopes. We become dry in our hearts. We die inside, so we look for life in the things we do. All of these are dead works, and they produce death. We cannot change our lives by merely changing our actions. We need a healing inside! We need a change in our hearts. We need to come alive inside to the life of God's Spirit! We need the power of His grace! When we find the grace of God's Spirit, we find that life happens! Something living begins to grow inside of us. Living things bear fruit!

Gal. 5:22 But the fruit of the Spirit is love, joy, peace, longsuffering, kindness, goodness, faithfulness, 23 gentleness, self-control. Against such there is no law.

The fruit of the Spirit is not something we can do. It is living and it grows out of a living heart. The grace of the Spirit of the Lord makes us alive in our hearts toward God. The desires of our hearts change! Against the fruit of the Spirit there is no law, because those things are alive, and they cannot be overpowered my mere things. They are a freedom, not a rule! They are an act of passion, not an act of discipline. They are the result of a changed life by the power of God's life-changing grace!

It is the grace of the Spirit of the Lord that changes our hearts. He returns us to our first love! He literally gives us God's desires within our hearts. Without God in our hearts, we are left with a path that seems right to us, but it ends in death (Pr. 14:12). To repent, we must acknowledge our need to repent, but God is the one who changes our hearts unto repentance.

> *Rom. 3:20 For no one can ever be made right in God's sight by doing what his law commands. For the more we know God's law, the clearer it becomes that we aren't obeying it. 21 But now God has shown us a different way of being right in his sight-not by obeying the law but by the way promised in the Scriptures long ago. 22 We are made right in God's sight when we trust in Jesus Christ to take away our sins. And we all can be saved in this same way, no matter who we are or what we have done. 23 For all have sinned; all fall short of God's glorious standard. 24 Yet now God in his gracious kindness declares us not guilty. He has done this through Christ Jesus, who has freed us by taking away our sins. 25 For God sent Jesus to take the punishment for our sins and to satisfy God's anger against us. We are made right with God when we believe that Jesus shed his blood, sacrificing his life for us. God was being entirely fair and just when he did not punish those who sinned in former times. 26 And he is entirely fair and just in this present time when he declares sinners to be right in his sight because they believe in Jesus. NLT*

Repentance is not something a human can do on his own. The information of being wrong is not enough to change our lives. The Law was sufficient to show us where we were wrong, but it could never make us right with God. It is a relationship with God in Christ that makes us come alive unto life! Jesus didn't come so that we would know what was wrong in our lives. He came to change our hearts! He came to anoint us to choose life! God has set before us life and death, and the Holy Spirit is here to anoint us to choose life (Deut. 30:19).

NOTE: Once again, I recommend you stop and allow the Holy Spirit to minister to you in regard to the subject of this chapter. Ask the Spirit of the Lord to minister to you as a grace given by God.

Chapter 1.5

The First Eye of Grace

We are very often ignorant to the power of God's grace, because we are so used to a world of information. We think that if we have the right information, we will be able to make correct decisions in life. This is the government of the knowledge of good and evil. Jesus didn't come so that we would know what to do. He came so that we would become a spiritual house for His presence (1 Pet. 2:5). Jesus came so the "want to" of our hearts would change! He came to empower us to love God and to love others as we love ourselves.

> *Heb. 8:10 "For this is the covenant that I will make with the house of Israel: After those days," says the Lord, "I will put My laws in their mind and write them on their hearts; and I will be their God, and they shall be My people. 11 None of them shall teach his neighbor, and none his brother, saying, 'Know the Lord,' for all shall know Me, from the least of them to the greatest of them. 12 For I will be merciful to their unrighteousness, and their sins and their lawless deeds I will remember no more." 13 In that He says, "A new covenant," He has made the first obsolete. Now what is becoming obsolete and growing old is ready to vanish away.*

Jesus didn't come so that we would know what to do. The nation of Israel knew exactly what to do. The real problem with humanity was their hearts. Jesus came so that we would know God. He didn't come so we would repent from being evil. He came so that we would repent from not knowing God. The only way we can know God is to be alive unto Him in the Spirit. It is an act of God's grace! Repentance is not something we do by our own human strength. Repentance is a gift; it is something granted. Israel knew they needed to change in their ways, but Jesus had to come to "give" to them the gift of repentance.

> *Acts 5:31 "Him God has exalted to His right hand to be Prince and Savior, <u>to give repentance</u> to Israel and forgiveness of sins."*

Jesus didn't just come to give the gift of repentance to those who knew what to do; He came to give the gift of repentance to those who didn't even know what to do. He came to become the light of life within the hearts of all people (Jn. 1:4). The first step in the process is to receive the grant of the Spirit of the Lord, a grace gift to repentance from dead works. It is the eating of the Tree of Life and the beginning of life and peace in Him (Rom. 8:6). The power of the Holy Spirit in the life of Cornelius and his family was a testimony to heaven's "grant" of grace!

> *Acts 11:18 When they heard these things they became silent; and they glorified God, saying, "Then God has also granted to the Gentiles repentance to life."*

This process is not just true for us in our initial conversion experience. It is true throughout our entire lives as believers in Christ. Even though we have been made alive in Christ, there are still areas in our hearts that are dead to God. This is why we must work out our own salvation with fear and trembling before God (Phil. 2:12). Apostle Paul told Timothy to correct those who oppose the faith of Christ in a spirit of humility so that God might "perhaps grant them repentance". The implication is that repentance might not be "granted" to them. Repentance is not the remorse for being wrong. It is the power of God's grace to change our hearts!

> *2 Tim. 2:24 And a servant of the Lord must not quarrel but be gentle to all, able to teach, patient, 25 in humility correcting those who are in opposition, if God perhaps will grant them repentance, so that they may know the truth...*

I like to think of it as a "government grant". On my own I was bankrupt. I didn't have any possible means of delivering myself. I could not change my heart. I did not have God's character, nature, way, power, or authority in my life. I knew I needed something, but only God had what I needed. I needed a "grant" from the "government of life". I didn't need a loan! My credit report was a disaster! I could not pay the debt of my sins. I couldn't change my desires. I needed a "grant" from heaven that would never need to be paid back. I needed freedom, not bondage! God gave me that "grant" in His Son Jesus Christ. I knew it was real. He touched my heart, and I was pierced to brokenness.

For many generations, people had the knowledge of good and evil. They had all the information necessary to conclude the need to repent. They lacked the power to repent. Repentance isn't a matter of information. It is a matter of intimacy! It is a matter of love for God and love for others. True repentance is a grace gift from heaven. It comes from the government of God. It comes from the government of grace. It is an administration suitable for the summing up of all things in Christ (Eph. 1:10). It is a heavenly government that changes our hearts to a heavenly condition. It is not imaginary! It is real!

Repentance is not simply being sorry for things that we do wrong. Repentance of dead works is the repentance of a dry place. It is the repentance of a dead place in our lives that allows a changed condition within. It is the power of God that changes a dry dead place to a well-watered place of life. One of the ingredients in the incense of the altar of incense was an ingredient called galbanum (Ex. 30:34). It was an herb root that was very hard and bitter. It was difficult to break, but when it was broken it would release a resin that could be dried and burned. The Israelites would burn this resin to repel snakes and lizards in the dry places of the wilderness. This ingredient in the incense revealed a secret to the deliverance from dry places in our hearts. Dry places are the strongholds of demonic influences. Only true brokenness of the heart repels the influence of demonic strongholds in our lives. The application for a grant of repentance is to truly have a broken or contrite heart.

2 Cor. 7:9 Now I rejoice, not that you were made sorry, but that your sorrow led to repentance. For you were made sorry in a godly manner, that you might suffer loss from us in nothing. 10 For godly sorrow produces repentance to salvation, not to be regretted; but the sorrow of the world produces death.

I have experienced the grace of the Spirit of the Lord and the gift of repentance from dead works many times in my life. On every occasion, I experienced a sorrow that led to the grant of repentance. It is kind of like the application form for the government grant. We do not qualify for a grant from the government of life unless we fill out the right application form. The application form begins with a sorrow in our hearts. We have to want the grant of repentance from the source of those dead works in our lives. We must desire the change. That desire must come from deep within our hearts.

I used to have a problem with anger. I am not the kind of guy that gets angry often, but when I would get angry it would be a doozy! My anger problem didn't just disappear when I became a Christian. I had been delivered from drugs and alcohol. I had been delivered from smoking. I had been delivered from pornography and many areas of carnal mindedness. Even though I had experienced the grace of repentance from dead works in many areas of my life,

The Seven Eyes of Grace

I still had a problem with the dead work of anger. I consistently experienced outbursts of wrath in my life. It was almost always when I had a legitimate reason to be angry. However, my legitimate reasons didn't justify my illegitimate actions. I remember one time driving down the road as a young single man. I had known Jesus for a few years. I was frustrated because of work, because of having to live with other single guys, because of life! I remember hitting the dashboard of my truck in my fit of anger. When I did, the dashboard cracked from front to back. I felt terrible! I asked God for forgiveness and even experienced tears of sorrow. As sorry as I was, I couldn't change my heart. My anger problem continued into my married life. There were occasions where my anger scared my family. It wasn't often, but on a wrong day in a wrong circumstance my outburst of wrath would manifest on some tool, some bucket, or some thing that would be thrown across a room or into the yard. I had a dead area in my heart that was filled with the dead work of anger. Although I was sorry in my heart, I hadn't really come to the place of a broken or contrite heart. I remember a particular event that took place. It was instrumental in bringing me to the place of true brokenness. I had been working on building a log house that I built from scratch in the middle of the woods in the mountains. It was a frustrating day. Nothing was going right. I was angry! My tractor wasn't cooperating with my need at the time. The battery had died and it wouldn't start! It was a moment in the day that was the culmination of a day that "nothing was going right". I had a bad attitude, and I knew it. Something caught my attention from the corner of my eye. I looked to the corner of the house and there was my five-year-old boy on his knees praying. I was broken! I knew I was an idiot! I was a jerk, and I was not being a good example to that little boy that was expressing his love for his daddy and his appeal to God for help. I knew he was praying my tractor would start. I confessed to God, "I'm an idiot. I don't deserve anything from You, but that's Your son praying over there. Don't start this tractor for me. Start this tractor for Your son over there." I hit the starter button on the tractor one more time. It started immediately! I knew it was an act of God's love for me and my son. I was broken in my heart. I knew I needed the grace of a changed heart. There were a few times after that I had a moment of anger, but that moment was a key to the process of receiving the grant from heaven to repent of the dead work of anger. God delivered me by the power of His grace, but I had to fill out the application for His grant of grace. I had to come to the place where I wasn't just sorry. I had to come to the place my heart was broken.

NOTE: It is time to allow the Holy Spirit to help you apply the reality of the material found in this chapter. Let him transform any dry places of your heart to life-giving places by His grace.

Chapter 1.6

The First Eye of Grace

The grant of the grace of repentance from dead works doesn't just come to our lives because Jesus paid the price for it to happen. We also have to be in agreement with the conditions for the grant. We cannot just believe for the gift of a changed heart. We must also renounce our old way!

> *Ps. 119:58 I entreated Your favor with my whole heart; Be merciful to me according to Your word. 59 I thought about my ways, and turned my feet to Your testimonies. 60 I made haste, and did not delay to keep Your commandments.*

> *2 Cor. 7:11 Just see what this godly sorrow produced in you! Such earnestness, such concern to clear yourselves, such indignation, such alarm, such longing to see me, such zeal, and such a readiness to punish the wrongdoer. You showed that you have done everything you could to make things right. (NLT)*

We must make a confession with our mouths and with the actions of our lives that are in agreement with the grant of repentance given to us from heaven's throne of grace (Heb. 4:16). God gives us the grace of repentance, but we must be willing to follow through with actions that agree with His grant of repentance to our lives. We cannot despise the grace that He gives. We must never receive His grace in vain (2 Cor. 6:1). It is possible to fall short of the grace of God, so we must stand on His word and the leading of His Spirit in the process of His transformation (Heb. 12:15; Rom. 12:1, 2). If we are obedient to our confession of His grace of repentance from dead works, we will be recipients of the same. There is a demonstration of power that comes into our lives when His repentance is granted to us. REPENTANCE leads to FORGIVENESS through JESUS CHRIST and a changed life. A revelation of FORGIVENESS also leads to the empowerment of REPENTANCE.

45

The Seven Eyes of Grace

1 Jn 1:9 If we confess our sins, He is faithful and just to forgive us our sins and to cleanse us from all unrighteousness.

Ps. 32:1 Blessed is he whose transgression is forgiven, whose sin is covered. 2 Blessed is the man to whom the LORD does not impute iniquity, and in whose spirit there is no guile. 3 When I kept silent, my bones grew old through my groaning all the day long. 4 For day and night Your hand was heavy upon me; my vitality was turned into the drought of summer. Selah 5 I acknowledged my sin to You, and my iniquity I have not hidden. I said, "I will confess my transgressions to the LORD," and You forgave the iniquity of my sin. Selah

Rom. 5:8 But God demonstrates His own love toward us, in that while we were still sinners, Christ died for us.

John the Baptist preached repentance according to the Law. Unfortunately, many times believers seek to be people of the "book" and forget that it is a heartfelt relationship with God in Christ that transforms us. We must never be content to be a PERSON OF THE BOOK! We must desire HIS WAYS more than an INTRODUCTION to who He is. We must desire FELLOWSHIP WITH Him as a person, more than KNOWLEDGE ABOUT Him. Anything short of intimacy with God in Christ is less than true Christianity. We will be no different than the Pharisees of Jesus' day. It is not the knowledge of good and evil that changes our lives. It is intimacy with the Tree of Life! Grace is a power of heaven sent to change our lives! The Spirit of the Lord is a grace of the Holy Spirit in our lives sent to transform us into the brightness of the Father's glory and the express image of His person (Heb. 1:3). Our lives must increasingly become a testimony of being the weight of the Father's influence and the substance of His person to others in the world in which we live.

Jn. 5:39 "You search the Scriptures, for in them you think you have eternal life; and these are they which testify of Me."

REPENTANCE is 'a change of mind' which allows God to change our hearts, resulting in a changed life. The process is simple and yet profound. To receive the grace of repentance from dead works, we have to present our bodies in the right place. We have to make a commitment to truth, and then understand that it is God's part to transform our thinking by the power of His Spirit. The transformation comes by the renewing of our minds. The renewing of our minds is like the metamorphosis of a butterfly. There is actually a physical and spiritual change that takes place! One thing becomes another! Our old minds become our new minds in Christ by the power of Christ's Spirit within us. It is only possible when we present our bodies to God as living sacrifices. We must be committed to the Spirit, not merely committed to being delivered from our past.

> *Rom. 12:1 And so, dear Christian friends, [12:1 Greek brothers.] I plead with you to give your bodies to God. Let them be a living and holy sacrifice-the kind he will accept. When you think of what he has done for you, is this too much to ask? 2 Don't copy the behavior and customs of this world, but let God transform you into a new person by changing the way you think. Then you will know what God wants you to do, and you will know how good and pleasing and perfect his will really is. (The Message)*

Let's review the process of repentance from dead works. Our problem is not that we are evil. Our problem is that we are a habitation for evil things. Areas of our hearts are dead unto God and have therefore become resting places for strongholds of earthly, sensual, and demonic influences. We cannot possibly change by receiving the right information of good or evil. We can only change by the empowerment of life in Christ! We need to repent from being dead! This is humanly impossible, but heavenly real for all who come to God in Christ. The Holy Spirit has come to convict our heart of sin (Jn. 16:8). It is sin to be separated from our life source, which is God. We live and move and have our being in Him. We were created to live on the expressions that come from Him. We must be joined to Him in every way. The dead areas of our hearts keep us separate from Him and His life. We need to be reconnected to Him unashamedly and in every way!

When the Holy Spirit convicts our hearts, we are prompted to consider our ways. We are moved in our hearts with sorrow for our transgressions toward God. We experience brokenness in our hearts. Our response is to renounce our old ways and to ask God that He would grant us a change of heart. God acts by granting us a power from heaven! It is not earned on our part. It is simply properly applied for. It is free to us from heaven's bank of glory! It is not a loan! It is not purchased! It is a GRANT from God that changes our hearts. It is the grace of the dominion of the Spirit of the Lord! It happens by presenting our bodies as a living sacrifice and a demonstration of our trust that God will grant us the grace of the Spirit of the Lord to change our hearts. We need to have new desires within us, not actions about us. We must present our bodies to receive the change. The change doesn't happen because we present our bodies. The change comes because God grants us repentance unto life. Repentance is God's response of grace when we ask Him for His power of grace. It is a commitment on our part to stay in relationship with Him. It is a first love response. We give our lives to Him! We present our bodies to Him! We choose to enter the chamber of change where God changes our ways.

Having been a pastor of a congregation of believers, I have found there are many times that relationships get broken because of misunderstandings and offenses of some kind. I have been wounded and hurt many times over the years by people misunderstanding me, speaking evil of me, and ultimately leaving me and the ministry God has entrusted to my care. It has been very difficult at times, but it is a part of "church life". Every pastor experiences the pain and suffering of broken relationships. I have little control over the decisions that people make, but I do have charge of my response to the decisions they make. I have learned to practice forgiving people in my heart. I have practiced believing the best for those who have left my life for wrong or confused reasons. Even though I know all the right things to do, I have to rely upon God's grace to empower me to move on when I am wounded. There have been a couple of times where I have been tempted to quit everything and forget about caring for the flock of God. I have been tempted to get a secular job and walk away from it all. When I have entertained these thoughts, I have practiced sin. I have practiced allowing my heart to die to God and to the wonderful responsibility He has given me. There have been times where the warfare in my mind has become so intense, I could hardly stand it. I had one such time where I entertained thoughts ranging from quitting the ministry, pursuing other ministry, getting a job, and even committing suicide. All of those thoughts were dead works formulating from a dead area in my heart. They were the fruit of being dead to God and the vision He had given me. I am not condoning them; I am confessing them for your sake. I found a key to the amazing grace of the Spirit of the Lord and repentance from dead works. I had to be broken in my heart and make a commitment to God's will in my life. In one such case it included selling my house and buying a new house in my city. I had to make a fresh commitment to presenting my body a living sacrifice in the place that God has joined me. I couldn't just say that I would stay committed to the people and the vision God had entrusted to me. I had to actually buy a new house and confess a permanent commitment to the place of my planting. When I took that action, God miraculously changed my heart! He granted the grace of repentance from my dead works! I fell in love with the people again. I fell in love with God again! I fell in love with my calling in Him again! It was a grant from heaven. I didn't earn it! I didn't pay for it! I simply positioned myself to receive it, but it included making a commitment. I had to present my body a living sacrifice in order to receive a changed mind and a changed heart!

When the Holy Spirit convicts our hearts, we must make a commitment to God. We must present our bodies as living sacrifices to Him. We must put our minds to the place of our commitment. Then we must allow God to bring us through the chamber of change. We must allow God to GRANT us new desires in our hearts.

Make a Commitment

A presented body = a changed mind = a changed heart = a changed action = a changed reality

It is the GRACE of THE SPIRIT OF THE LORD, A burnt offering – A LIVING SACRIFICE!

NOTE: Take time to meditate again on the subject of repentance and the Spirit of the Lord. Allow the Holy Spirit to minister to you in a personal way throughout your day.

49

Chapter 1.1 – 1.6 - The First Eye of Grace

Statements and Questions to Consider for a Group Discussion:

1. Read Heb. 10:5-7; 6:1, 2; Deut. 12:5, 6 & Acts 2:37, 38. Discuss how these Scriptures relate to one another. Discuss the differences of an administration of information and an administration of transformation.

2. What does it mean for the Christian believer to find the place that God chooses for them to go and for His name to abide?

3. When we find the divine place of God's choosing, we can experience the full dynamic of seven offerings. The first of those offerings is the "burnt offering". Discuss this level of relationship in the Body of Christ.

4. What is the difference between Conscience & Law and Grace? Define Grace.

5. What is the first of the sevenfold graces of God? Define "repentance" as a group.

6. What is the difference between repentance in the Old Covenant and repentance in the New Covenant? John's message of repentance concerned the requirements of the Law. Jesus commands repentance in accordance with the power of His grace. How do these two differ?

7. Why is it that repentance is not merely an act of the human will? What does it mean for repentance to be by the empowerment of God's grace within the human heart? What are some personal examples in the group?

8. Repentance from dead works is not the repentance from evil. It is the repentance of the resting place of evil. Dead places are dry places. Discuss what those dry places look like. Are there any personal testimonies in the group?

9. Repentance is not merely a confession of our mouths; it is an act of grace on God's part in changing the desires of our hearts. It is a transformation of the dead heart to come alive in Christ. Are there any personal testimonies in the group?

10. Discuss how repentance is not merely a change of our actions. It is a change of character, nature, and way.

11. The Law was sufficient in telling us what to do. It was sufficient in knowledge, but it lacked intimacy with God. It was perfect information, but it lacked the ability to bring God's transformation to our lives. What is the difference between knowing what to do and knowing God the person?

12. The grace of the Spirit of the Lord makes us alive in our hearts toward God. It is the grace of the Spirit of the Lord that changes our hearts. He returns us to our

first love. Has anyone returned to his or her first love this week?

13. The first step in the process of repentance is to receive the grant of the Spirit of the Lord, a grace gift to repentance from dead works. Repentance comes by eating of the Tree of Life and it brings life and peace in Him. What does this look like?

14. Repentance is a matter of love for God and love for others. The application form for repentance begins with a sorrow in our hearts. Discuss this type of sorrow and its effects.

15. The grant of the grace of repentance from dead works doesn't just come to our lives because Jesus paid the price for it to happen. We must also renounce our old ways. How do we renounce our old ways?

16. It is possible to fall short of the grace of God, so we must stand on His word and the leading of His Spirit in the process of His transformation. What does that look like in the process of the grace of the Spirit of the Lord and repentance from dead works? We must be committed to the Spirit, not merely committed to being delivered from our past.

17. Our problem is not that we are evil. Our problem is that we are a habitation for evil things. Areas of our hearts are dead unto God and have therefore become resting places for strongholds of earthly, sensual, and demonic influences. Read Jam. 3:13-18 & Eph. 5:8-21 and discuss what this looks like.

18. When the Holy Spirit convicts our hearts, we are prompted to consider our ways. We are moved in our hearts with sorrow for our transgressions toward God. We experience brokenness in our hearts. Are there any experiences in the group of sorrow to brokenness?

19. Repentance is the grace of the dominion of the Spirit of the Lord! It happens by presenting our bodies as a living sacrifice and a demonstration of our trust that God will grant us the grace of the Spirit of the Lord to change our hearts. What does presenting our bodies as a living sacrifice look like?

20. When the Holy Spirit convicts our hearts, we must make a commitment to God. We must present our bodies as living sacrifices to Him. We must put our minds to the place of our commitment. Then we must allow God to bring us through the chamber of change. We must allow God to GRANT us new desires in our hearts. Discuss how a presented body = a changed mind = a changed heart = a changed action = a changed reality.

51

Chapter 2.1

The Second Eye of Grace

- The Spirit of Wisdom

In these next five chapters we will look at the second of the *Seven Eyes of Grace*. The second grace is the Spirit of Wisdom. It is a grace of the Holy Spirit at work in our lives allowing us to do works that speak of our faith. Whereas the Spirit of the Lord reveals that we are justified by faith, the Spirit of Wisdom anoints and activates us to do works that speak of our faith. In the Old Testament, the book of Proverbs is known as the book of wisdom. It is filled with many proverbs and practical instructions given by Solomon pertaining to the wisdom of God. In the New Testament the book of James is filled with instructions concerning the wisdom of God. The book starts by encouraging anyone who lacks wisdom to ask for it from God (Jam. 1:5). All of the chapters of the book of James are filled with instructions pertaining to doing works that speak of our faith. We must again remember that it is not works that justifies any of us. We must also know that if in fact we are justified by faith in Christ, the lives we now live we should live by faith in Christ. James says that our faith is revealed by our works, for without works faith is dead (Jam. 2:20, 26). It is interesting to note that the two earliest writings of the New Testament are the books of Galatians and James. One deals with being justified by faith and the other deals with doing works that speak of our faith. The two books do not contradict one another, for Paul was not saying that the church of Galatia should not do works. He was simply correcting them for thinking that works are necessary in order to be justified. It is by faith that we are saved! James was not saying that works would substitute faith. He was saying that faith is proved to be real by the actions we take and the works that we do that testify of our faith. In either case, works justify no one, but works will testify to the fact that we have been justified.

We must again understand that this second grace is a power of transformation given to us by God in Christ. It is not merely doing works. It is doing works that are anointed and motivated by the Spirit of Wisdom. This *Eye of Grace* is part of the perfecting anointing of the Holy Spirit in and upon our lives as members of the Body of Christ. Let us refresh our minds to know God's real desire of us. He never desired sacrifices and offerings. He wanted a Body. He wanted a place for His presence to abide. God has always desired a spiritual house wherein He could dwell.

> *Heb. 10:5 Therefore, when He came into the world, He said: "Sacrifice and offering You did not desire, but a body You have prepared for Me. 6 In burnt offerings and sacrifices for sin you had no pleasure. 7 Then I said, 'Behold, I have come—in the volume of the book it is written of Me—to do Your will, O God.'"*

To understand the grace of the Spirit of the Lord and repentance from dead works, we looked at the offering of the Old Testament known as the "burnt offering". We saw how the "burnt offering" testified of our love relationship with God in Christ. It revealed that Jesus died once for us all that we might no longer be bound to the life of the flesh, but that we might be motivated by the Spirit of the Lord to present our bodies as living sacrifices to God in Christ. The "burnt offering" of the Old Testament was nothing more than the shadow cast from heaven concerning the living Body of Christ and a level of relationship made known when we return to our first love. Paradise has been restored in Christ whereby we may freely eat of the Tree of Life and know that we are justified by faith. The desires of our hearts can be made new in Christ. We can receive the desires of God within us that will motivate us to love Him. God has given to us an administration of grace. We are not seeking to repent from being evil. We are empowered by the grace of God to repent from being dead. The dead works of our old life in First Adam are exchanged with a passion to love God in the Last Adam. The first foundation of grace that we find in our relationship with God in Christ is that of the Spirit of the Lord and repentance from dead works (Heb. 6:1).

The *Second Eye of Grace* is the Spirit of Wisdom. It directly relates to the foundation found in Christ known as "faith toward God" (Heb. 6:1). It is not a doctrine concerning what we believe about faith toward God. It is actual "faith toward God". It motivates us to do works that speak of our faith. It is the grace of the Spirit of Wisdom that allows us to do things we've never seen, heard, or thought of before. To understand this grace, we must look at the shadow cast from the Body in heaven to the Old Testament requirements of the past. Remember, the Old Testament was a shadow of that which is made real in Christ. It was a shadow of things yet to come. That shadow was merely an imprint of information concerning the real image in heaven. The light of God shown through the image of life and cast an exact imprint called the shadow of the truth of Christ. We can see this clearly in the seven sacrifices and offerings that were required in the place where God chose His name to abide for each of the tribes of Israel.

> *Deut. 12:5 "But <u>you shall seek the place where the LORD your God chooses, out of all your tribes, to put His name for His habitation; and there you shall go</u>. 6 There <u>you shall take</u> your [1]<u>burnt offerings</u>, your [2] <u>sacrifices</u>, your [3]<u>tithes</u>, the [4]<u>heave offerings</u> of your hand, your [5]<u>vowed offerings</u>, your [6]<u>freewill offerings</u>, and the [7]<u>firstlings of your herds and flocks</u>. 7 And there you shall eat before the LORD your God, and you shall rejoice in all to which you have put your hand, you and your households, in which the LORD your God has blessed you."*

The second of the required offerings was one known as "sacrifices". What kind of sacrifice does God require? The only true sacrifice that God desires is a sacrifice of faith. Faith is testified by acts of love. Faith works by love (Gal. 5:6). To understand this act of "sacrifices", we must also understand that it is a gift of grace. Sacrifices are not merely works we decide to do. These are not works that we do in an attempt to be justified. They are not works that we do in an attempt to be loved. We are not trying to earn God's acceptance. We have God's acceptance! When Jesus was baptized by John in the River Jordan, the heavens opened up and the voice of God was heard.

> *Mt. 3:16 Then Jesus, when He had been baptized, came up immediately from the water; and behold, the heavens were opened to Him, and He saw the Spirit of God descending like a dove and alighting upon Him. 17 And suddenly a voice came from heaven, saying, "This is My beloved Son, in whom I am well pleased."*

The baptism of Jesus was a work that spoke of His faith toward God. He didn't get water baptized that He might be clean. He didn't get water baptized so that He would be saved. He got water baptized so that all righteousness might be fulfilled (Mt. 3:15). He did it so that His relationship of faith toward God might be known. When Jesus completed this act of obedience to faith, God's voice was heard announcing His favor. Jesus hadn't healed a single sick person. He hadn't preached a single sermon. He hadn't raised anyone from the dead. He hadn't turned water to wine, walked on water, or made known that He was the Living Water sent from heaven. God's favor was not upon the life of Jesus as a MAN because of the things that He had done. God's favor was simply upon His life; therefore, Jesus could freely walk by faith and consistently and continually do works that spoke of His faith. He was anointed with the grace of the Spirit of Wisdom.

I believe we can correlate this grace of the Spirit of Wisdom and faith toward God to another action found in Acts, Chapter Two. Acts Chapter Two reveals the testimony of the anointing of the Body of Christ upon the earth from the throne of grace in heaven. The Spirit poured out upon the Church was the sevenfold Spirit of God's grace. It was the presence, anointing, and power of the Holy Spirit upon the Branch (Isa. 11:1, 2). Holy Spirit is a Spirit of Jubilee for all who find themselves as members of the Body of Christ. This is confirmed in the fact that the Holy Spirit was poured out upon the full flesh Body of Christ at the culmination of the feast of Pentecost. Let's add a second level of relationship to the anointing of the Body of Christ:

> *Acts 2:38 Then Peter said to them, "<u>Repent</u>, and let every one of you be baptized in the name of Jesus Christ for the remission of sins"...*

Peter addressed the crowd and testified that those who believe in Christ must "be baptized in the name of Jesus Christ for the remission of sins". Water baptism is an act of faith. We are not justified through water baptism. We are justified by the grant of repentance from dead works that comes by grace. It is the grace of the Spirit of the Lord that transforms us from a life of dead works to a born-again life of love for God. That love for God inspires us to faith. Just as the Holy Spirit's expression of the Spirit of the Lord changes the desires of our hearts, the Holy Spirit's expression of the Spirit of Wisdom inspires our hearts to do works that speak of our faith toward God. Water baptism is a first work of faith and is to be one act among countless acts of our faith toward God. Water baptism reveals the truth of every act of faith we do in Christ. Water baptism testifies to the fact that we died in Christ, were buried in Christ, and have risen to a new life in Him (Rom. 6:4)! That new life has no fear of death, since water baptism is an act that testifies of the once-for-all death of Christ. By this act of faith, we can know that every action we take of faith toward God has no fear of death in it. Not even the second death, the final eternal death, has any power over us (Rev. 2:11). Works that speak of our faith are acts of relationship that testify of "sacrifices" of faith. We depend upon the wisdom of God! Experience is not our best teacher. The Holy Spirit is! He is revealing things to us we have not seen, heard, or thought of before. We are inspired by the grace of the Spirit of Wisdom. No one is saved by water baptism. We are saved by the grace of the Spirit of the Lord! Water baptism is important, however. It is a work that speaks of our faith! I was water baptized eight months after my "born-again" experience. I didn't understand then what I do now concerning this essential act of faith. My action was one of faith, however. It didn't justify me before God. It testified to God, to angels, and to men that I was a member of the Body of Christ. I wanted to declare that the life I now live, I live by faith in Christ (Gal. 2:20). My actions in this life are motivated by the grace of the Spirit of Wisdom from the throne of grace in heaven.

We have faith toward God by the Spirit of Wisdom at work in our lives. Faith toward God is faith filled and fear empty. Faith toward God is not the fear of circumstances. Many people confuse faith toward God with the fear of circumstances. They read their Bibles, because they believe they are in trouble if they don't. They pray, because they are afraid something bad will happen if they don't. They tell others about Jesus, because they believe they will be in trouble if they don't. Do you see the pattern here? I don't read my Bible because I am in trouble if I don't. I read my Bible, because I live on every word that comes from the mouth of God! Reading my Bible helps me hear His voice! I don't pray because I am in trouble if I don't. I pray, because I have faith to develop my relationship with God in this life! I don't tell others about Jesus because I am in trouble if I don't. I tell people about Jesus, because He is wonderful!

I was part of a ministry at one time that had some very strict requirements of discipleship. Anyone who was involved in any service of ministry had to read a minimum of five chapters of the word each day and pray for a minimum of one hour. It wasn't a bad idea, but it ended up being something of law and legalism. It was void of the grace of the Spirit of Wisdom. Many of us would quickly cram at the end of a day to be sure we got our chapters of the word read or our hour of prayer in. We didn't do it because we had faith toward God in our action. We did it, because we knew we were in big trouble if we didn't! Now, that's not to say that reading five chapters of the word a day and praying for an hour is a bad thing. It could be a very good thing! The key is the source of our motivation. Actions of faith are motivated by the grace of the Spirit of Wisdom. Actions that are merely required actions are ones that are motivated by fear and lead to bondage (Rom. 8:15).

NOTE: I recommend you stop and allow the Holy Spirit to minister to you throughout your day in regard to the grace of the Spirit of Wisdom and faith toward God.

Chapter 2.2

The Second Eye of Grace

The grace of the Spirit of Wisdom correlates to the foundation found in Christ of "faith toward God" (Heb. 6:1). Faith toward God is faith filled and fear empty. FAITH toward God is THE SECOND STEP toward living in the blessings of God's kingdom. It is not enough to be justified by faith; we must do works that speak of our faith. As believers in Christ, we have experienced a first resurrection; therefore, the second death has no power over us (Rev. 2:11).

Eph. 2:1 And you He made alive, who were dead in trespasses and sins, 2 in which you once walked according to the course of this world, according to the prince of the power of the air, the spirit who now works in the sons of disobedience, 3 among whom also we all once conducted ourselves in the lusts of our flesh, fulfilling the desires of the flesh and of the mind, and were by nature children of wrath, just as the others. 4 But God, who is rich in mercy, because of His great love with which He loved us, 5 even when we were dead in trespasses, made us alive together with Christ (by grace you have been saved), 6 and raised us up together, and made us sit together in the heavenly places in Christ Jesus, 7 that in the ages to come He might show the exceeding riches of His grace in His kindness toward us in Christ Jesus.

Jn. 5:24 "Most assuredly, I say to you, he who hears My word and believes in Him who sent Me has everlasting life, and shall not come into judgment, but has passed from death into life. 25 Most assuredly, I say to you, the hour is coming, and now is, when the dead will hear the voice of the Son of God; and those who hear will live."

Rom. 6:4 Therefore we were buried with Him through baptism into death, that just as Christ was raised from the dead by the glory of the Father, even so we also should walk in newness of life.

The Seven Eyes of Grace

Our lives have been made to be brand new in Christ (2 Cor. 5:17)! We can be assured that everything in life will end in increasing power of life on our behalf. We need not fear any power of death. You cannot kill a dead man! We died in the flesh in Christ, but the life that we live in the flesh we live by faith in Christ. Jesus said that we would be in the world, but we would not be of the world (Jn. 17:11-14). The second curse of the fall of man was the temptation of the fear of death. The woman was marked with a worrisomeness in pregnancy and great pain in child delivery. These things symbolize the fact that life is accompanied with the temptation of the fear of death. For the believer, life can even be filled with pain and suffering, yet we have the hope of His grace of wisdom in all things. We need not fear death, for though we are in the world, we are not of the world. In the world we will have tribulation, but we can be of good cheer for Christ has overcome the world (Jn. 16:33). We can do works that speak of our faith in all situations! We are marked with the testimony of Christ's life. Faith is the motivator of our works.

In the Old Testament Law there was a ceremonial washing that took place by the priest for anything or anyone that had been touched in some way by death. That death could have been the touching of a dead body, the stain of mildew or mold, or some other form of death's degradation. The ceremony involved the sprinkling of water that included the ashes of a red heifer (Num. 19:17). There were two parts to the ceremonial washing process. The first was to wash the contaminated person or object and then to examine it again for a second washing after seven days (Lev. 13:3-6). We have already passed from death to life in Christ. We can rest assured that Jesus is both the sprinkled blood for our death and the sprinkling of the ashes of the red heifer for our sanctification in life (Heb. 9:13, 14). We do not do works to be sanctified; we do works because we are sanctified! He has already washed us and He has sanctified us to live for Him while in this life of the flesh! When it is all said and done, it will be revealed that we are clean, and the second death has no power over us!

Heb. 9:13 For if the blood of bulls and goats and the ashes of a heifer, sprinkling the unclean, sanctifies for the purifying of the flesh, 14 how much more shall the blood of Christ, who through the eternal Spirit offered Himself without spot to God, purge your conscience from dead works to serve the living God?

1 Jn. 3:14 We know that we have passed from death to life, because we love the brethren. He who does not love his brother abides in death.

58

We must do works in Christ from simplicity and godly sincerity. Our works are motivated by the grace of the Spirit of Wisdom. Carnal wisdom is based upon experience. There is an old saying that says that 'wisdom is the best teacher'. That is not true! Human wisdom is a teacher, but it is not the best teacher. The best teacher is the Holy Spirit. He wants to give us things we haven't seen, heard, or thought before (1 Cor. 2:9, 10). He reveals them to us and then He motivates our hearts to act upon that which we know by faith. Human experience will most often prove to influence us in a way that causes us to restrain our hearts and live our lives within the boundaries of fear. We will refuse to do some things, because experience tells us that those things didn't work. We may emulate or copy the experiences of others in the hope that we will get the same positive results we feel they have obtained. In either case, fear is the motivation of our actions. We fear we might die if we do, or we fear we might die if we don't. Unfortunately, this is the same principle upon which many people who claim to be Christians live their lives. Whole books and seminars have been devoted to fear-based principles. They have been packaged in the veneer of faith, but in the core of their substance they are fear-based principles.

> *2 Cor. 1:12 For our boasting is this: the testimony of our conscience that we conducted ourselves in the world in simplicity and godly sincerity, not with fleshly wisdom but by the grace of God, and more abundantly toward you.*

This Scripture reveals that, we have passed from death to life and the evidence is a life of *Faith Toward God*. We were in bondage, but Jesus made us free! We now live by the grace of the Spirit of Wisdom (Rom. 5:9-17)! We have been justified to live through the shed blood of Jesus Christ. We never need to fear the wrath of God again! We are not God's enemies! We are His friends! Jesus reconciled us to God our Father while we were still sinners, so how much more will we not be blessed while we are children of God? God even promises that bad things in our lives will work out for good (Rom. 8:28). We used to have the curse of death in our lives. It was viable for us to fear death, because death held dominion in our world. We have now been translated from that darkness into the power of the kingdom of the love of God's Son (Col. 1:13). Death used to reign in our lives, but now we are under the dominion of life in Christ! It is a free gift of grace! It is a gift of righteousness in Christ. We need not fear death again. Our lives do not come from our past or from our past experiences. Our lives come from our future, which is hidden in Christ. Only the Spirit of Wisdom can make known to us the will of God. We can trust Him and do works that speak of our faith. The Spirit of Wisdom causes us to be a faith-filled people. Faith-filled people are God-seekers. Fear-filled people are self-seekers. It has to do with God's Spirit of Wisdom. It is a gift of grace!

Jam. 3:13 Who is wise and understanding among you? Let him show by good conduct that his works are done in the meekness of wisdom. 14 But if you have bitter envy and self-seeking in your hearts, do not boast and lie against the truth. 15 This wisdom does not descend from above, but is earthly, sensual, demonic. 16 For where envy and self-seeking exist, confusion and every evil thing will be there. 17 But the wisdom that is from above is first pure, then peaceable, gentle, willing to yield, full of mercy and good fruits, without partiality and without hypocrisy. 18 Now the fruit of righteousness is sown in peace by those who make peace.

The evidence of true wisdom is our conduct. Wisdom motivates our actions. The wisdom of the world motivates our actions to be those that take life from others. We are tempted to take life from others because we fear we lack life, or we fear losing life in some way. The motivation behind this wisdom is the fear of death. We act in human wisdom because we fear death. The opposite of faith is often thought to be fear, but fear is not the opposite of faith. The opposite of faith is natural sight (2 Cor. 5:7). Natural sight often inspires our hearts to fear. Life-giving faith comes by hearing the word of God (Rom. 10:17). When we act in human wisdom, we become bound to a natural mind-set. We begin to judge things by what we naturally know or by what we naturally see (Jude 10). We begin to be motivated by emotions. We trust our feelings more than the promise of God's love. We even yield to demonic influences because we are starving for some form of inspiration or facsimile of life. Human wisdom is steeped in human confusion. The wisdom that comes from God is pure, peaceable, gentle, willing to yield, full of mercy and good fruits, and is without partiality or hypocrisy. It is faith-filled wisdom! God's wisdom inspires sacrifices of faith. Those works are made real by the grace of the Spirit of Wisdom.

When we are motivated in our hearts by the wisdom of God we will always be inspired to walk by faith. Our faith will be seen in the works that we do. Those works will be sacrifices empowered by grace! That grace is the Spirit of Wisdom. We have a great example in the Scriptures. The story is one of Daniel, Hananiah, Mishael, and Azariah. These four Hebrew men had been taken captive into Babylon. They had been made eunuchs in the king's court. A eunuch is not just someone who is unmarried. In the day of these men's captivity in Babylon, a eunuch was someone who went through a surgical procedure to assure they would never seek marriage or be able to father children. It was a permanent action, and it changed the entire future of those who were required to undergo such a procedure. This was the world of Daniel, Hananiah, Mishael, and Azariah. They had no more hope of the 'Jewish dream' of a family and future generations to their name. They were prisoners in Babylon, and they were bound to the hopes and dreams of Babylon. It sounds to me like the temptation of the fear of death could have been very powerful in their lives. However, these men were men of faith toward God. Their lives reveal to us the attributes of the Spirit of Wisdom and faith toward God. You can find the story in Daniel, Chapter 1.

The king of Babylon had put out a decree for these men to be a part of His wise counsel. They were forced to go to several years of school to learn the language, ways, and customs of Babylon. It was not their native tongue, custom, or culture. It was no doubt an intimidating situation, but these men chose to have faith toward God. They chose not to fear their circumstances. They requested that they be put to a test. They petitioned their king's steward to allow them to be given vegetables to eat and water to drink for ten days. This is a testimony to their faith. They didn't request Israelite vegetables or Israelite water. They looked at the Babylonian provisions before them and decided to consume only that which they had the faith to consume. They had faith to eat the vegetables and to drink the water. The steward agreed to their test. At the end of the ten days these men were found to have better countenances than any of the other wise men. The Scripture says that "God gave them knowledge and skill in all literature and wisdom; and Daniel had understanding in all visions and dreams" (Dan. 1:17). These men were promoted in their land of captivity and were known to be "ten times better than all the magicians and astrologers" in matters of wisdom and understanding (Dan. 1:20). These men had faith toward God, but their faith was made evident by their works.

I was part of a mission trip one time that involved going into Kosovo with some money to buy food to feed the poor, a young pastor to plant a church, and a plan to provide provision for the poor of a particular community for an extended period of time. We had to drive from Albania, through Macedonia, and then into Kosovo. As we approached the border of Kosovo on the northern edge of Macedonia, the Macedonian government began to bomb some of the boarder villages. According to the Albanians, the fighting was against the Albanian "freedom fighters". According to the Macedonian government, the bombing was on the "Albanian terrorists". We were obviously in an area of danger and conflict. At one point we stopped our vehicle and watched the bombing of a village about a mile from where the bombs were landing. Things seemed to be uncertain, but we knew that God had a plan. We drove a bit further and spent the night in a city in Macedonia. The plan was to go through the border and into Kosovo the following morning. There was a problem that we didn't know about. The border was completely closed. Our leader, and driver, obviously had a sense of the Spirit's direction. He began to drive down a gravel road in a direction we perceived might be the border. I, speaking a minimal number of Macedonian words, got out and asked a community resident if the border was in that direction. The person I had asked said something about the border being a ways down the road across the river. We continued to drive in that direction. We finally came to a "T" in the road. To the right was a gravel road and to the left was a dirt trail. We at first turned to the right on what seemed to be the most driven path. We ended up in a gravel pit. There were some workers there and our driver asked them for directions. They pointed back in the direction that we came from. After a couple of attempts at driving in circles, we felt the unction to try the dirt trail. We entered into a huge garbage dump. As we came around the corner of a huge pile of garbage, we saw a very narrow and rickety metal bridge crossing the river. Our vehicle barely fit on the bridge and it made quite the noise as we drove across. Upon crossing the river, we came upon a main road. There were three United Nation soldiers there, waiting for some sort of supply delivery. We stopped and asked them where the border might be. They responded by telling us that the border was closed. They wondered how we got to the point we were on the road, for the police had completely closed the highway. They told us we could try the border, but they had no assurance we would get through. Our driver clipped a homemade humanitarian aid badge on his collar. As we approached the border there were military tanks and trucks everywhere! There were no civilian vehicles in sight. The guard at the post took one look at us and immediately allowed us to cross the border. He assumed the police had let us through and that we must be some people of importance. We crossed that border and in that week we accomplished all that God had sent us to do. Faith toward God is seen in our actions. The Spirit of Wisdom is a grace from God, and He will empower our sacrifices of faith in Christ! We need never fear death, but only respond to the wisdom of God in the actions we make in life.

NOTE: Stop and consider acts of faith toward God. Let the Holy Spirit minister to you once again as you meditate throughout the day.

Chapter 2.3

The Second Eye of Grace

In the Christian faith, the first work that speaks of our faith is that of water baptism (Acts 2:38). It correlates directly to the second foundation of New Covenant Life, "Faith Toward God" (Heb. 6:1). It is not a doctrine. It is a reality found in Christ. We either have faith toward God, or we don't. It is the key to our works in Christ. We must do works that are motivated by faith, not works that are motivated by death. Water baptism is not only the first work of such actions, it is also a work that is symbolic and prophetic of every work we will do as members of the Body of Christ. It is a direct testimony to our relationship with God through Jesus Christ. A relationship with God through Jesus Christ will cause us to do works that speak of our faith. It is not only God's wisdom; the Spirit of Wisdom also inspires it. The Spirit of Wisdom is the second *Eye of Grace* found in the Holy Spirit of God. The grace of the Spirit of Wisdom is sent to anoint us to do works founded in God's wisdom. They are works that speak of our faith and they will open the door to our futures in Christ. God's wisdom will give us a future in Him. Human wisdom binds us to a selfish human future, which is nothing other than failure, self-bankruptcy, and death.

Jam. 3:13 Who is wise and understanding among you? Let him show by good conduct that his works are done in the meekness of wisdom.

As Christians, we have experienced a first resurrection and the second death has no power over us. The actions of our lives will now be works of faith and not of fear. Although we were justified to live through the blood of Jesus Christ, it is not enough to say we are justified by faith. We must also do works that speak of our faith!

Jam. 2:14 What does it profit, my brethren, if someone says he has faith but does not have works? Can faith save him? 15 If a brother or sister is naked and destitute of daily food, 16 and one of you says to them, "Depart in peace, be warmed and filled," but you do not give

them the things which are needed for the body, what does it profit?
17 Thus also faith by itself, if it does not have works, is dead. 18 But
someone will say, "You have faith, and I have works." Show me your
faith without your works, and I will show you my faith by my works.
19 You believe that there is one God. You do well. Even the demons
believe—and tremble! 20 But do you want to know, O foolish man, that
faith without works is dead? 21 Was not Abraham our father justified
by works when he offered Isaac his son on the altar? 22 Do you see
that faith was working together with his works, and by works faith was
made perfect? 23 And the Scripture was fulfilled which says, "Abraham
believed God, and it was accounted to him for righteousness." And he
was called the friend of God. 24 You see then that a man is justified by
works, and not by faith only. 25 Likewise, was not Rahab the harlot
also justified by works when she received the messengers and sent
them out another way? 26 For as the body without the spirit is dead,
so faith without works is dead also.

The only 'sacrifices' that God accepts are ones of faith. We must learn to make faith-filled sacrifices. Water Baptism is a first 'act' of a lifestyle of 'acts' of faith. The Greek word for baptism means "immersion". It implies an immersion, a submersion, and emergence. The elements of its meaning describe the process of coming to faith in Christ. Christ died for our sins, was buried for the punishment of our sin, and rose from the dead to give us His resurrected life of righteousness.

Acts 19:4 Then Paul said, "John indeed baptized with a baptism of
repentance, saying to the people that they should believe on Him who
would come after him, that is, on Christ Jesus." 5 When they heard
this, they were baptized in the name of the Lord Jesus. 6 And when
Paul had laid hands on them, the Holy Spirit came upon them, and
they spoke with tongues and prophesied.

Notice, in this Scripture there is a difference between the baptism of John and the baptism of Christ Jesus. To be "baptized" is to be "immersed" into something. They had been "immersed" into the name of John, but they had not been "immersed" into the name of Jesus. To be baptized into Jesus is an act of faith granting us identification with the Body of Christ. It is to be immersed into the sacrifice of His death, submerged in His burial, and to emerge to a faith-filled life of His resurrection power. Having been "submerged" into the name of the Lord Jesus, they were able to receive the identification of Christ's

Spirit upon their lives. They spoke with other tongues and prophesied. It wasn't water baptism that submerged them in the Holy Spirit's anointing, but it was water baptism that identified them in the Body of Christ. Their act of faith was a work that confirmed they were the place of Christ's habitation in the earth. A name includes the character, nature, way, power, and authority of someone. To be baptized into the name of the Lord Jesus is to be "submerged" into His character, nature, way, power, and authority. The grace of the Spirit of Wisdom is present, since Christ is seated in heavenly places. Jesus has been exalted to the right hand of the Father as Lord of lords and King of kings. To become identified in Him is to become joined with Him in His future and His hope. It frees us from the power of death and joins us to the presence of His resurrection victory. It is not just an identification with who He is; it is a full immersion into all that He is! This includes all that He has done and all that He will do!

Many denominations teach that water baptism is to be practiced by parents in the christening of their baby children. It has been thought in many traditions, that unless you are baptized in water you cannot be saved. This teaching has also evolved to where many believe that one is saved when they are baptized. There were perhaps good intentions in the root thinking of this process, but it misses the point of this amazing work that speaks of our faith.

Let me address those who may still adhere to this practice, or who may know of those who do. I grew up in a denomination that practiced infant water baptism. It wasn't really a baptism, since the word baptism means "immersion" or "to be fully submerged". The act that my parents authorized, and the minister of God performed, was a sprinkling of water upon my head. It was an act of faith on the part of my parents. For that I am grateful! I believe that God looks at those acts and sees them as moments of dedication. Again, there is a difference between an act of faith and an act of fear. I believe it is honorable to act in faith on behalf of our children. I believe my infant water baptism was an act of dedication on the part of my parents. I do practice baby and children dedications. I have often laid hands upon infants and children and dedicated their lives to God. This is an act of faith on behalf of a family and a congregation. It is a powerful thing! Infant water baptism could be like that. It could also be merely an act of fear. It could be a vain action, for fear of hell if it is not performed. Do you see the principle? There is a difference between fear-based actions and faith-filled ones. However, we must all understand that water baptism by immersion is commanded in the Scriptures. It would be good to mention at this point as well, that the act of water immersion is not the most important point. It is an act of faith that identifies the individual with the death, burial, and resurrection of Christ. It is a work that speaks of one's faith. The act of water baptism is not only an action of faith, it is also a prophetic demonstration of everything represented in a work of faith. It would be quite impossible for someone restricted to a hospital bed, a paraplegic, or in some other handicapped restriction to fulfill the letter of the requirement. The principle is more important than the legalism of the method of the act.

Mt. 28:19 "Go therefore and make disciples of all the nations, baptizing them in the name of the Father and of the Son and of the Holy Spirit"...

There is much more to the command of, "baptizing them in the name of the Father and of the Son and of the Holy Spirit". I believe it is much more than just the act of submerging someone in water and saying the name of "Jesus" over the act. Churches have split over that issue. Great debates have developed that have caused some to say that this act is in "Jesus' name only" and others to say with passion that it must be performed in the name of "the Father, the Son, and the Holy Spirit". What does it really mean to be "baptized into the name"? I believe the act of submerging someone in water is an essential act of faith, but I don't believe that is the entirety of what Jesus commanded. Let me propose that Jesus was saying something like this:

Since all authority in heaven and earth has been given to Me, go and make disciples of all nations. Bring them under the discipline of My grace! Don't just gather a few converts or a meager number of followers. Go change the world! Submerge the nations and the peoples of the nations into My name. Let My character, nature, way, power, and authority swallow up the old nature of the nations. Go and cause the nations to find their identity in Me.

Everyone who receives the grace of the Spirit of the Lord and God's government grant of repentance from dead works must be submerged into the name of Christ. The Body of Christ is the place of Christ's habitation. It is the Body that Jesus said would do greater works than He (Jn. 14:12). We must all do works that speak of our faith. The first work is to be submerged in water as an act of faith in identifying in Jesus' name. It is an act of faith that initiates the grace of the Spirit of Wisdom in the life of the believer. Through baptism we identify with Christ that we might walk in newness of life in Him.

Water Baptism is symbolized in Scripture by the crossing of the Red Sea and should be exercised in faith as a complete release of the believer from the bondage and afflictions of his or her past life. It should be an act of faith that is a first step toward receiving all that God has for him or her in their new life in Christ.

> *1 Cor. 10:1 Moreover, brethren, I do not want you to be unaware that all our fathers were under the cloud, all passed through the sea, 2 all were baptized into Moses in the cloud and in the sea, 3 all ate the same spiritual food, 4 and all drank the same spiritual drink. For they drank of that spiritual Rock that followed them, and that Rock was Christ.*

Those who went through the sea were baptized into the name of Moses. They identified in the Torah (Law), the covenant of Law to God's chosen people. Under the government of the knowledge of good and evil, the children of Israel chose to find the pure "information" or pure "knowledge" of good. The rest of the nations were led by their consciences that were continually hardened toward God (Rom. 1). The children of Israel crossed the Red Sea not just to get away from their Egyptian pursuers. They crossed the Red Sea to get to the place of preparation for the Promised Land. They didn't just cross the Red Sea to get away from Egypt; they crossed the Red Sea to get to the place that Egypt could be removed from their hearts. For the Christian believer, water baptism into the name of Jesus is the same. We get baptized in order to position our lives for the inheritance of the future, not merely to get rid of the strongholds of our past. However, we should expect the strongholds of our past to be broken through our act of faith in water baptism. Just as the Israelites saw the Egyptians dead along the shore of the sea, so we should see our past lives as dead to our present lives in Christ (Ex. 14:30). Our act of being water baptized is an act of faith so that we can position ourselves for the things that are not of faith to be removed from our hearts. Instead of being submerged into the government of Law, as they were with Moses; we become submerged into the government of grace (Jn. 1:17). Having received our deliverance that came by the government grant of repentance from dead works, we take the first step of increasing grace. That grace is the Spirit of Wisdom that requires our acts of faith to acquire all that God has for us in Christ. It puts us in the right place for the work of Christ in our lives. It positions us to receive a changed character, nature, way, power, and authority in His NAME!

Water baptism is a first act of faith that 'engulfs' or 'submerges' the believer into a lifestyle of faith and inheritance in Christ. The believer's commitment to Christ allows the Spirit of the Lord to grant a change of mind and heart to the believer. John's baptism was commanded as an obedient act for repentance from evil according to the LAW of good (Lk. 3:3). Our act of water baptism is a demonstration of faith, according to God's government of grace.

NOTE: Stop and consider your own water baptism and what this act of faith meant in your own life. Let the Holy Spirit speak to you in regard to your lifestyle of faith toward God and works that speak of your faith in Him.

Chapter 2.4

The Second Eye of Grace

The Grace of the Spirit of Wisdom is the power by which God determines the future of the world. He does not judge by what He naturally sees or by what He naturally hears (Isa. 11:3). He decides by what His wisdom decrees. He makes decisions for the world based upon what He possesses, and He empowers the transformation of mankind by the power of His grace that He gives to us (Isa. 11:5). This is the wisdom that Jesus exercised when He endured the cross for the joy that was set before Him. He was not afraid of death. He knew the wisdom of His Father would reveal the full glory of His resurrection (1 Cor. 2:7, 8). Jesus knew that pain and suffering was not a sign of death, but the testimony of a new day (Heb. 12:2). That same wisdom will anoint us to do acts of faith toward God in the world, to transform the nations in which we live. Water baptism is the first act that speaks of our faith. It is an activating catalyst to the world changing power of God's Spirit of Wisdom in our lives. It is a prophetic testimony, and it activates the power of a life lived with faith toward God!

It is interesting to note there are three types of experiences with believers and water in the Scriptures. The first is the act of God to flood the earth. The flood on the earth was the result of man's decision to choose the knowledge of good and evil over a trust relationship of love with God. Man's inability to handle the knowledge of good and evil, quickly developed into a mass of humanity whose consciences were seared to God (Gen. 6:1-6). God sent a flood upon the entire earth to wash it of man's wickedness. The creation that we now see is not the creation as it was in the beginning. It is the creation that is the result of the effects of a global destruction by water (2 Pet. 3:5, 6). During that act, God preserved the lives of eight souls to propagate a new beginning for man in the earth. Noah and his family were instructed to build an ark. That ark carried those eight souls "on top" of the water of the judgment of God (1 Pet. 3:20). Man's adherence to evil under a government of the knowledge of good and evil resulted in the destruction of all flesh upon the earth. God made a provision "on water" to save a remnant for a new beginning in the earth. The earth was left covered with the evidence of that judgment and the testimony that eight souls had survived within the boundaries of Noah's ark. The government of the earth was one of the knowledge of good and evil. God had placed it inside the heart of man to know that there was a God (Rom. 1:19), but the administration of conscience proved to activate only eight souls to do works that spoke of their faith. Their work of faith toward God by building the ark and entering into it, was the result of the discipline of conscience. The government of the earth was still one of the knowledge of good and evil, but God had found a remnant that would "call on the name of God" (Gen. 4:26). God made a covenant with Noah's family in the earth. He promised to never again destroy the earth with a flood, but He set His rainbow in the heavens as the testimony of the day when God would transform the human world by the power of His *Seven Eyes of Grace* (Gen. 9:13-17).

Noah's salvation was "on water". In the years that followed, God established a covenant with Abraham, and later with Israel. In a world governed by the knowledge of good and evil, God called one man to birth a nation that would be given the perfect knowledge of good. That nation was comprised of the tribes of Israel. Their "passing through" the Red Sea was a prophetic sign that God would give them a testimony that would be salvation to them in a world governed by the knowledge of good and evil. They were given the testimony of that which was the fullness of all that is good in a government that required the knowledge of good. They were brought "through water" as a testimony to the world of what happens when men trust God who is good. They were saved "through water" both in their passing through the Red Sea and their entrance into the Promised Land (Ex. 14:21, 22; Josh. 3:14-16). The "ark of the covenant", which contained the Torah (Law) of God, allowed them to enter the Promised Land in the day of the knowledge of good and evil. They were preserved as a holy nation before God amidst the wickedness of the world. It was a government of the knowledge of good and evil. The administration of the Law was a ministry of condemnation, and it could never transform the lives of those who believed (2 Cor. 3:9). The testimony within the Ark of the Covenant informed the world of all that was good, but it could not transform the world to become good. It could pass "through water", through the judgment of man's doing in the earth, but it could not heal the earth of the curse of the fall of man. A nation was saved under the discipline of the Law. Their obedience to the Law was an act of faith toward God, but it could not save the world. It served only to fully clarify the need for God's power of grace!

The ark of Noah was God's provision for a human race with no Law. The Ark of the Covenant was God's provision for a people with the Law. One saved mankind on water and one allowed man to be preserved through water. Neither of these healed the cause of the bitter waters of the flood. Conscience and Law were God's provisions for man only until the day of His GRACE. Both the ark of Noah's flood and the Ark of the Covenant testified of the reality of a place of God's habitation in the earth. That place is the living Body of Christ, the house of God's habitation. This is the New Covenant testimony of grace. The ark of the Body of Christ is not like the shadow seen in Noah's day that saved a remnant on water. It is not like the ark of His testimony that saved a nation to testify of God who is good in a time of the Law. The ark of the New Covenant is the Body of Christ. It is an "ark of God's presence" that comes "out of water". It is the place of God's overcoming grace (Rev. 2 & 3). It is through the testimony of God's grace at work in the Body of Christ that the nations will finally come alive in God. The earth will be covered with the knowledge of the glory of God as the waters presently cover the sea (Isa. 11:9; Hab. 2:14). Men will not be inspired or controlled by mere conscience or law. They will be made fully alive by the power of God's grace! The evidence of what Jesus did will outweigh the evidence of what Adam did at the fall of man.

The Body of Christ is anointed with the power of God's transforming sevenfold grace. It is not merely the salvation of eight souls, or of one nation. The ark of the Body of Christ is an overcoming place of God's grace for all nations! It is through rising out of the waters of baptism that we proclaim we are members of the ark of the Body of Christ. It is an act of faith that testifies the earth will finally be filled with a human race that is fully alive to God! The Body of Christ will emerge from the nations (out of water). The rudiments, the elements, the beginning things of conscience and law; will be consumed by the fire of grace. True faith toward God is empowered by the grace of the Spirit of Wisdom. That grace will empower the nations to do works that speak of their faith!

> *1 Pet. 3:20 ...who formerly were disobedient, when once the longsuffering of God waited in the days of Noah, while the ark was being prepared, in which a few, that is, eight souls, were saved through water. 21 There is also an antitype which now saves us, namely baptism (not the removal of the filth of the flesh, but the answer of a good conscience toward God), through the resurrection of Jesus Christ...*

Noah's act of faith was to build an ark. It took Him 120 years to construct it in obedience to God (Gen. 6:3). Moses was 120 years old when the mantle was passed to Joshua and the Ark of the Covenant was carried across the Jordan River (Deut. 31:2). The Body of Christ began with 120 souls in an upper room in Jerusalem. They were clearly identified as the "Body of Christ" with the out-pouring of the Holy Spirit (Acts 2). When we are water baptized, we identify with the safe place known as the "Body of Christ". It is the ark of God's salvation for the nations of the world. As members of the Body of Christ we do not merely believe to be saved out of the world, but to see the nations saved in Christ! Our testimony is that the evidence of what Last Adam has done will outweigh the evidence of the decision of First Adam in the earth. The testimony of coming up "out of the water" is a testimony of victory, triumph, and the overcoming power of God's amazing grace. When Jesus came up out of the waters of baptism, He was led into the wilderness by the Spirit of God and made known to the world in the fullness of the power of the Spirit of Christ.

I am now going past my 49th year as a Christian. I am not just someone who believes in Christ. I am an active member of the Body of Christ. I was water baptized as an act of faith toward God. The overcoming power of coming out of water has been very true for me. The One who began a good work in me is being faithful to complete that work (Phil. 1:6). I am experiencing continued transformation in my life as an identifiable member of the Body of Christ. I was submerged by faith into a house of destiny! The earth will be changed from that place! I have had many opportunities to seek to isolate from the Body of Christ and become merely a believer in Jesus. I have resisted those temptations, because my life is filled with works that speak of my faith. I am not interested in being saved "on water". I am not interested in just "passing through water". I am interested in being the source of a different kind of water. I am interested in being a part of the living Body of Christ! From within the corporate Body of Christ flow rivers of living water (Jn. 7:37-39; Rev. 22:1)! That water is the water of life. It is not like the salt water of the sea. It is not like the dark descending waters of the Jordan. It is the water of heaven that has come to the earth. I believe the testimony of that water is evident in the earth. The world changing, nation-transforming power of God is in the ark of His Body in the earth! I am part of God's covenant plan for the earth. I have acknowledged the death that was due me as per the government of the knowledge of good and evil. When I went down into the waters of baptism I identified with my death, which is found in Christ. My life that was bound to the lifeless rules of conscience and law was transformed by my identification with Christ in baptism. When I came out of that water, I came out in the identity of the true ark of life. I am part of the Body of Christ that will fill the earth with the testimony of Christ! I know that the temptation of the fear of death has no power over me. My testimony is life forevermore in the Body of Christ.

Water baptism is an act of faith, and it testifies of a life in Christ that can be filled with countless acts of faith. My life is filled with acts that speak of my faith. I have done some things in presumption of God's word, but there are countless times where I have responded to the word of the Lord with actions of faith toward God. Many are the everyday acts of faith of caring for the needy, committing to a lifestyle of prayer, diligently studying God's word, fasting for many days, and hours of worshipping God. Some acts were major decisions that have affected my life forever. In 1981 I, and my family, moved to a place that was over 2000 miles away from our home in Texas. We went to a place we had never been before to be a part of starting a new ministry. We had no clue what to expect, but by faith we sold all we had and moved to a place not knowing where we were going. It was an act of faith toward God, and it was a direct response to God's word of wisdom in our lives. In 1988 I became a minister of the gospel of Jesus Christ in direct response to the wisdom of the Lord. In 1990 I went full-time into the ministry in obedience to the word of God in my life. I remember thinking that my partial retirement plan would possibly meet our needs for a while. God instructed me to give my entire retirement as an offering to Him. By faith I obeyed, and He has always met my needs. In 1991 I became the senior minister of the ministry I led for 20 years. In 1992 I took my first trip to Eastern Europe, of which I now travel around 200,000 miles each year in ministry service to many parts of the world. I have done all these things to identify with the Body of Christ. I haven't done them to find my own ministry. They are acts that speak of my faith and they have all served to increase my claim of covenant with the Body of Christ and her many members.

NOTE: Once again consider your life of faith toward God. Let the Holy Spirit touch you with His grace of the Spirit of Wisdom and faith toward God.

Chapter 2.5

The Second Eye of Grace

The believer's commitment to Christ allows the Spirit of the Lord to grant a change of mind and heart to the believer. Repentance is the act of receiving a "changed mind" and is granted to us by God, but water baptism is a physical demonstration that goes beyond repentance. It is an act of faith. When we are pierced in our hearts to repentance toward God, the obedient act of baptism brings us to identification with Christ. We are baptized unto a person, who is a personal leader. We become identified with Him in His presence and authority. It is not merely an act of being submerged in water. It is not simply a sacrament preformed so that we can be called Christians. Baptism is an act of faith that identifies us in a living relationship with a real person. Being baptized in the name of Jesus means being baptized in the name of God's fullness. That is to be baptized in the name of the Father, the Son, and the Holy Spirit (Mt. 28:19). Being baptized into the name of the Lord Jesus is to enter a life of 'faith toward God'. It is not a lifeless action. It is a demonstration of power put into motion as an act of faith toward God. Water baptism is an act inspired and anointed by the grace of the Spirit of Wisdom. Our act of faith in water baptism gives each of us an entrance into a lifestyle of obeying God's voice in all things. Water baptism is an act of faith granting us an identity in the Body of Christ.

One cannot be water baptized without first fulfilling the condition of qualification. The Word says we must believe and be baptized.

Mk. 16:16 "He who believes and is baptized will be saved; but he who does not believe will be condemned."

Acts 18:8 Then Crispus, the ruler of the synagogue, believed on the Lord with all his household. And many of the Corinthians, hearing, believed and were baptized.

Many people believe unless one is water baptized, they are not saved. It is true to say that without acts of faith our faith is dead. Since water baptism is an act of faith toward God, it should be the first act of faith toward Him as believers in Christ. It is our relationship with God in Christ that grants us the grace of repentance from dead works. To be granted repentance from dead works is also to be granted life in Christ. This makes our salvation secure and needs nothing more. We are justified by faith! However, water baptism is part of our salvation plan, since salvation is the complete process of God in our lives. The entrance to that process is first made known by our ability to repent and believe on the Lord Jesus Christ. Once we believe, we can enter into the process of receiving God's full salvation plan for our lives. Water baptism is the first step in that salvation plan. It places us into the realm of FAITH. It is a living demonstration of the grace of the Spirit of Wisdom at work in our lives. It is the Holy Spirit's work of the Spirit of Wisdom that procures our inheritance in Christ. It is the key to the place of our future destinies in Him.

Water baptism demonstrates the removal of our past and causes us to be positioned for our future in Christ. If we believe with all our hearts that Jesus Christ is the Son of God, we may be baptized.

> *Acts 8:36 Now as they went down the road, they came to some water. And the eunuch said, "See, here is water. What hinders me from being baptized?" 37 Then Philip said, "If you believe with all your heart, you may." And he answered and said, "I believe that Jesus Christ is the Son of God." 38 So he commanded the chariot to stand still. And both Philip and the eunuch went down into the water, and he baptized him.*

Water baptism is the outward act of faith proclaiming our circumcision in Christ. It is a lifestyle of faith that testifies we are a part of the Body of Christ. Water baptism is the act of the Christian faith that marks us as part of the Body of Christ. It is a testimony of the circumcision of our hearts toward God.

> *1 Pet. 2:9 But you are a chosen generation, a royal priesthood, a holy nation, His own special people, that you may proclaim the praises of Him who called you out of darkness into His marvelous light; 10 who once were not a people but are now the people of God, who had not obtained mercy but now have obtained mercy.*

What is the process of Water Baptism? When we are pierced in our hearts to repentance toward God, and have accepted the Spirit of the Lord Jesus

Christ to grant us repentance unto life, the obedient act of baptism brings us to identification with Christ. We become one with Christ in His death that we might be one with Him in His life. It is an act of faith that proclaims our death in Him. It is also an act of grace that actually joins us to Him as a person. He is the one who died, was buried, rose from the dead, and is seated at the right hand of the Father in heaven. When we are baptized into His name, we join ourselves to His death, His burial, His resurrection, and His ascension into the heavenly place. We are made free from every fear of death! We experience the deliverance from death, having already died in Him. We experience freedom from all condemnation, having already been condemned in His descending to the depths of judgment. We also experience the power and authority to live a life in this world that is filled with the grace of the Spirit of Wisdom and accompanying acts of faith toward God. We are guaranteed the resurrection of our physical bodies and the complete eternal habitation of all that is eternal in Christ.

Rom. 6:3 Or do you not know that as many of us as were baptized into Christ Jesus were baptized into His death? 4 Therefore we were buried with Him through baptism into death, that just as Christ was raised from the dead by the glory of the Father, even so we also should walk in newness of life. 5 For if we have been united together in the likeness of His death, certainly we also shall be in the likeness of His resurrection, 6 knowing this, that our old man was crucified with Him, that the body of sin might be done away with, that we should no longer be slaves of sin. 7 For he who has died has been freed from sin. 8 Now if we died with Christ, we believe that we shall also live with Him, 9 knowing that Christ, having been raised from the dead, dies no more. Death no longer has dominion over Him.

In water baptism our old man is put to death with Jesus on the cross, buried with Jesus in the tomb, and raised with Jesus in the power of His resurrection. What a wonderful testimony of grace!

Col. 2:11 In Him you were also circumcised with the circumcision made without hands, by putting off the body of the sins of the flesh, by the circumcision of Christ, 12 buried with Him in baptism, in which you also were raised with Him through faith in the working of God, who raised Him from the dead.

Because our old self has been put to death, we can now, by faith, become

CLOTHED IN CHRIST to a new life.

Gal. 3:27 For as many of you as were baptized into Christ have put on Christ.

Salvation is not through baptism but through belief in Jesus Christ. Water baptism opens the door for the process of God's inheritance in our lives. It is a first work that speaks of our faith!

1 Pet. 3:18 For Christ also suffered once for sins, the just for the unjust, that He might bring us to God, being put to death in the flesh but made alive by the Spirit, 19 by whom also He went and preached to the spirits in prison, 20 who formerly were disobedient, when once the longsuffering of God waited in the days of Noah, while the ark was being prepared, in which a few, that is, eight souls, were saved through water. 21 There is also an antitype which now saves us, namely baptism (not the removal of the filth of the flesh, but the answer of a good conscience toward God), through the resurrection of Jesus Christ, 22 who has gone into heaven and is at the right hand of God, angels and authorities and powers having been made subject to Him.

Water baptism is a foundational experience of FAITH. It is the first step of the testimony of the Spirit of Wisdom at work in our lives. When we do works of faith, God performs an operation upon our hearts. The significance of this act is found as being an 'ACT OF FAITH'. It is not a ceremonial cleansing. It is not an act to make us sanctified or holy. It is an act of faith done as a demonstration to the fact that we are sanctified and holy! It is like a key in the lock to the door of our inheritance that activates the furtherance of the grace of the Spirit of Wisdom at work in our lives.

Water baptism acknowledges our acceptance of Jesus as Lord and is an act of faith whereby we confess the Lordship of Jesus in our lives. It is an ACT OF FAITH that allows God to circumcise our hearts for new lives in Him as new creations in Christ (2 Cor. 5:17). Water baptism is a memorial. It identifies the believer with the death of Jesus Christ. It is an acceptance of the Lamb of God as the sacrifice for our sins. It is a confession of our death in Him, our burial in Him, our resurrection in Him, and our new lives lived in Him by faith. This act of baptism declares a solemn determination to leave our old lives behind and to put on our new lives in Christ. It announces our separation from our old lives of sin. Through water baptism we accept our new identities in Christ. We are no longer sinners, but "saints". We are set apart to God to live our lives in Christ. Like Abraham, we become children of faith and receive the circumcision of our hearts to live as members of the SEED of God's promise in the earth.

> *Rom. 2:28 For he is not a Jew who is one outwardly, nor is that circumcision which is outward in the flesh; 29 but he is a Jew who is one inwardly, and circumcision is that of the heart, in the Spirit, and not in the letter; whose praise is not from men but from God.*

It is through our acts of faith toward God that we put on Christ. Water baptism is the first act of this process. It is a prophetic act to the full process. It actually joins us to the person Jesus Christ who has already entered into the full glory of this process made complete. It joins us to Him in heaven and His Body in heaven and earth. When we are baptized, we confess our membership in the Body of Christ.

> *1 Cor. 12:13 For by one Spirit we were all baptized into one body— whether Jews or Greeks, whether slaves or free—and have all been made to drink into one Spirit. 14 For in fact the body is not one member but many.*

When we are water baptized, we present ourselves before God, His angels, the powers of darkness, the demonic strongholds of our past, and all the witnesses gathered to observe our confessions of faith. As we identify our lives in Christ, we can expect that the full authority of God is present to break off the power of the enemy in our lives. Like the children of Israel, as they crossed the dry land of the Red Sea, we will cross the path prepared for us that declares our futures in Christ. When the children of Israel crossed the Red Sea, their enemies were destroyed. The dead bodies of their enemies were seen along the shore. They were not able to forget their past, but rather were able to remember it as "dead". God intends for us to remember our lives of sin as "dead" and "no more" forever.

Water baptism is an act of faith toward God. Acts of faith testify of a new life in Christ! Our acts of obedience to be water baptized are a confession of God before men. Through this act we make a confession that Jesus is Lord of our lives. We confess that we are free from the sins of our past and from the sin nature that was against us. We are free from the power of the enemy! We are one with Christ and with His Body. We are eternally living members of the Body of Christ!

Mt. 10:32 "Therefore whoever confesses Me before men, him I will also confess before My Father who is in heaven. 33 But whoever denies Me before men, him I will also deny before My Father who is in heaven."

All of our actions must be faith-filled actions. Faith-filled actions will build a faith-filled house. Faith-filled actions will produce faith-filled generations. Fear-filled actions will build a fear-filled house. Fear-filled actions will build fear-filled generations. A fear-filled house is always afraid of the trespasser, but a faith-filled house always knows they are test-passers.

NOTE: Allow the Holy Spirit to minister to you one more time in regard to the Spirit of Wisdom and faith toward God. This is a growing grace in your life so let Him touch you today.

Chapter 2.1 – 2.5 - The Second Eye of Grace

Statements and Questions to Consider
For a Group Discussion:

1. Read James 2:14-26. The second grace is the Spirit of Wisdom. The Spirit of Wisdom anoints and activates us to do works that speak of our faith. Discuss what works of faith look like.

2. The grace of the Spirit of Wisdom correlates to the foundation found in Christ of "Faith Toward God". It is not enough to be justified by faith; we must do works that speak of our faith. The testimony of Faith Toward God is not merely about doing works. It is doing works that are anointed and motivated by the Spirit of Wisdom. What is the difference between the wisdom of the world and the wisdom of God?

3. The second of the required offerings of Deuteronomy, Chapter 12, was one known as "sacrifices". What is the difference between a sacrifice of fear and a sacrifice of faith? What are some examples of each?

4. Faith is testified by acts of love. Is there a difference between acts of service and acts of performance? What do you think those differences might be?

5. The baptism of Jesus was a work that spoke of His faith toward God. He didn't get water baptized so that He might be clean. He didn't get water baptized so that He would be saved. He got water baptized so that all righteousness might be fulfilled.

6. God's favor was not upon the life of Jesus as a MAN because of the things that He had done. God's favor was simply upon His life; therefore, Jesus could freely walk by faith and consistently and continually do works that spoke of His faith.

7. As believers in Christ, we have experienced a first resurrection; therefore, the second death has no power over us. We can be assured that everything in life will end in increasing power of life on our behalf. We need not fear any power of death. There are more types of death than merely the physical expiration of our bodies. What are some examples of death?

8. We have already passed from death to life in Christ. We can rest assured that Jesus is both the sprinkled blood for our death and the sprinkling of the ashes of the red heifer for our sanctification in life. We do not do works to be sanctified; we do works because we are sanctified! What is the difference between doing works from sanctification and works to be sanctified?

9. Human wisdom can be a teacher in our lives, but human wisdom is based upon experience. The best teacher is the Holy Spirit. He wants to give us things we haven't seen, heard, or thought before. Are there any group examples?

10. Faith-filled people are God-seekers - Fear-filled people are self-seekers. Read James 3:13-18. Discuss carnal wisdom and wisdom of the Spirit of God.

11. The opposite of faith is natural sight. Are there any examples in the group of how natural sight has opposed faith in their lives?

12. To be baptized into the name of the Lord Jesus is to be "submerged" into His character, nature, way, power, and authority. Discuss what this looks like.

13. Water baptism is a first act of faith that 'engulfs' or 'submerges' the believer into a lifestyle of faith and inheritance in Christ. Discuss water baptism and what kind of spiritual realities are given in the act of water baptism.

14. The grace of the Spirit of Wisdom is the power by which God determines the future of the world. God makes decisions for the world based upon what He possesses, and He empowers the transformation of mankind by the power of His grace that He gives to us. Discuss what it is that God possesses and how our works of faith might grant us the substance of His possessions.

15. God desires for all to be made fully alive by the power of God's grace! The evidence of what Jesus did will out-weigh the evidence of what Adam did at the fall of man. How is this working in your life now? Are there any group examples? Discuss this.

16. Water baptism is the outward 'ACT OF FAITH' PROCLAIMING our circumcision in Christ. It is a lifestyle of faith that testifies we are a part of the Body of Christ. When the Spirit circumcises our hearts, does it motivate us to actions of faith? Without actions of faith is there really a circumcision of heart? What are some thoughts on this?

17. In water baptism our old man is put to death with Jesus on the cross, buried with Jesus in the tomb, and raised with Jesus in the power of His resurrection. Because our old selves have been put to death, we can now, by faith, become CLOTHED IN CHRIST to a new life. What does this look like?

18. Salvation is not through baptism but through Jesus Christ. Water baptism opens the door for the process of God's inheritance in our lives. It is through our acts of faith toward God that we put on Christ. Water baptism is the first act of this process. It is a prophetic act to the full process.

19. A faith-filled house always knows they are test-passers. Are there any "test-passing" testimonies in the group?

Chapter 3.1

The Third Eye of Grace
- The Spirit of Understanding

In these next five chapters we will describe the third grace of the *Seven Eyes of Grace*. This third grace is the Spirit of Understanding. It is a grace of the Holy Spirit at work in our lives as the teacher who transforms us. Remember, a grace is not merely a pardon from our failure. Grace is the empowerment of God in our lives that increasingly transforms us to the glory of God. Grace is the power of God's life within us.

The Old Covenant pertained to a government of the knowledge of good and evil. The government of the New Covenant is one of intimacy with God in Christ and the Tree of Life. It is a government of grace. It begins with a pardon from our failures and proceeds to grow in the ability to change our lives. The teachers of the Old Covenant were the Law and the Prophets. Preceding the Old Covenant, and for the nations outside of the Covenant of Israel, the teacher was the consciences of men. These teachers were teachers of information. They were rudiments, or beginning things, given to inform us of God who is good. They revealed our need for change, but they could never eternally change us. They had the power of "information" but lacked the power of "transformation" in our lives.

The New Covenant is a covenant of transformation. We are being transformed into the brightness of the Father's glory and the express image of His person in Christ (Heb. 1:3). We are becoming the weight of the influence of the Father and the substance of His person in this world. There is only one teacher able to do that! He is the Holy Spirit of God! He teaches us by the grace of the Spirit of Understanding. We become transformed by His presence in and upon our lives. This grace of the Spirit of Understanding corresponds to the foundation truth of the doctrine of baptisms (Heb. 6:2). It is not the doctrine about baptisms. It is the <u>doctrine of baptisms</u>. It is not what we believe about baptisms, but rather what happens when we are submerged in His anointing.

The word baptism means to be "submerged" or completely "immersed" in something. The doctrine of baptisms is the transformational teaching that comes into our lives when we are "submerged" or "immersed" into the anointing of the Holy Spirit and His grace of the Spirit of Understanding. This is the only one of the seven graces described as a "doctrine" in the foundation of Christ (Heb. 6:1, 2).

We have all heard teachings on the "doctrines of the Christian faith". We have perhaps taught those things. This book by itself is mere information concerning the truth that is found in the sevenfold transforming grace of Christ. The actual power of the Holy Spirit at work in our lives is more important than the information of this book. The information of this book is only intended to reveal the truth of the Holy Spirit at work in our lives. This book cannot change our lives, but the grace of the Holy Spirit as described in this book can transform our lives to the likeness and image of our Father in heaven! It is not what we teach about repentance, faith, baptism, the laying on of hands, the resurrection of the dead, eternal judgment, or perfections that matters. It is the transformation that comes by the grace of God in all of these truths that matters. The reason that "baptisms" is listed as a "doctrine" is because that is how the Holy Spirit teaches us. The word "doctrine" means, "teaching". This grace is the teaching that comes by being submerged in the Spirit of Understanding. Holy Spirit takes what is of Jesus and the Father and reveals it to us (Jn. 16:14). He doesn't reveal His teaching to us as "information". He doesn't come to "inform" us of anything. He comes to change our lives! He comes to "transform" us. He comes as the Spirit of revelation to open up the eyes of our hearts to know the hope of Christ's calling and the riches of His inheritance in us (Eph. 1:18). That is the kind of teacher He is! He is the facilitator of the covenant of grace. Grace is the power of the Holy Spirit's presence to change our lives! The Holy Spirit is the only teacher of the New Covenant.

1 Jn. 2:20 But you have an anointing from the Holy One, and you know all things.

1 Jn. 2:27 But the anointing which you have received from Him abides in you, and you do not need that anyone teach you; but as the same anointing teaches you concerning all things, and is true, and is not a lie, and just as it has taught you, you will abide in Him.

To understand this grace of the Spirit of Understanding (Isa. 11:2), we must again look at the Old Testament shadow of the living relationships found in the Body of Christ. This truth was seen as sacrifices or offerings in the place that God chose for His name to abide for each of the tribes of Israel. God did not desire sacrifices and offerings, so the truth of those things commanded was really a type of the anti-type revealed as levels of "relationship" in the Body of Christ.

> *Heb. 10:5 Therefore, when He came into the world, He said: "Sacrifice and offering You did not desire, but a body You have prepared for Me. 6 In burnt offerings and sacrifices for sin you had no pleasure. 7 Then I said, 'Behold, I have come—in the volume of the book it is written of Me—to do Your will, O God.'"*

Let's look at the requirement of the Law that speaks of the "doctrine of baptisms" and the grace of the Spirit of Understanding:

> *Deut. 12:5 "But you shall seek the place where the LORD your God chooses, out of all your tribes, to put His name for His habitation; and there you shall go. 6 "There you shall take your 1)burnt offerings, your 2)sacrifices, your 3)tithes...*

The third requirement to be given, in the place that God chose His name to abide, for any tribe of Israel was the requirement of the "tithe". Tithe is hugely misunderstood in the Body of Christ. Many believe that tithe has been done away with in the New Testament. If tithe was merely an offering of money, this would be true, but tithe was never intended to be about money. Tithe includes money, but it is a testimony to a relational truth found in Christ. It was an act of responding to God, not obedience to the Law. Tithe of substance to God did not initiate in the priesthood of Aaron. It initiated in the priesthood of Melchizedek.

> *Gen. 14:18 Then Melchizedek king of Salem brought out bread and wine; he was the priest of God Most High. 19 And he blessed him and said: "Blessed be Abram of God Most High, Possessor of heaven and earth; 20 And blessed be God Most High, Who has delivered your enemies into your hand." And he gave him a tithe of all.*

The word "tithe" means, "tenth". It is impossible to "tithe" more or less than 10%. Tithe is either tithe (10%) or it is not tithe (10%). Abram didn't tithe (10%) to Melchizedek so that God would bless the remaining 90% of his possessions. He didn't keep a single thing of the spoils of his victory. Abram didn't tithe to God so that God would do something for Him. He tithed in response to what God had done for him. He was responding to Melchizedek's gift of bread and wine. He tithed to Melchizedek because He was the giver of bread and wine. I believe Abram tithed because he recognized the presence of the Lord. He knew that the presence of God in his life was the key to everything. He understood what the testimony of the word (bread) and the Spirit (wine) meant for his life. Abram was quickened by the Spirit of Understanding to realize that the bread and wine given to him by Melchizedek was only a gratuity of all that God possessed. He somehow knew in his spirit that God's gift of bread and wine to him was a small measure of God's love to Him and it represented the full measure of all that God had for Him. Abram responded to God by giving Melchizedek a gratuity (tithe) of all that he possessed. His love response to Melchizedek was a key to releasing the fullness of the inheritance that God had for him.

In the next chapters I will relate this offering of tithe to the receiving of the gift of the Holy Spirit and the doctrine of baptisms. In this chapter I will begin by giving the clear reasons for tithe in any covenant with God. Let's begin by looking at Jacob's account of tithing:

Gen. 28:10 Now Jacob went out from Beersheba and went toward Haran. 11 So he came to a certain place and stayed there all night, because the sun had set. And he took one of the stones of that place and put it at his head, and he lay down in that place to sleep. 12 Then he dreamed, and behold, a ladder was set up on the earth, and its top reached to heaven; and there the angels of God were ascending and descending on it. 13 And behold, the LORD stood above it and said: "I am the LORD God of Abraham your father and the God of Isaac; the land on which you lie I will give to you and your descendants. 14 Also your descendants shall be as the dust of the earth; you shall spread abroad to the west and the east, to the north and the south; and in you and in your seed all the families of the earth shall be blessed. 15 Behold, I am with you and will keep you wherever you go, and will bring you back to this land; for I will not leave you until I have done what I have spoken to you." 16 Then Jacob awoke from his sleep and said, "Surely the LORD is in this place, and I did not know it."

The first revelation that was revealed to Jacob was that the place he rested in was the place of the Lord's presence. Jacob recognized that the Lord was in the place where he rested. This stirred Jacob's heart toward the awe of what that place really was. Jacob thought he had merely found a place to sleep. God was revealing to Jacob a New Covenant truth of God inhabiting the human house that rests in, and because of, His presence.

> _Gen. 28:17 And he was afraid and said, "How awesome is this place! This is none other than the house of God, and this is the gate of heaven!"_

Jacob not only recognized that God was awesome, he recognized the place he was in was awesome! It was a place of God's presence! He acknowledged that the place was "God's house". He recognized that it was the key to accessing heaven for the earth. He saw that angels were released from there and that they went into heaven's storehouse to bring back what was needed for the house of God's presence in the earth. What a truth! Angels don't begin in heaven. They are ministering spirits sent unto those who inherit salvation (Heb. 1:14). Angels begin in the "house of God". They are sent to heavenly storehouses when a heavenly place is found in the earth. This truth is about the Body of Christ. When the corporate place of God's habitation is found in the earth, angels "ascend" and "descend" to bring heaven's supply! It is like rain. Rain doesn't begin in heaven. Rain begins in the earth! When vapors ascend to heaven, they meet certain conditions in heaven and return back to the earth as rain.

> _Ps. 135:7 He causes the vapors to ascend from the ends of the earth; He makes lightning for the rain; He brings the wind out of His treasuries._

> _Jer. 10:13 & Jer. 51:16 When He utters His voice, there is a multitude of waters in the heavens: "And He causes the vapors to ascend from the ends of the earth. He makes lightning for the rain, He brings the wind out of His treasuries."_

Angels are like rain. They don't begin in heaven; they are sent from the house of God to heavenly places on behalf of those who rest there. They are ministering spirits sent to those who "inherit" the things of God (Heb. 1:14). Jacob's ladder extended to heaven and the angels were seen "ascending" and "descending". They were not "descending" from heaven. Something was happening on the earth to make them "ascend" and then return with heavenly provisions from the heavenly storehouses!

> _Gen. 28:18 Then Jacob rose early in the morning, and took the stone that he had put at his head, set it up as a pillar, and poured oil on top of it._

Jacob took the stone he slept on. I believe that stone represented his old life.

His old life was dead, but God confirmed a house of a new creation set before him. The pillow became a pillar. It became a portal (pillar) to the destiny of Jacob's seed. He was awakened to destiny! He poured oil on the rock. Oil represents the manifest presence of Christ. He submerged (baptized) the rock in oil. His act was symbolic of the submergings (baptisms) of the Holy Spirit in our lives. It is like the oil on Aaron's head (Ps. 133) as the testimony of Zion's presence. Oil is the manifest presence of Christ that breaks every yoke (Isa. 10:26). Jacob recognized that the house of God was the place of Christ's manifest presence. All these things were prophetic in Jacob's time, but his physical acts reveal the true meaning of the baptism of the Holy Spirit and the grace of the Spirit of Understanding in and on the Church.

Jacob's rock represented the stone not cut with human hands seen by the prophet Daniel (Dan. 2:35). It represented the house of God on the Rock of Christ (1 Cor. 3:11). It was symbolic of the mountain destined to fill the earth with God's glory (Dan. 2:45). Jacob confirmed that the rock testified of the manifest presence of Christ when he changed the name of the place from Luz to Bethel.

Gen. 28:19 And he called the name of that place Bethel; but the name of that city had been Luz previously.

The name Luz means, "isolation" or "separation". The name Bethel means, "house of God". Jacob no longer saw the place as a place of isolation or separation (Luz). He saw it as a place of being joined to God. He saw it as the house of God (Bethel), a place where God's presence abides.

Gen. 28:20 Then Jacob made a vow, saying, "If God will be with me ¹, and keep me in this way that I am going ², and give me bread to eat ³ and clothing to put on,

Jacob's actions were prophetically profound. He revealed the testimony of the Holy Spirit in and upon the Body of Christ (the house of God). His actions testified of that which is the inward evidence of God in his house (bread – the word of God – a changed heart). His act was also a witness to the outward evidence (clothing – charisma and fruit) that he was the house of God.

Gen. 28:21 ...⁴"so that I come back to my father's house in peace, then the LORD shall be my God."

Jacob proclaimed the testimony that God and man tabernacle together. He was proclaiming by a prophetic action and word that his descendants of faith would know the inward evidence of God in his house (Passover), the outward evidence of the Holy Spirit as a spill-over from their lives (Pentecost), and that there would be a full return to the Father's house where men and God live fully together (Tabernacles).

> *Gen. 28:22 "And <u>this stone</u> which I have set as a pillar shall be God's house, and of all that You give me I will surely give a tenth to You."*

Jacob's stone represented the place of God's manifest presence in the earth. It represented the place of bread and wine. It was symbolic of the place of being in a right relationship with God (righteousness – God is our God) with no separation between men and God (we are God's people). Jacob's promise to tithe was not because of financial increase. His tithe was to be of all his increase, but it wasn't to be given because he had received increase. It was a first spill-over to God because he was a part of the manifestation of the house of God in the earth! His tithe was merely the evidence of being God's house. It was the loosing of the vapor of inheritance from the gate of heaven. His spilling over to God was a testimony to the fact that all he had received had come from God. That testimony was one of being an inheritor of the things of God. Angels are ministering spirits sent unto those who inherit salvation (Heb. 1:14). When Jacob tithed his substance to God, he released vapors of inheritance to heaven. This clearly identified him as an inheritor of God. Like vapor ascends for rain, angels ascend for the heavenly blessing on behalf of the inheritors of God. Jacob's spill-over of tithe identified him as a recipient of inheritance. Jacob's promise of tithe was a level of relationship with God to spill-over from the house of God with a testimony that his house was God's house.

> *Mal. 3:10 Bring all the tithes into the storehouse, that there may be <u>food in My house</u>, and prove Me now in this," says the LORD of hosts, "If I will not <u>open for you the windows of heaven</u> and pour out for you such blessing that there will not be room enough to receive it. 11 And I will <u>rebuke the devourer for your sakes</u>, so that he will not destroy the fruit of your ground, nor shall the vine fail to bear fruit for you in the field," says the LORD of hosts; 12 <u>And all nations will call you blessed, for you will be a delightful land</u>," says the LORD of hosts.*

Tithe is a testimony to a spill-over grace that confirms we are God's house. It is a testimony to the spill-over evidence of God's grace of the Spirit of Understanding testifying:

1 – He is with us - an open heaven - angels ascending and bringing blessing.

2 – He keeps us in the way - rebukes the devourer on our behalf.

3 – He gives us bread - food in His house - a changed character, nature, and way of our hearts.

4 – He gives us clothing - outward evidence - nations call us blessed.

Tithe is a recognition of God's house. It acknowledges that His house is the gate of heaven. It is the key to the storehouses of heaven and a loosing of the ability for angels (sent ones of God) to go into the heavenly places of God and bring back spiritual blessings to the earthly habitation of God (the Church, the Body of Christ, the place of God's manifest presence in the earth). Tithe is the acknowledgment of bread and wine from the Melchizedek King. It is a spill-over offering testifying of the presence of the testimony of the Word (bread) and the Spirit (wine) in God's house. In an even greater sense, tithe is a level of relationship with God that spills over with the testimony that comes when the Word and the Spirit come together in our lives (1 Jn. 4:2).

When we tithe, we acknowledge that the Word of God (living bread) and the Spirit of God (wine) have come together in our flesh, and it is changing the place that we live. We are being revealed as the place where God lives. When the Word (true knowledge) and Wisdom (true Spirit) come together in our lives, we come to Understanding. When Moses (the Word) and Elijah (the Spirit) were seen together with Jesus on the Mount, Jesus became a manifestation of the house of God's glory (Mt. 17:1-3; Mk. 9:2-4). He was transfigured. He became a living testimony of the house of God in the earth. A tithe level of relationship with God is our access to heaven's provision as Abrahamic sojourners of faith. We don't tithe because we receive an increase of money. We tithe because we recognize we are the place where the Melchizedek King brings bread and wine. We tithe because we are the house of God.

We tithe money, attitude, time, etc. – because we recognize the place of God's manifest presence in the earth. Tithe looses angels to the storehouses of God. It doesn't bless the remaining 90% of our earthly possessions. It gives us access to 100% of God's provision for us in heaven. What we possess is not enough to fulfill the testimony of all God has for us from heaven. Only what God possesses is enough to fulfill the testimony of God in our lives. That inheritance is loosed by an encounter with the Melchizedek King that involves a spill-over of our possessions to the King of righteousness and peace. It in turn invites a perpetual habitation and relationship with the Melchizedek King. It looses on earth what has already been loosed in heaven and thus it is loosed from heaven. It is fully seen in our encounter with Jesus as the Melchizedek King when His Spirit is poured out upon our lives. It is then that we spill over with the fruit and charisma of the Spirit, which guarantees us full access to all the Spirit has for us in heavenly places.

NOTE: Stop and let the Holy Spirit help you digest the subject matter of this chapter. Consider the Spirit of Understanding and your relationship with Jesus the Melchizedek King.

Chapter 3.2

The Third Eye of Grace

The third *Eye of Grace* is the grace of the Spirit of Understanding. It directly relates to the doctrine of baptisms and a tithe relationship with God in heaven. We find the New Testament correlation to this power of grace at the anointing of the Body of Christ in Acts, Chapter 2.

Acts 2:38 Then Peter said to them, "Repent, and let every one of you be baptized in the name of Jesus Christ for the remission of sins; and you shall <u>receive the gift of the Holy Spirit</u>."

This was the third instruction of Peter to the crowd in Jerusalem. Those who believe in Jesus are to receive the "gift of the Holy Spirit". The word for "gift" here is not the Greek word "charisma". It is the word "dorea". It is not the charisma of the Holy Spirit; it is the "gratuity". A "gratuity" is like a tithe. The word tithe means, "tenth". The "gratuity" of the Holy Spirit here is like the tithe. Tithe is not a spill-over of what we naturally possess. It is a spill-over of what God possesses on our behalf. We spill-over, of our natural possessions to the place that God chooses His name to abide on our behalf, not to get God's blessing on the remaining 90% of our natural possessions. We spill-over 10% of all that we possess to God, because we are His house. We are acknowledging that all we possess comes from God in heaven and not from our natural accounts in the earth. The tithe is not merely 10% of our natural possessions; it is a "gratuity" of all of our inheritance in heaven. We are acknowledging that we are God's house in the earth, but the full house is heavenly. It is not earthly! We are empowered with gifts from on high! Angels are ascending to God's heavenly storehouses and descending with heaven's provisions on our behalf. The tithe of the Old Covenant is a type and shadow of something hidden in the receiving of the gratuity of the Holy Spirit.

This "gratuity" is the gift of the Holy Spirit Himself. He is the "gift" and He is very "charismatic" in power and "fruitful" in His character. He is in us, upon us, and He is also fully in heaven. He has come to grant us the grace of the Spirit of Understanding so that we will spill-over (tithe) with the gratuity of all that He is in the heavenly place. He is God in and upon our lives! The "gift" of the Holy Spirit upon our lives is the evidence of an open heaven over our lives. He is the one who gives us understanding. He transforms our lives with the nature of God and the power of God by His grace of the Spirit of Understanding. The Spirit of Understanding is one of His *Seven Eyes of Grace* given to perfect our lives in Christ. It is like the practical applications of tithe, but tithe is not just an act we do before God. Tithe is a level of relationship with God that is inspired by the grace of the Spirit of Understanding. When the Holy Spirit was poured out upon the Church in Acts Chapter 2, there was an evidence of this tithe level of relationship. There was a spill-over of the charisma of the Holy Spirit. They began to speak in heavenly anointed tongues and prophecy. Heaven inspired words and substance began to spill-over from their hearts. Tithe is not 10% of our possessions. It is the first 10% spill-over of all of our increase. The Church in Acts, Chapter 2, was experiencing an increase of the testimony of God in their lives. They began to "spill-over" to God with the evidence of this heavenly increase. It was made possible by the grace of the Spirit of Understanding.

The Spirit of Understanding is found "in God". The gift of the Holy Spirit is the gift of God in and upon our lives. He makes it possible for us to be one with God's house in heaven. When we receive the gift of the Holy Spirit there is a "spill-over" of the life of God from within our hearts.

Jn. 4:24 "God is Spirit, and those who worship Him must worship in spirit and truth."

2 Cor. 3:17 Now the Lord is the Spirit; and where the Spirit of the Lord is, there is liberty.

The Spirit of Understanding gives an outward expression of the life of Christ within us. It is foundational to the doctrine of baptisms. It is the engulfing of the Holy Spirit that teaches us. He doesn't teach us in the same way as the Law or conscience teaches men. He doesn't come to inform us of what we must do. He empowers us to become who we must be as the house of God in the earth. He teaches us with the power of transformation. He activates the outward evidences of what is hidden within. Christ in us is our hope of glory (Col. 1:27). Holy Spirit comes to reveal that power hidden in our earthen vessels of clay.

2 Cor. 4:7 But we have this treasure in earthen vessels, that the excellence of the power may be of God and not of us.

I experienced the grace of the Spirit of the Lord and repentance from dead works on May 12, 1973. Two weeks after my conversion in Christ, I experienced the gift (gratuity) of the Holy Spirit. I believe the Holy Spirit was already inside my heart as the Spirit of the Lord and I had even experienced the grace of the Spirit of Wisdom in that I was immediately motivated to do works that spoke of my faith. I had already been delivered from cursing in my common language. I had been delivered from alcohol, drugs, and cigarettes. I saw amazing changes each and every day of my life upon my conversion to Christianity. The Spirit of the Lord was motivating my heart to Love God. The Spirit of Wisdom was granting me the grace to do new works that were speaking of my faith. But more grace was given to me when I experienced the gift of the Holy Spirit "upon" my life. It happened two weeks after my "born-again" experience in Christ.

When I was saved, I sought out the group of girls who I had previously called "Jesus freaks". They were very encouraged by my conversion. Several of my friends were being saved at that time as well and one of my friends came with me one evening to meet this group of girls in a place that changed my life forever. There was an older couple near my home that had converted a garage into a little chapel. They would let the Christian young people come and pray there anytime they liked. This group of Christian girls would go there each evening and pray and worship God. One evening they invited my friend and me to come along. We gladly went. When we arrived, we were amazed! Several of the girls were praying for one of the other girls. They began to minister to her with words of knowledge given by the Holy Spirit. I knew there was no way they knew naturally the things they were sharing with this girl. The girl they were ministering to was being amazingly touched by the love of God. It was powerful and obvious! I knew there must be something more to this Christian life I had just begun to experience. My friend was impressed as well. We both asked them about this obvious power evident upon their lives. They explained to us that it was the baptism of the Holy Spirit. We were both eager to receive this gift from heaven. The grace of the Spirit of Understanding was ready to give us the ability for the power of God inside of us to be known visibly to the world around us. The Holy Spirit's power from within caused us to become anointed to be witnesses of Christ. We were not to be merely witnesses "about" Him. We were anointed to become witnesses "of" Him. His anointed presence and the power of His resurrection began to "spill-over" from our lives. We were "submerged" in His presence! We both received a heavenly language that night. It wasn't very elegant! I think my greatest word was "scaw" and his greatest word was "raw"! It wasn't the clarity of the language that amazed me. It was the power and the presence of the Holy Spirit that accompanied those words! We were both intoxicated in the presence of God.

I remember the joy that was spilling-over from within me. It was only a matter of days that my new prayer language became fluent and took on many new words of expression, but it wasn't the words themselves that were amazing. It was the power and presence of the Holy Spirit! I began to experience new revelation from God each day. I experienced a grace of the Holy Spirit's charisma of the discerning of spirits. Every evening for the next weeks, we would gather to pray and worship God. The Holy Spirit would almost always tell us to go to some town and we would share our testimony. I led many people to Jesus during that time. I was being anointed to be a witness of Jesus Christ and the power of His resurrection!

Lk. 24:49 "Behold, I send the Promise of My Father upon you; but tarry in the city of Jerusalem until you are endued with power from on high."

Acts 1:8 "But you shall receive power when the Holy Spirit has come upon you; and you shall be witnesses to Me in Jerusalem, and in all Judea and Samaria, and to the end of the earth."

Receiving the "gift of the Holy Spirit" didn't mean the Spirit of the Lord was not within my heart at the moment I accepted Jesus Christ. I had experienced God in my heart the moment I asked Him to come into my life. I believe that every believer has the ability to cast out demons, speak with new tongues, break the power of the enemy's deceptions, have victory over every deadly thing, be kept safe by the power of God, lay hands on the sick for their recovery, and anything that Christ has obtained for us as a MAN. However, I don't believe that all believers live with these things evident in their lives. These things are not manifested by the right instruction or information given to us. They are made known by the power of Christ's anointing that comes to us by the grace of the Spirit of Understanding and the gift of the engulfing presence of the Holy Spirit upon our lives. When we are submerged in Him, He releases the things of heaven in our hearts to become a "spill-over" of Christlike evidence upon our lives. The baptism of the Holy Spirit is the key to releasing the power of Christ hidden within us!

Mk. 16:16 "He who believes and is baptized will be saved; but he who does not believe will be condemned. 17 And these signs will follow those who believe: In My name they will cast out demons; they will speak with new tongues; 18 they will take up serpents; and if they drink anything deadly, it will by no means hurt them; they will lay hands on the sick, and they will recover."

When we experience the power of this grace of the Spirit of Understanding, we receive the BOLD outward evidence of God's character and power in our lives. The more we experience the true Teacher of "transformation", the more we become changed in Him. We receive a personal testimony in Christ. The evidence of the inward teacher becomes a personal testimony that others can see.

1 Jn. 5:9 If we receive the witness of men, the witness of God is greater; for this is the witness of God which He has testified of His Son. 10 He who believes in the Son of God has the witness in himself; he who does not believe God has made Him a liar, because he has not believed the testimony that God has given of His Son. 11 And this is the testimony: that God has given us eternal life, and this life is in His Son. 12 He who has the Son has life; he who does not have the Son of God does not have life.

The Spirit of Understanding outwardly reveals the mysteries within. The things within us come from the power of Christ who is in our hearts. The gate of heaven is found in our hearts. God wants to release the mystery, the power, and the inheritance of heaven through the gate of heaven found in our hearts. It is the same as the principles seen in the offering of tithe. There is a spill-over to God of the things that come from God because we are the house of God. Oil is poured out upon the Rock of Christ! There is an open heaven and the evidence of spiritual bread (inward change) and spiritual clothing (outward evidence) are manifested in our lives. We receive things by God's Spirit that go beyond our human abilities. We begin to understand God in a way that exceeds our human limitations of understanding.

NOTE: Stop and practice the spill over relationship of the Holy Spirit in your life. Spend time praying in the Spirit today and let the Holy Spirit minister to you in regard to the Spirit of Understanding.

Chapter 3.3

The Third Eye of Grace

The grace of the Spirit of Understanding is the testimony of the engulfing of the Holy Spirit. It is the baptism of the Holy Spirit that quickens our new nature in Christ and reveals His resurrection power through our lives. As I stated earlier, the word baptism means to "engulf" or to "immerse completely". To be baptized in the Holy Spirit is to be "engulfed" in the Spirit of Christ. How do we receive the fullness and the power of the Holy Spirit? The baptism of the Holy Spirit comes from Jesus Himself.

Mt. 3:11 "I indeed baptize you with water unto repentance, but He who is coming after me is mightier than I, whose sandals I am not worthy to carry. He will baptize you with the Holy Spirit and fire."

Jn. 1:32 And John bore witness, saying, "I saw the Spirit descending from heaven like a dove, and He remained upon Him. 33 I did not know Him, but He who sent me to baptize with water said to me, 'Upon whom you see the Spirit descending, and remaining on Him, this is He who baptizes with the Holy Spirit.' 34 And I have seen and testified that this is the Son of God."

John the Baptist submerged people in water as a testimony of repentance from an old life, but Jesus is the one who "submerges" us in the Holy Spirit for a testimony of our new lives in Christ. The Holy Spirit is the witness of Jesus in His resurrection. He has come to reveal who He is in our lives. He has also come to reveal who He is in the corporate life of the Church. He comes to teach us with power and life! He does not come with information from heaven, but with the power of transformation. He brings to us the grace of the Spirit of Understanding to give to us a name that is new by Christ's life. The grace of the Spirit of Understanding comes upon our lives to give us a personal testimony in Christ. He changes our character, nature, way, power, and authority to reveal our new lives hidden in Him. Peter instructed the

96

crowd in Acts, Chapter 2, to "receive the gift of the Holy Spirit". Is there a difference between the Holy Spirit within us and the Holy Spirit upon us?

> *Jn. 14:16 "And I will pray the Father, and He will give you another Helper, that He may abide with you forever, 17 even the Spirit of truth, whom the world cannot receive, because it neither sees Him nor knows Him; but you know Him, for He dwells with you and will be in you."*

Jesus told His disciples that the Helper, the Holy Spirit, would both be "in them" and "with them". He was with them in the form of the Body of Jesus Christ the man, but He would come to them as the Spirit who would abide in their hearts and who would also be with them in the Body of Christ, the Church. Jesus completed the first part of this promise after His resurrection from the dead. He came to them as the Spirit of the Lord and the giver of life. They were hiding in a room for fear of death and Jesus came to give them the overcoming power of life!

> *Jn. 20:19 Then, the same day at evening, being the first day of the week, when the doors were shut where the disciples were assembled, for fear of the Jews, Jesus came and stood in the midst, and said to them, "Peace be with you." 20 Now when He had said this, He showed them His hands and His side. Then the disciples were glad when they saw the Lord. 21 Then Jesus said to them again, "Peace to you! As the Father has sent Me, I also send you." 22 And when He had said this, He breathed on them, and said to them, "Receive the Holy Spirit."*

When Jesus appeared to His disciples after His resurrection, He breathed upon them and said to them, "Receive the Holy Spirit". I believe that Jesus breathed on His disciples just as God did with First Adam (Gen. 2:7). Jesus gave to them the true breath of life! It was only after seeing Jesus, after His resurrection, that the disciples were able to receive the Holy Spirit. Jesus said that unless we are born-again we cannot see the kingdom of God (Jn. 3:3). When we are "born-again", we become able to see the life of God's kingdom by His Spirit. Just like the disciples, we received the Holy Spirit within us when we became "born-again". After Jesus appeared to the disciples, He spoke to them concerning a greater fulfillment of the Holy Spirit in their lives. Just like He did for the early disciples, Jesus has a plan concerning our lives and the fullness that He intends for every believer to have. This fullness of the New Covenant promise comes when we receive the Holy Spirit upon us to become a powerful witness of the power of His resurrection and the authority of His name to the world. We find a record of Jesus talking to his disciples further in the book of Luke in regard to this fullness. His recorded instruction given to them was after He had appeared to them and breathed on them to "receive the Holy Spirit". Jesus then told these same disciples to wait in Jerusalem until they would receive the promise, which He had spoken about. This promise was the Holy Spirit whom Jesus said would come upon them with power.

Lk. 24:49 "Behold, I send the Promise of My Father upon you; but tarry in the city of Jerusalem until you are endued with power from on high."

Jesus told them to go and wait in Jerusalem until they would be endued with power from on high. To be "endued" is to be fully "clothed". Jesus told them the Holy Spirit would come upon them and would "clothe" them. He was testifying that the Holy Spirit would not only be "in them", but that He would also be "with them". He would come "upon them". How can the Holy Spirit be within and upon us? I believe the best way to understand this is to understand a mystery revealed by Jesus. One day, a man named Nicodemus approached Jesus. Nicodemus had assumed that Jesus was a great teacher sent by God, since supernatural things were happening as a result of His ministry. When Nicodemus made His statements to Jesus, Jesus responded by saying that unless one is "born-again" he cannot see the kingdom of God (Jn. 3:3). Nicodemus had a hard time with Jesus' words. Jesus was trying to reveal to Nicodemus that being born-again was an earthly experience through a heavenly encounter with God. Jesus made a powerful statement to him when He made a statement alluding to a heavenly mystery.

Jn. 3:12 "If I have told you earthly things and you do not believe, how will you believe if I tell you heavenly things? 13 No one has ascended to heaven but He who came down from heaven, that is, the Son of Man who is in heaven."

Jesus was saying to Nicodemus, "You're having a hard time with something earthly, Nicodemus. What will you do if I tell you something heavenly? I am the one who has ascended to heaven, I came from heaven, and I am in heaven right now." How could this be possible! How could Jesus be in all three places at the same time! Jesus was revealing to Nicodemus that He was God. He was not limited to the realm of time and space, as human beings know it. Jesus was in all three places at the same time and in all three places at different times. He had ascended to heaven, though He had not ascended. He had come from heaven, yet He was in heaven. He could do this because Jesus was God! How can the Holy Spirit be in us and upon us? The Holy Spirit is like Jesus. He is God!

The promise of the Father spoken through Jesus was that God would be in us, and upon us. We would know God in us and we would know God with us. Jesus Promised to send the Holy Spirit to ALL Believers!

> *Acts 1:8 "But you shall receive power when the Holy Spirit has come upon you; and you shall be witnesses to Me in Jerusalem, and in all Judea and Samaria, and to the end of the earth."*

> *Lk. 24:49 "Behold, I send the Promise of My Father upon you; but tarry in the city of Jerusalem until you are endued with power from on high."*

Jesus paid the full price for us all to be brought near to God (Eph. 2:13). Now that we have been brought near to God, He desires for us to become a witness of His resurrection life. To make this possible, God desires to place His Holy Spirit upon us. When we asked Jesus into our hearts, we became born-again. It was God's Holy Spirit who caused the regeneration of our spirits to give us new life through Jesus Christ. God's Holy Spirit now lives within us. Now that God lives within us, He desires that we have all the fullness of Him with us here on earth. Not only does He desire to live within us, He also desires to be upon us. John the Baptist testified that Jesus would do two things; 1) take away the sins of the world; and 2) baptize with the Holy Spirit. As the Lord, Jesus has taken away our sins. As Christ, He desires to baptize us with the Holy Spirit. Jesus promised that the Father would not leave us comfortless, but that He would send us the Comforter who is the Holy Spirit.

> *Jn. 14:26 "But the Helper, the Holy Spirit, whom the Father will send in My name, He will teach you all things, and bring to your remembrance all things that I said to you."*

The Holy Spirit has come that He might make known the things of God to us. He is the Spirit of God sent to our lives in order to release the authority of Christ Jesus through us to the world. Before Jesus ascended to the Father, He spoke of the promised Holy Spirit. He told the disciples to remain in

99

Jerusalem until they would receive power from on high.

> *Acts 1:5 "For John truly baptized with water, but you shall be baptized with the Holy Spirit not many days from now."*

You may ask, "Am I a Christian if I'm not baptized in the Holy Spirit?" The answer to that question is most definitely YES! Your next question may be, "Why do I need the baptism of the Holy Spirit if I am already a Christian and already saved?" The question is not whether you are or are not a Christian. It is only a question of how effective you are as a Christian. How effective is your witness to the world of the resurrection anointing of Christ? The grace of the Spirit of Understanding is one of the *Seven Eyes of Grace* of God given to perfect the Church. The Holy Spirit is in us as the Spirit that cries out Abba, Father, to God in Heaven (Gal. 4:6). He is upon us to testify that Jesus is both Lord and Christ (Acts 2:36)! Just as Jesus testified of the Father through the many miracles, signs, and wonders performed through Him in His ministry; the Holy Spirit testifies of Jesus in our lives through miracles, signs, and wonders of His resurrection life!

NOTE: Stop again and let the Holy Spirit minister to you in regard to the material in this chapter.

Chapter 3.4

The Third Eye of Grace

It is the Holy Spirit, in His grace of the Spirit of Understanding, who gives the prophetic power of a new testimony in Christ. He is at work in our lives as the teacher who carries the power of transformation to the testimony of a new life in Christ. He also has the power to create a new reality in the world we live in. The outpouring of the Holy Spirit in Acts, Chapter 2, was the fulfillment of a prophetic word given through the mouth of the prophet Joel.

> *Joel 2:28 "And it shall come to pass afterward that I will pour out My Spirit on all flesh; your sons and your daughters shall prophesy, your old men shall dream dreams, your young men shall see visions; 29 And also on My menservants and on My maidservants I will pour out My Spirit in those days."*

The prophet Joel prophesied that the Spirit that would come upon God's people would anoint them to become prophetic. They would proclaim prophetic words of life. They would be anointed to have prophetic dreams and prophetic visions. I like to define prophecy as, "God speaks, life happens!" The Holy Spirit's anointing upon our lives is prophetic. He anoints us to become God's voice in the earth. He speaks His voice to us and "life happens"! We speak "His voice" to the world and "life happens"! The Holy Spirit gives us prophetic understanding and a prophetic anointing to speak God's words of life. He anoints us with the third *Eye of Grace* known as the Spirit of Understanding. His prophetic anointing doesn't just affect us. It has the power to change the world! When Peter explained to the crowd in Acts, Chapter 2, what this prophetic Spirit was about, he included the world changing aspects of Joel's prophecy (Acts 2:19-21).

> *Joel 2:30 "And I will show wonders in the heavens and in the earth: blood and fire and pillars of smoke. 31 The sun shall be turned into darkness, and the moon into blood, before the coming of the great and terrible day of the LORD. 32 And it shall come to pass that whoever*

> *calls on the name of the LORD shall be saved. For in Mount Zion and
> in Jerusalem there shall be deliverance, as the LORD has said, among
> the remnant whom the LORD calls."*

Many have taught that Peter was testifying of the second coming of
Jesus in his prophetic revelation. They believe he was testifying of the "end
times" to come. I believe Peter was testifying of the "last days" that had come
to the earth in the first century. I believe he was referring to the "last days" that
come in every century since that time. In order to truly be Scripture, Peter's
words had to apply to the day he spoke, and to the days that would follow
(2 Tim. 3:16, 17). He was speaking to real people gathered in a real crowd
in Jerusalem. In the Scripture certain phrases mean certain things. It is God's
way of revealing His heavenly language to an earthbound people. There is a
consistency throughout the word of God (Heb. 13:8). Certain biblical phrases
have always meant the same thing throughout Scripture. The phrase, "the sun
shall be turned to darkness", has always meant the same thing throughout all
of Scripture. It means the end of a natural kingdom. It was used for the fall of
Egypt, the fall of Edom, the fall of Babylon, and the then coming fall of Israel
as the nation of God among the nations of the world. The "moon turned to
blood," testifies of the fact that the life of the flesh is lost for a nation, a people,
or even a person. The life of the flesh is in the blood (Lev. 17:11), and it is
indicative of a society's priesthood, social order, or culture. The "sun turned
to darkness" and the "moon turned to blood" are expressions that reveal what
happens to a natural nation or people when the presence of the Lord comes to
them. These were expressions true of natural kingdoms and societies in the
day of the Lord. The day of the Lord is not just a day to come. It is a day that
has come for many throughout the generations of humanity. For the righteous
it is blessing, and for the unrighteous it is judgment. There are many Scripture
examples of the day of the Lord in terms of both blessing and judgment: For
the righteous - Isa. 58:13, 14; For Babylon - Isa. 13:6, 7; Described - Isa. 2:12;
For Egypt - Jer. 46:10; Ezek. 30:3; And False Prophets - Ezek. 13:5; Judah -
Joel 1:15; 2:1, 11; For Pharisaic Israel - Joel 2:31; For the Northern Kingdom
- Amos 5:18, 20; For Edom - Obad. 1:15, 16; For Judah - Zeph. 1:7, 14; For
Jerusalem - Zech. 14:1; For the Pharisaic day - Mal. 4:5; Acts 2:20;
1 Thes. 5:1-9; Rev. 6:12-17.

The other phrase that needs to be defined in this Scripture in Joel and Acts
is the phrase, "before the coming of".

Joel 2:31 The sun shall be turned into darkness, and the moon into blood, before ~~the coming of~~ the great and terrible day of the LORD.

The Hebrew word for "before", as it is found in the book of Joel, is the word "paniym". It means, *the face (as the part that turns); used in a great variety of applications (literally and figuratively); also (with prep. pref.) as a prep. (before, etc.).* The Hebrew word for "day" is the word "yowm". It means, *a day (as the warm hours), whether lit. (from sunrise to sunset, or from one sunset to the next), or fig. (a space of time defined by an associated term), [often used adv.]* So, the word "before" can imply a progressive process and the word "day" describes a season of process or time as well. Neither of these words implies just a "moment" in time. I don't believe this is just the coming event of Christ's second return, but it is "in the face of" every part of the continual, increasing coming of Christ. On the day of Pentecost in Acts, Chapter 2, the cloud of the Lord's presence came upon the Body of Christ. The Body of Christ in the form of the man Jesus had physically risen into heaven ten days earlier, but now the presence of heaven was poured out upon the Body of Christ in the form of the Church in the earth. Maybe this is why the angels told the disciples to get to Jerusalem and wait for the promise, for He would return in "like manner" as He went (Acts 1:11). Jesus ascended into the cloud of heaven in Bodily form, and He began an unstoppable, perpetual, ever increasing return as the cloud of heaven's grace upon the Body of Christ on the day of Pentecost. The Holy Spirit can be understood as the rainbow promise of God to change the nations, and not destroy them (Gen. 9:11-16). This was happening in the day of the first century Church. It is still happening today! It will continue to happen until the fullness of Christ has come! We are living in both the "last days" in the earth and the "eternal day of the Lord" in the Body of Christ. The grace of the Spirit of Understanding has come to end all "natural kingdoms" and to subdue them under the dominion of Christ's life and His eternal kingdom. When we are "engulfed" or "submerged into" the presence of the prophetic Spirit of God, our worlds change! Jesus becomes our light of life and our old kingdom rule ceases and desists to be as it was. We receive a new name by the testimony of the grace of the Spirit of Understanding and the doctrine of baptisms.

Isa. 60:19 "The sun shall no longer be your light by day, nor for brightness shall the moon give light to you; but the LORD will be to you an everlasting light, and your God your glory. 20 Your sun shall no longer go down, nor shall your moon withdraw itself; for the LORD will be your everlasting light, and the days of your mourning shall be ended. 21 Also your people shall all be righteous; they shall inherit

> *the land forever, the branch of My planting, the work of My hands,*
> *that I may be glorified. 22 A little one shall become a thousand, and*
> *a small one a strong nation. I, the LORD, will hasten it in its time."*

It was the unity of man in the flesh that resulted in a world that is divided and confused. The Tower of Babel (Babel means, confusion) was the result of man's attempts at building his own heavenly kingdom (Gen. 11:2-9). The Holy Spirit is the asked of seed in Babel. He was symbolized in the governor in Nehemiah's day known as Zerubbabel. Zerubbabel means, "seed in babble". He was the son of Shealtiel - meaning, "asked of or lent of God". The governor Zerubbabel was symbolic of the government of grace given to us when we ask the Holy Spirit to come into our lives (Lk. 11:9-13). The Holy Spirit has been sent to bring the unity of God the Father to the scattered and confused nations of the world.

When the Holy Spirit was poured out on my life in 1973, I was a relatively confused person. My life had been consumed with desires of my own kingdom. I could have been known as "King Ted" with the "kingdom of Ted". I lived my life for me, and I had developed a certain culture about myself. The Holy Spirit introduced King Jesus to my life and the kingdom of Ted bowed the knee to His amazing grace. I began to pursue the life of the Spirit, rather than the life of my own flesh. I found that it was a progressive work in my life. I began to grow quickly as a Christian, but not as quickly as I perhaps thought. I used to bind things that should be loosed and loose things that should be bound. I used to believe fear based doctrines and legalistic practices. Even in my ignorance God blessed me, but most of all He blessed me with more of the presence of the grace of His Spirit of Understanding. My old traditions began to be transformed by the transformations of the Holy Spirit. I find this true today. I have been a Christian for more than 49 years, but I am expecting more changes in my life this year by the "engulfing" of the Holy Spirit and His grace of the Spirit of Understanding. I am being confirmed as a member of the house of God. His anointed presence (oil) is being poured out upon the rock of my life. There is an open heaven over my life. The devourer is being rebuked on my behalf. The word of God is becoming more real in my heart year by year. The daily bread of God's word to my heart is being confirmed by His voice speaking inside my heart. I am coming alive in Him! The outward evidence of His power and authority is causing other people's lives to be touched by His life in and upon me. I have laid hands on numerous people and seen them healed. I have cast out numerous devils. I pray in tongues daily and prophesy the same. The charisma and the fruit of the Spirit are becoming more real in my life, year by year. If this is true for my individual life, it must also be true for the life of the corporate Church. We can expect the increasing testimony of the grace of the Spirit of Understanding in the life of the Church. It is a "tithe" level relationship that spills over with His gifts from heaven. It confirms we are the place of His habitation. We are the inheritors of His kingdom and of His will! We are the Body of Christ!

As a young man I used to find my identity in music. I got my first guitar when I was 13 years old. It was more than a guitar to me. It was a dream of becoming someone in life. I used to practice daily. I was part of a rock band in the world and used to spend my weekends filled with performances in the midst of a drunken and loose lifestyle. When I asked Jesus to come into my heart and be the Lord of my life, this insecurity in identity was still an issue in my life. I changed my style of music, but I hadn't yet changed my source of identity. The Holy Spirit was in my heart and upon my life. I would write songs on a weekly basis and play my songs on the streets, in coffee shops, and in church environments. I did this for a couple of years as a young Christian. The Holy Spirit began to touch my heart about music and my looking to music as a source of identity. Although I felt I was inspired to write songs by the leading of the Holy Spirit, there was something greater that the Holy Spirit wanted to do in my life. He wanted me to find my identity in my Father in Heaven. He began to convict my heart of my wrong motives. One day He told me not to play my guitar anymore. It was hard to obey at first, but the Holy Spirit gave me the grace to release it from my life. I soon found that I didn't need to play music to be secure in whom I was as a person. I found my love for God as my Father was increasing. A couple of years later, as I was going to sleep one night, the Holy Spirit put a song in my spirit. I began to sing the song. The Holy Spirit told me to get my guitar and write the song. It was a worship song to my Father in heaven. That very week, my pastor approached me about leading worship in a small group. I felt led by the Spirit to do so. I began a brand-new journey in my life. I was a worship leader for the next fifteen years in various measures of responsibility. Everything was new! The kingdom of Ted Hanson had been subdued by the grace and love of the kingdom of Jesus Christ. I no longer got my identity out of music, but I could present my gift of worship to the One in whom I did identify! The Holy Spirit had submerged my life to transform my identity. It was the grace of the Spirit of Understanding at work in my life.

NOTE: Please stop again and allow the Holy Spirit to speak to you throughout this day. Invite the grace of the Spirit of Understanding to work in your life.

Chapter 3.5
The Third Eye of Grace

Just like tithe, the receiving of the baptism of the Holy Spirit is not something that just automatically comes to our lives. The first initiation of the out-pouring of the Holy Spirit came to 120 people who diligently sought God's presence in an upper room in Jerusalem. Their hunger for God proved to position them for the giving of the gift of the promise from heaven. They gathered in an upper room because they believed the promise would come. They believed there was an open heaven over their lives. They weren't testing to see if it was open or not. They were expecting the Spirit to be poured out. When the day of Pentecost fully came, they received the Holy Spirit.

Acts 2:4 And they were all filled with the Holy Spirit and began to speak with other tongues, as the Spirit gave them utterance.

The crowd was amazed with the evidence of the resurrection power of Christ poured out upon the 120 in the upper room. The people pressed the apostle Peter to know what this astonishing display was all about. Peter instructed the crowd concerning the testimony of a prophetic Spirit prophesied by the Prophet Joel. He instructed the crowd in Jerusalem to repent, be baptized in the name of Jesus, and to "receive" the gift of the Holy Spirit.

Acts 2:38 Then Peter said to them, "Repent and let every one of you be baptized in the name of Jesus Christ for the remission of sins, and you shall receive the gift of the Holy Spirit."

This was the third grace of the Holy Spirit's sevenfold power of grace. The result was obviously a grace from heaven. God confirmed Peter's words by baptizing thousands in the crowd with the Holy Spirit.

Acts 10:44 While Peter was still speaking these words, the Holy Spirit fell upon all those who heard the word. 45 And those of the circumcision who believed were astonished, as many as came with Peter, because the gift of the Holy Spirit had been poured out on the Gentiles also. 46 For they heard them speak with tongues and magnify God...

There are times where God acts in His sovereign ability to fulfill His promises in our lives, and surely this experience in Jerusalem was one of those times. We must remember that this was the first experience of what was expected to be a continual experience in the world. I know of testimonies like these. I know of a man who was baptized in the Holy Spirit and spoke in other tongues before he even knew what happened to him. He had been on a two-year journey in pursuit of "truth". At the end of his journey, he felt prompted to read the Bible one more time. He had read it already, along with the Koran, the writings of Buddha, and other religious manuscripts. He felt compelled to give the Bible one more reading. As he began in the book of Genesis, he read the story of the fall of man. When he read the part where the woman and the man ate of the tree of the knowledge of good and evil, he felt as though the bottoms of the souls of his feet had opened to a hole and energy began to drain from his body. He went to sleep, only to awake the next morning with the same experience continuing to happen. He drove to the country where some friends of his lived in the hope of asking them for help in explaining what he was experiencing. When he arrived at their property, he had to walk across a meadow to get to their house. As he did, he experienced a bright light, and he began to feel as though he was being filled up with abundance of life. He began to speak in tongues. He had no idea what was going on in his life. No one was home at the house so he got in his car and began to drive to a nearby town that he thought his friends might be in. The whole time he was being filled with great joy and this strange language continued to bubble up from within him. When he arrived at the town, he amazingly ran into the man that he had been traveling with for two years in his search for "truth". When he approached the man, out of his own mouth came the words, "I have ended my pursuit of truth and I have found the love of the Lord Jesus Christ!" That was the first moment that he actually knew what had happened to him. Jesus had come into his life, and he didn't even know what had happened until the Holy Spirit confessed from his own mouth the truth of his experience. I believe the key for this man was in the fact that he had been searching for truth for two years. He was a hungry soul who had found what he was looking for in the true source of life.

HOW can someone RECEIVE? The Bible teaches that we are to ask to receive the Holy Spirit. Sometimes asking comes in the form of intently seeking, like the 120 in the upper room or like the case of my friend. Sometimes it is simple. It is simply asking. A key to asking is found in the passion to ask.

Lk. 11:5 And He said to them, "Which of you shall have a friend, and go to him at midnight and say to him, 'Friend, lend me three loaves; 6 'for a friend of mine has come to me on his journey, and I have nothing to set before him'; 7 and he will answer from within and say, 'Do not trouble me; the door is now shut, and my children are with me in bed; I cannot rise and give to you'? 8 I say to you, though he will not rise and give to him because he is his friend, yet because of his persistence he will rise and give him as many as he needs."

I believe the person asking for the bread in this story represented the Gentile nations of the world. The nation of Israel had been given the word of God and His covenant among all the nations of the world. The problem when Jesus came was that the nation of Israel was asleep. The nations were hungry, but Israel was asleep to who God really was. I believe this story can apply to our lives today, but it definitely applied to the lost nations in the day of Jesus' first coming. They needed "three loaves". The number "three" is commonly significant of "God" in the Scriptures. The implication is that no other bread could satisfy. Friends were coming and the man had nothing to give them. This is the state of our lives apart from Christ. Only the bread of God's living word in our hearts gives us what is needed to meet the needs of the world. I would like to also point out here that Jesus said the promise would be given so that we could be witnesses of Him to the world (Acts. 1:11). This is the life of the Holy Spirit given through us to the world we live in. The story progresses to reveal further truth of receiving the Holy Spirit.

Lk.11: 9 "And I say to you, ask, and it will be given to you; seek, and you will find; knock, and it will be opened to you. 10 For everyone who asks receives, and he who seeks finds, and to him who knocks it will be opened. 11 If a son asks for bread from any father among you, will he give him a stone? Or if he asks for a fish, will he give him a serpent instead of a fish? 12 Or if he asks for an egg, will he offer him a scorpion? 13 If you then, being evil, know how to give good gifts to your children, how much more will your heavenly Father give the Holy Spirit to those who ask Him!"

Several things are seen in this Scripture. We see that God is a Father and He gives good gifts. The source of all of the perfect gifts that He gives is the gift of His Holy Spirit. He is the grace of the Spirit of Understanding who comes as a gratuity into our lives when we ask for Him. He is like the tithe that releases angels on our behalf to bring to us everything that is needed from the heavenly storehouses. He is the presence of God that confirms we are God's children. We also see that He is ready for us to ask, and He is ready to give. The key is that our asking involves an asking, a seeking, and a knocking. We must know we need Him, we must pursue finding Him, and we must expect that He will answer.

When we were born-again, the Holy Spirit came within us. When Jesus baptizes us with the Holy Spirit we become "clothed with power from on high" (Lk. 24:49). The Greek word for "clothed" is ENDUO, which means, *"to invest with clothing (lit. or fig.): array, clothe (with), endue, have (put) on"*. The Father sends the Holy Spirit as the clothes of Christ upon our lives to confirm that Christ lives in us. He comes upon us, because He is already in us. This can happen simultaneously, but we find an example in the book of Acts, where a group received the baptism of the Holy Spirit having already been believers in Jesus Christ.

> *Acts 8:15 ...who, when they had come down, prayed for them that they might receive the Holy Spirit. 16 For as yet He had fallen upon none of them. They had only been baptized in the name of the Lord Jesus. 17 Then they laid hands on them, and they received the Holy Spirit.*

This group of people was in Samaria and had received the word of the Lord through Phillip. When the apostles heard about the fact these Samarians had received the word of the Lord, they sent Peter and John to them to minister the Holy Spirit to them. Peter and John laid hands on them, and they received the baptism of the Holy Spirit. They were willing and asking, and Peter and John were simply giving them what they possessed. From this, we can also know that when the Holy Spirit is upon our lives, we can in turn release His presence to come upon others.

> *Acts 19:6 And when Paul had laid hands on them, the Holy Spirit came upon them, and they spoke with tongues and prophesied.*

When the Holy Spirit comes upon our lives there is a testimony of His presence. Just like we tithe of our money to reveal that we have been increased in our money, the Holy Spirit comes to spill-over with charisma and fruit to reveal that we have received an increase of the grace of the Spirit of Understanding. In the Second Chapter of Acts, those baptized in the Holy Spirit were filled with the fruits of love and joy, but also the charisma of other tongues and prophecy. There are several things that happen in our lives as a result of the transformation teaching power of the Holy Spirit and the grace of the Spirit of Understanding.

When we receive the baptism of the Holy Spirit, we have the power of the Spirit. He gives us the ability to pray when we don't know how.

Rom. 8:26 Likewise the Spirit also helps in our weaknesses. For we do not know what we should pray for as we ought, but the Spirit Himself makes intercession for us with groanings which cannot be uttered. 27 Now He who searches the hearts knows what the mind of the Spirit is, because He makes intercession for the saints according to the will of God.

He speaks a language that we don't understand. That language reveals the mysteries of heaven in the midst of the natural world we live in. It is not a bad idea to have the mysteries of heaven when we are limited by the patterns of our past!

1 Cor. 14:2 For he who speaks in a tongue does not speak to men but to God, for no one understands him; however, in the spirit he speaks mysteries.

He gives us the ability to build ourselves up for the sake of the Body of Christ, and the ability to build up the other members of the Body. He literally enables us to be like spiritual architects or builders. He enables us to give God's expressions (words) of life to others so that they will be further joined to the roof of the house of God. That "roof" is the headship of Jesus Christ in the Church.

1 Cor. 14:3 But he who prophesies speaks edification and exhortation and comfort to men. 4 He who speaks in a tongue edifies himself, but he who prophesies edifies the church.

1 Cor. 14:13 Therefore let him who speaks in a tongue pray that he may interpret. 14 For if I pray in a tongue, my spirit prays, but my understanding is unfruitful. 15 What is the result then? I will pray with the spirit, and I will also pray with the understanding. I will sing with the spirit, and I will also sing with the understanding.

Jude, revealed to us that praying in tongues will build up our most holy faith. The context of Jude is when people speak evil of us according to what they don't understand, or what they only understand naturally. When we are being spoken of wrongly, it is good to pray in tongues. The source of faith is not praying in tongues. The source of faith is hearing God (Rom. 10:17), but praying in the Holy Spirit (tongues) can position our spirits to hear God's word to our spirits and not the accusations against our souls. What a simple, yet wonderful gift!

> *Jude 20 But you, beloved, building yourselves up on your most holy faith, praying in the Holy Spirit...*

The Holy Spirit gives the ability to pray and to know what is the will of God in our lives (1 Cor. 2:6-13). He gives us the power to intercede (pray) for one another (Eph. 6:18). He gives us times of rest and refreshing (Isa. 28:11, 12). It's from within that He gives the ability to bear the fruit of God (Gal. 5:22, 23). The fruit of the Holy Spirit reveals the personality of the Holy Spirit. The fruit testifies of the presence of God in our lives.

The manifestations of the Holy Spirit are given as power for the believer, and for the benefit of all. The Holy Spirit was poured out upon the Body of Christ to confirm we are the corporate house of God. The manifestation of the Spirit is not just given for us as individuals. The manifestation of the Holy Spirit is given to each of us for the profit of the other members of His house (1 Cor. 12:7). The charismas of the Spirit are the WORKING POWER OF GOD. They TESTIFY that JESUS IS LORD (1 Cor. 12:1-11). They are His personal endowment of revelation, power, and utterance to the believer. They are a divine enablement whereby each believer may minister with wisdom, power, or speak beyond their own abilities. The charisma of the Spirit can be defined in three groups of three. There are three revelatory charismas (gifts), there are three power demonstration charismas, and there are three utterance or speaking charismas. We must always remember that the gift God gives to us is the Holy Spirit Himself. The gifts that He manifests are manifestations of Him in our lives. We will probably excel in the charismas of the Spirit that match our motivational gifting given to us by our Father and the callings we have in Christ. If we are evangelists, we will more than likely excel in the power charismas. If we are intercessors, we will probably excel in the revelatory charismas. If we are prophets, it will be a combination of the speaking and revelatory charismas. We must all understand that the Holy Spirit could manifest any of the nine charismas, or even all of the charismas, in our lives whenever it is necessary. Some people believe the Holy Spirit only gives us certain charismas, and that those charismas are the gifts we receive from God. I believe the gift we receive is the Holy Spirit and that He is very charismatic in His abilities. He comes as a Helper to us, and He will manifest in a way that fits our motivational giftings from our heavenly Father (Rom. 12:6-8), and any equipping graces given us in our calling in Christ (Eph. 4:11, 12). The charismas of the Holy Spirit often manifest in a way that is a combination of several charismas. It is sometimes difficult to tell which is working. An example would be to think of it in this way; what charismas are needed to raise someone from the dead? It is obviously a miracle (miracles), there may need to be a healing charisma (since disease, wounding, or sickness may have killed them), and it may take a gift of faith to activate belief. The individual charismas needed are not as important as the gift (dorea or gratuity) of the Holy Spirit that is needed. The Holy Spirit is the gift that is given to us; and He is very gifted in whom He is and what He does.

1. REVELATION - REVEAL
   a. Word of Knowledge
   b. Word of Wisdom
   c. Discerning of Spirits

2. POWER - DO
   a. Faith
   b. Miracles
   c. Gifts of Healings

3. UTTERANCE - SAY
   a. Prophesy
   b. Tongues
   c. Interpretation of Tongues

The charismas of the Holy Spirit are His personal endowments of revelation, power, and utterance to the believer. They are a divine enablement whereby a believer may minister with wisdom, power, or speak beyond their own abilities. They are the testimony of Christ in His resurrection power upon our lives as members of the Body of Christ. They are part of the spill-over testimony of God's inheritance in our lives as His house!

NOTE: Stop and spend time with the Holy Spirit today. Let Him move through you in the gifting of His charisma.

Chapter 3.1 – 3.5 - The Third Eye of Grace

Statements and Questions to Consider
For a Group Discussion:

1. This third grace is the Spirit of Understanding. It is a grace of the Holy Spirit at work in our lives as the teacher who transforms us. Discuss the difference between information and transformation.

2. This grace of the Spirit of Understanding corresponds to the foundation truth of the doctrine of baptisms. It is not the doctrine about baptisms. It is the doctrine of baptisms. What is meant by the doctrine of baptisms?

3. The Holy Spirit confirms the presence of the house of God in the earth. Discuss how the spill-over of tithe and the spill-over of the Spirit relate to one another.

4. Angels begin in the "house of God". They are sent to heavenly storehouses when a heavenly place is found in the earth. Do you think the spill-over of the Holy Spirit and angelic activity are related to one another in any way?

5. Tithe is a spill-over grace that confirms we are God's house. It is the spill-over evidence of God's grace testifying:

    1 – He is with us - open heaven -
       angels ascending & descending to bring blessing

    2 – He keeps us in the way - rebukes the devourer on our behalf

    3 – He gives us bread - food in His house - a changed character,
       nature, and way of heart

    4 – He gives us clothing - outward evidence - nations call us blessed

       -- Relate these things to the baptism of the Holy Spirit.

6. When we tithe, we acknowledge that the Word of God (living bread) and the Spirit of God (wine) have come together in our flesh, and it is changing the place that we live. We are being revealed as the place where God lives. How do the Holy Spirit's baptisms (submersions) relate to bread and wine?

7. Peter told the crowd in Jerusalem that those who believe in Jesus are to receive the "gift of the Holy Spirit". The word for "gift" here is not the Greek word "charisma". It is the word "dorea". It is not the charisma of the Holy Spirit; it is the "gratuity". What is the difference between "charisma" and "dorea"?

8. The tithe is not merely 10% of our natural possessions; it is a "gratuity" of all that is in heaven. How do you think this relates to the baptisms (submersions) of the Holy Spirit?

9. The Church in Acts, Chapter 2, was experiencing an increase of God in their lives. They began to "spill-over" to God with the evidence of this heavenly increase. Are there any personal testimonies in the group?

10. Receiving the "gift of the Holy Spirit" doesn't mean the Spirit of the Lord was not within your heart at the moment you accepted Jesus Christ. When we are submerged in the Holy Spirit, He releases the things of heaven in our hearts to become a "spill over" evidence upon our lives. The baptism of the Holy Spirit is the key to releasing the power of Christ hidden within us! What are some testimonies in the group?

11. The Holy Spirit is the witness of Jesus in His resurrection. How does He do this?

12. To be "endued" is to be fully "clothed". Jesus told them the Holy Spirit would come upon them and would "clothe" them. He was testifying that the Holy Spirit would not only be "in them", but that He would also be "with them". He would come "upon them". Discuss the difference between the Holy Spirit within us and upon us.

13. The Holy Spirit is at work in our lives as the teacher who carries the power of transformation to the testimony of a new life in Christ. What are some testimonies of His transformation anointing in the group?

14. Read Acts 2:1-21. The Holy Spirit's anointing upon our lives is prophetic. The Holy Spirit's prophetic anointing doesn't just affect us. It has the power to change the world! Discuss this.

15. Just like tithe, the receiving of the baptism of the Holy Spirit is not something that just automatically comes to our lives. Read Luke 11:5-13 and discuss what it means to ask.

16. Discuss some of the things that praying in tongues accomplishes. It reveals the mysteries of heaven in the midst of the natural world we live in. Examples: It builds us up for the sake of the Body of Christ, and the ability to build up the other members of the Body. Praying in the Holy Spirit (tongues) can position our spirits to hear God's word and not the accusations against our souls. It gives the ability to pray and to know what is the will of God in our lives. He gives us the power to intercede (pray) for one another. It gives us times of rest and refreshing.

17. The Holy Spirit testifies of Jesus in our lives through miracles, signs, and wonders of Christ's resurrection life! Read 1 Cor. 12:1-11 and discuss the nine manifestations of the Spirit. There are three revelatory charismas (gifts), there are three power demonstration charismas, and there are three utterance or speaking charismas.

18. We will probably excel in the charismas of the Spirit that match our motivational gifting given to us by our Father and the callings we have in Christ. Discuss this. Our motivation giftings are described in Rom. 12:6-8.

Chapter 4.1

The Fourth Eye of Grace

In these next five chapters, I will present the fourth of the *Seven Eyes of Grace*. This grace is perhaps one that we are less likely to be familiar with. We are at least prone to not recognize this grace, since it involves the subject of "apostolic teaching" and "submission one to another" in the Body of Christ. In the past three decades of the Church, there are a couple of buzzwords that have come to the forefront in the Church. These are the buzzwords of the "prophetic" and the "apostolic". These are not new truths, but they are areas of interest that have come to the forefront of focus in many parts of the Church in the past few decades. Whenever something is rekindled, rebirthed, or renewed in the Church it often becomes over emphasized or off focus in some way. This has no doubt been true for these two areas of ministry. We tend to exalt a "gift", rather than appreciate the fruit that comes from a gift given. I have found that most of the time something is actually happening in the Church before we know what it is called. When we finally do know what it is called, we tend to over emphasize it enough to distort what it was really intended to be in the first place. I believe that has been the case for these two areas of ministry. These two areas of ministry were very clearly operating in the first century Church. We will look at the area of "apostolic teaching" in these next chapters.

In the second chapter of the book of Acts, Peter instructed the crowd to: 1) repent, 2) be baptized for the remission of sins, and 3) receive the gift of the Holy Spirit (Acts 2:38). After these three instructions of entrance to the Body of Christ, there were four acts of relationship that continued to be practiced in the Body of Christ. We will look at the first of these four practices.

Acts 2:42 And they continued steadfastly in the apostles' doctrine (instruction taught them by the apostles) and fellowship, in the breaking of bread, and in prayers.

Here we see that the Church continued in the apostles' doctrine, they continued in fellowship, they continued in the breaking of bread, and they continued in prayers. In these next five chapters, I will address the subject of continuing in the "apostles' doctrine". To understand this truth, we must look at the Old Testament type and shadow. Remember, sacrifices and offerings were not what God desired. It was a "Body" that He desired. Since a "Body" was equated to "sacrifices and offerings", we can only truly understand the sacrifices of the Old Testament in light of "relationship" in the Body of Christ. We can also conclude that in understanding the sacrifices and offerings of the Old Testament we can understand the various levels of relationship in the Body of Christ.

> _Heb. 10:5 Therefore, when He came into the world, He said: "Sacrifice and offering You did not desire, but a body You have prepared for Me. 6 In burnt offerings and sacrifices for sin you had no pleasure. 7 Then I said, 'Behold, I have come—in the volume of the book it is written of Me—to do Your will, O God.'"_

I will again relate this fourth grace, as revealed in Acts, Chapter 2, to one of seven offerings given in Deuteronomy, Chapter 12. This is again one of _Seven Eyes of Grace_ at work in the Body of Christ (Isa. 11:2; Heb. 6:1, 2). This grace is another attribute of the Holy Spirit's work in the Church. It is the grace of the Spirit of Counsel (Isa. 11:2). It is a foundation grace enabling the ministry of the "laying on of hands" in the Body of Christ (Heb. 6:2). To understand this grace, we must again look at the shadow that was cast to the earth in the Old Covenant sacrifices. The Body of Christ that existed in the eternal truth of Christ cast a shadow through the Old Covenant system of the Law (Torah) and gave us information for our learning. That information merely reveals a testimony attributed to Christ's power of transformation made possible to us through the sevenfold Spirit of Christ. This is the Holy Spirit's power revealed in His _Seven Eyes of Grace_ (Isa. 11:2; Zech. 3:9; 4:10; Rev. 5:6). It is the grace of the Spirit of Counsel that enables us to keep in the apostolic teachings given to us in Christ. This grace also relates to the fourth truth found in the foundation of Christ. This is the "laying on of hands" (Heb. 6:2). Again, the "laying on of hands" is not a doctrine. It is a reality found in the relationship and function of the Body of Christ. It is not what we believe about the "laying on of hands" that counts. It is whether or not we are actually functioning as those who perform the work of Christ or not. The hands represent our ability to receive instruction and perform work (1 Chr. 28:19; Job 4:3; Heb. 12:12; Mk. 8:25). The laying on of hands imparts the blessings of the Father (Num. 27:23; Deut. 34:9; Mk. 10:16; Acts 8:17; 19:6). It is by the laying on of hands that someone is sent forth in authority (Num. 27:23; Deut. 34:9; Mk. 16:18; Acts 13:3; 1 Tim. 5:22). Are we receiving the instruction of the Spirit and are we performing the works of Christ that testify of that instruction? Are we being sent forth by God's authority for His corporate purpose in the earth? All authority comes from being under authority. Unless we are under authority we cannot be sent in and with authority. We can find the type and shadow of this fourth grace and its practice in the book of Deuteronomy.

> *Deut. 12:5 "But you shall seek the place where the LORD your God chooses, out of all your tribes, to put His name for His habitation; and there you shall go. 6 "There you shall take your ¹⁾burnt offerings, your ²⁾sacrifices, your ³⁾tithes, the ⁴⁾heave offerings of your hand, your ⁵⁾vowed offerings, your ⁶⁾freewill offerings, and the ⁷⁾firstlings of your herds and flocks. 7 And there you shall eat before the LORD your God, and you shall rejoice in all to which you have put your hand, you and your households, in which the LORD your God has blessed you."*

The fourth offering that God instructed the children of Israel to bring to the place He chose for His name to abide for them was the "heave offering". What was the "heave offering"? In the Old Testament, the "heave offering" was brought as an offering to the priest. This offering was a choice piece of meat. It was either the right shoulder or thigh of the animal sacrificed. It would be placed into the hands of the priest and the priest would lift it before the Lord. It was an offering that was "lifted up" or "heaved" to the Lord (Lev. 7:28-34). After the priest had lifted the offering up before the Lord the offering would be again lowered. That choice piece of the "body" of the sacrificed animal would then become food provision for that priest and his family. The symbolism was that of submission. As the offering was taken, lifted up to the Lord, and lowered to become the provision of the priest and his home, it was a symbolic statement of; "I submit to you as unto the Lord". This was symbolic of the Spirit of Counsel, a corporate grace of submission one to another in the Body of Christ. It testifies that God is the source of all authority, and we must recognize those sent by Him. It is through the act of submission to another that we receive authority for others.

The Body of Christ is the place of Christ's full expression of light to the world. Together we are the light of the world (Mt. 5:14; Jn. 9:5). We only experience the full light of God when we become the "city" of God (Mt. 5:14). We are not the fullness of the light of Christ by ourselves. We can only become the full light of Christ when we operate as the "Body" of Christ. This involves

117

a grace of submission one to another. This is not aimless submission. This is God ordained and God directed submission. It is an "apostolic" submission. The word apostle means "sent one". God is not interested in exalting apostles. He is interested in the fruit that is made known in the Body of Christ through "apostolic ministry". "Apostolic ministry" is the true ministry of Christ that "sends" us forth for the full purpose of His calling. It is given so that the Body of Christ can become unified in the faith and accomplish Christ's corporate purpose in the earth.

In Acts, Chapter 2, the Church was said to have continued steadfastly in the apostles' doctrine (teaching). What was that apostolic teaching? It is interesting to note that the second chapter of the book of Acts occurred around A.D. 30 of the first century. The first books of the New Testament were not written until around A.D. 50. The first two books were likely the book of James and Galatians. This means that the New Testament Church existed for twenty years before any New Testament Scriptures were written. This leaves us with a question. What does it mean when it says they continued steadfastly in the apostles' doctrine? It can't be something that didn't exist at the time the Church "continued in it". I believe the apostolic letters were part of their teaching, but this was not what was being referred to in Acts, Chapter 2.

I believe that the apostolic teaching was the relational teachings and examples of submission one to another as presented by Jesus to His disciples. The Body was meant to be relationally joined, not functionally motivated. They were joined in relationship one to another and that also joined them to the apostolic examples set before them. It was through submission to apostolic authority that full authority was given to the various members of the Body of Christ. "Keeping in the teachings of the apostles" is a fourth and essential relational ingredient toward living in the blessings of the kingdom of God. It is meant to be part of God's GRACE process in the Body of Christ today. Once again, remember that this grace is not merely the power of pardon from our failures. It is an empowerment to become all we are meant to be in Christ.

This grace given to us through the Holy Spirit's anointing upon our lives is not one of "accountability". It is one of "relationship", and because of divine connections we are easily "accountable". There are many people who want to be sure they are "accountable". Perhaps it is truer to say that many people want to be sure others are "accountable". My hand is not joined to my wrist so that it will be accountable. My hand is divinely attached to my wrist so that it can be healthy and alive! Because it is healthy and alive, it can do everything it was created to do. Keeping in the doctrine of the apostles is like that. Do you remember the old song, "You Send Me". It went something like, "Darling, you.... send me, Don't you know that you..... send me". It was something like that. The point of the song was that the woman of his dreams made him find his purpose in life. This is what submission one to another in the Body of Christ should be like. We should find our greater purpose in life when we are joined in proper relationship with others in the Body of Christ.

We are the Body of Christ, the evidence of Christ's resurrection in the earth. We are His word made flesh. We are His message made known. The Spirit of Counsel is God's power through us to do the will of God. Together we are the corporate manifestation of Christ's presence in the earth! The Body of Christ is made of many members. It is only when those members live in Christ's life together that we see the greater fullness of who Christ is. It is only then that the greater light of who He is can influence the darkness of the world.

1 Cor. 12:12 For as the body is one and has many members, but all the members of that one body, being many, are one body, so also is Christ. 13 For by one Spirit we were all baptized into one body—whether Jews or Greeks, whether slaves or free—and have all been made to drink into one Spirit. 14 For in fact the body is not one member but many.

Rom. 12:4 For as we have many members in one body, but all the members do not have the same function, 5 so we, being many, are one body in Christ, and individually members of one another.

God has made a way for us to become the corporate expression of who He is. Jesus told us that we would do greater works than He did while He was in the form of earthly flesh (Jn. 14:12). He said that because of His glory we would be anointed to do His works of life in this world. The Body of Christ is not without the sending power to accomplish all that is found in the destiny of His Body.

Isa. 9:6 For unto us a Child is born, unto us a Son is given; and the government will be upon His shoulder. And His name will be called Wonderful, Counselor, Mighty God, Everlasting Father, Prince of Peace. 7 Of the increase of His government and peace there will be no end, upon the throne of David and over His kingdom, to order it and establish it with judgment and justice from that time forward, even forever. The zeal of the LORD of hosts will perform this.

The promise given through the prophet Isaiah through the inspiration of the Holy Spirit was that there would be no end to the increase of the government and peace of God in our lives. This is true today! It has been true since the moment a Child was born and a Son was given. God's instruction comes by His Spirit through individual, as well as corporate grace and sent instructions. Paul wrote concerning this Spirit-empowered grace:

Rom. 1:5 ...through whom we have received grace and apostleship for obedience to the faith among all nations for His name,

The government of the Church must be focused on seeking and maintaining the Lordship and direction of Jesus Christ over His Body. Paul wrote that God had given two gifts for this purpose. These were the gifts of "grace" and "apostleship". He wasn't talking about his own ability to be an apostle. He was talking about the purpose of "apostleship". As Jesus was sent of the Father, we have been "sent" of the Son by the power of His Holy Spirit in and upon our lives. We have the grace of God at work within our hearts and upon our lives. We have the grace of those who are "sent" to us to empower us in being "sent" as the Body of Christ to fulfill the calling of Jesus in the Body of Christ (Eph. 1:18).

We are all members of the Body of Christ. We are part of the fellowship of the mystery (Eph. 3:9). Each of us as members must continually seek His mind and will, through His Spirit and the Word of God, in all actions and decisions. We can find His will and purpose through the grace at work in our lives and through those who have been sent as a "sending" authorities in our lives. These are those who help us find our place in the Body of Christ. These are those who set for us an example as to how to live as members of the Body of Christ. This includes those who are apostles (sent or sending ones) in the Body of Christ, but it also includes all of those who are "sent" to us by God to empower us to become who we are as a part of the fellowship of the Body of Christ.

NOTE: It is time to stop once again and consider the subject material of this chapter. Allow the Holy Spirit to minister to you in regard to being a part of the sent authority of God in Christ.

Chapter 4.2
The Fourth Eye of Grace

This grace of the Spirit of Counsel is a wonderful working power of the Holy Spirit in our lives. He knows who we each are, and He knows how to join us in the Body of Christ. I have seen this grace at work in my life for many years. I was blessed to be able to find a divine connection in the Church early on in my Christian conversion. Sometimes we confuse the wrong applications of authority with true applications. Sometimes we avoid true applications of authority in our lives because of wrong applications in our past. I have experienced my share of abuses in my Christian life, but I have never stopped believing in the principle of submission one to another for the corporate purpose of the Body of Christ. The abuse of "wrong use" is not an excuse for the abuse of "no use".

In the 1980's there was a great restoration of the prophetic ministry of Christ in the Body of Christ. During that time there were also a lot of abuses of authority and function in the Body. I have experienced my share of blessings and curses in the area of the prophetic. Let me relate one personal testimony. From 1988 through 1990 I was part of a prophetic ministry that was one of many emerging prophetic Churches in the 80's. I began as a participating member of that ministry through a practical application of a "street focused" ministry that operated strongly in prophetic gifts. I began by becoming involved in street evangelism. The ministry soon became a developing church body. I was soon asked to be the worship leader in that ministry. It was not long after that that I was also asked to become the youth pastor. My involvement in the ministry continued to progress and the ministry grew. I soon found myself in full-time ministry as an administrator and youth pastor. One day I was appointed as an associate minister in the ministry. Then my whole world changed! One of the other leaders in the ministry decided to split the fellowship. It was all orchestrated, planned, and implemented in its strategy in the name of "prophetic words" and "prophetic ministry". We were a congregation of 220 to 240 members. The "prophetess" who instigated the church split coordinated a church-wide phone campaign in the name of "prophetic warning". The church went from over 200 members to around 60 individuals. The rest had joined the church split or scattered into the city. The day after the split, the senior leader of the ministry made the decision to leave the city. I was left as the senior leader of 60 wounded and bleeding church members. I also became a target of accusation for many angry and scattered people in the community. Some became a part of a fellowship of believers who were very opposed to the ministry of which I had now become the inheritor. They were the split and were determined to "prophetically oppose" anything that was left of the original congregation. The leader who had split the church was "prophetic"! The senior leader who left the original church was also "prophetic"! I was also "prophetic"! I decided I didn't want anything more to do with the "prophetic". I hadn't asked to inherit the mess I was in! I took steps to become a nurturing pastor of the remaining 60 people in the ministry. Six months later I was on a fast, praying and seeking God for continued direction for the church. God confronted me in my confusion. He asked me why I was running from the "use" of the prophetic because of the "abuse". I made a commitment to Him that day to learn all I could from Him in regard to true prophetic ministry. I made a commitment to God that day that I would accept the responsibility of a father in facilitating the prophetic in the Body of Christ in a way that was life-giving and true.

Since then, I have discovered something about "abuse". The word abuse is made up of the root "ab" and the word "use". The preface of the word means, "to move away from". The word means to move away from proper use. There are two kinds of abuse. One is the wrong use of something. The other is the "no use" of something. This is true for anything in life. This is true for the function of authority in the Body of Christ. There are many types of abuse. There is "wrong use" and there is "no use". We must never seek to avoid something because of "wrong use". We must seek to find the true use and the full use as God intended it to be.

This same principle is true for properly understanding "apostolic ministry" and the submission of one to another in the Church. It is paramount to understanding proper submission to authority in every expression of the Church. All authority in heaven and earth is found in Jesus Christ (Mt. 28:18). Our first response to governmental function by those given authority to rule must be under the headship and direction of the Lord Jesus Christ.

Heb. 13:7 Remember those who rule over you, who have spoken the word of God to you, whose faith follow, considering the outcome of their conduct.

Let me expound this verse to read something like this:

Heb. 13:7 Remember (to exercise memory / to bear in mind, call to mind, to stay, to chew) those who rule (lead / bring, drive, induce) over you, who have spoken the word of God to you, whose faith follow, considering (to look again attentively / to be a spectator of / to look closely at) the outcome of their conduct.

All members of the Body of Christ are responsible for seeing their God-given leadership as a gift to them. Leaders are a source of authority in their lives. They are those to be thought of, considered, followed, and joined to. In this same chapter we find further instruction concerning submission and authority.

Heb. 13:17 Obey those who rule over you, and be submissive, for they watch out for your souls, as those who must give account. Let them do so with joy and not with grief, for that would be unprofitable for you.

Let me expound this verse to read:

Heb. 13:17 Obey (to convince; pacify; assent; rely on) those who rule (lead / bring, drive, induce) over you, and be submissive, for they watch out for your souls (they are awake concerning your souls), as those who must give account. Let them do so with joy and not with grief, for that would be unprofitable for you.

We can see that leadership is an awesome gift. It is not a control, but a source of activation and life-giving direction. Our destinies are directly connected to those God sends to us as a source of authority in our lives. Now let me give you the "Hanson Translation" of these verses combined:

Rely upon those who lead and induce you toward life, surrender yourself to them, for they are required to be awake concerning your souls, and they must give an account in thought and word for you. They will help keep you from falling into deception and will be alert to the life that God has for you. Let them do this with cheerfulness and joy and do not make them sigh and murmur because of you. Don't put them in straits, for if they are forced to live in a tight and narrow place because of you, it will only work against your gain and prove to cut your purpose short.

The Seven Eyes of Grace

Authority is given to us for our own benefit. It is given for the benefit of becoming the full manifestation of the light of Christ. Authority is a gift given to us from the headship of Jesus in heaven. Leadership is a grace gift given by God to the Body of Christ. Paul wrote to the church of Thessalonica in regard to submission to leadership in the Body of Christ. This is still true today! Let me give you the expounded version:

> *1 Thes. 5:12 And we urge you, brethren, to recognize (to see; know) those who labor among you, and are over you (stand before you or stand in front of you) in the Lord and admonish (to put in mind, caution / calling attention to; warning / to place in your intellect a knowing) you, 13 and to esteem them very highly in love for their work's sake. Be at peace among yourselves.*

The governing of the government of the Church comes through God's gift of grace and apostleship to the church. The Holy Spirit at work in the Body of Christ is the true government of grace. He is the power of the life of Christ within us. Leaders are a further expression of that grace. I like to think of leadership like a "governor" on a truck or tractor engine. The function and design of the engine is what gives it the ability to run. A fuel source to the engine is what gives it the source of energy it needs to run. Although the engine is perfect in its design, and empowered by its fuel source, there is a device on that engine that gives it the proper power of "restraint" or "focus" to allow it to accomplish the work it was designed to accomplish. That device is called a "governor". It doesn't' give the engine the ability to run. It gives a proper "restraint" or "focus" to run in a "work accomplishing" manner. I believe it is much the same in the Body of Christ. It is the grace of the divinely created and joined members of the Body of Christ that make it become what it is. It is the grace of the Holy Spirit within the Body of Christ that gives it the power to live and function. But it is the God sent leadership to the Body of Christ that gives it the proper "restraint" and "focus" to allow it to accomplish the work it was designed to accomplish. "God sent" leadership is half of the equation to our obedience to the faith.

> *Rom. 1:5 ...through whom we have received grace and apostleship for obedience to the faith among all nations for His name...*

I believe there is more to "apostleship" than "apostles". I believe that "apostleship" represents all "sent authority" in the Church. Jesus Christ is the "Apostle of our faith" (Heb. 3:1). He is the source of all authority in the Church and in the world (Mt. 28:18). I believe that there are "apostles" and even

124

believe myself to be one, but being an apostle is not the real point. The word apostle simply means "sent one". It implies the ability to activate the "sending" of others. I believe that apostleship represents the "sent ones" who carry the authority of Christ to assist the Body of Christ in being obedient to the faith. The government of the Church is both in the headship of Jesus Christ and in the full responsibility of Jesus Christ. It includes the grace of God within the Body of Christ. It includes the grace upon the Body of Christ. The government of the Church includes the grace that is upon the "governors" of the Body of Christ. These are God's sent leadership given to give proper "restraint" and "focus" to every corporate expression of the Body. God wants us to function as members of the Body of Christ for the hope of "His calling" and the riches of "His inheritance" in the Body of Christ. This Body is the "fullness of Him", not the fullness of ourselves. The Holy Spirit's grace of the Spirit of Counsel rests upon the Body of Christ (Branch – Isa. 11:2), for this reason.

Eph. 1:18 ...the eyes of your understanding being enlightened; that you may know what is the hope of His calling, what are the riches of the glory of His inheritance in the saints, 19 and what is the exceeding greatness of His power toward us who believe, according to the working of His mighty power 20 which He worked in Christ when He raised Him from the dead and seated Him at His right hand in the heavenly places, 21 far above all principality and power and might and dominion, and every name that is named, not only in this age but also in that which is to come. 22 And He put all things under His feet, and gave Him to be head over all things to the church, 23 which is His body, the fullness of Him who fills all in all.

Authority is not something we should fear. It is something we should all be eager to embrace. The only way we can embrace authority is to embrace every God-ordained opportunity to submit! We only have authority when we are "under authority" (Mt. 8:9; Lk. 7:8). Leadership is God's idea. Apostleship is God's gift to the Church to allow each and every body member to find his or her divine connection of relationship. When we find our proper places of submission, we contribute to the brightness of His glory. True authority is seen as the "fullness of" the Body of Christ. This is only possible when we submit to God's sent authority.

NOTE: Stop now and let the Holy Spirit speak to you today in regard to the authority of God. Consider the 'sent authority' in your own life.

Chapter 4.3

The Fourth Eye of Grace

God has given grace gifts of Christ's headship to His Church. These gifts are part of the whole "ship". They are part of the sent authority of Christ's headship to the Church. Each carries an anointing for the diverse members of the Body of Christ to come alive as the fullness of Christ's Body!

Eph. 4:11 And He Himself gave some to be apostles, some prophets, some evangelists, and some pastors and teachers, 12 for the equipping of the saints for the work of ministry, for the edifying of the body of Christ, 13 till we all come to the unity of the faith and the knowledge of the Son of God, to a perfect man, to the measure of the stature of the fullness of Christ; 14 that we should no longer be children, tossed to and fro and carried about with every wind of doctrine, by the trickery of men, in the cunning craftiness by which they lie in wait to deceive, 15 but, speaking the truth in love, may grow up in all things into Him who is the head—Christ— 16 from whom the whole body, joined and knit together by what every joint supplies, according to the effective working by which every part does its share, causes growth of the body for the edifying of itself in love.

As I read these verses, I find several things that are a part of this fivefold ministry of leadership grace given to the Church. These grace gifts of Jesus Christ:

1) Equip the saints for the work of ministry

2) Edify the Body of Christ

3) Cause the body members to come to the unity of the faith

4) Cause the body members to come to knowledge of the Son of God

5) Cause the body to become a perfect man, to the measure of the stature of the fullness of Christ

6) Prevent the body members from remaining little children, but to grow up in maturity

7) Protect the body from being tossed to and fro and carried about with every wind of doctrine

8) Protect the body from the trickery of men, who come in cunning craftiness by which they lie in wait to deceive

9) Teach the body members to learn to speak the truth in love

10) Produce a functioning body that grows up in all things into Him who is the head—Christ—

11) Cause the whole body to be properly joined

12) Cause the body members to be knit together

13) Cause every joint (body member) to supply life to one another

14) Cause everyone to find his or her place of effective working

15) Cause every part to do their share

16) Cause growth of the body

17) Cause the body to bring edification to itself in love

These all sound like essential benefits to me! I find no measure of control listed. I find elements of proper restraint and focus. I find attributes of impartation, activation, and facilitation to help the Body of Christ come to the fullness of Christ in the earth! These are gifts given to activate the level of relationship in the Body that was presented in the type and shadow of the "heave offering". These gifts inspire the Holy Spirit's grace of the Spirit of Counsel and the ministry of the laying on of hands of the Body of Christ. It is a testimony of Body ministry and submission of one to another.

God has a corporate purpose for the Body of Christ. Continuing steadfastly in the apostles' doctrine (instruction taught them by the apostles) is to keep in God's "sent word" to the corporate Body. God wants to accomplish the corporate ministry of the 'laying on of hands' through His Body. God wants to accomplish a 'corporate work' through His Body. He has a specific task for every corporate expression of His Body. The apostle Paul understood this when he wrote to the church of Corinth.

> *2 Cor. 3:2 You are our epistle written in our hearts, known and read by all men; 3 you are manifestly an epistle of Christ, ministered by us, written not with ink but by the Spirit of the living God, not on tablets of stone but on tablets of flesh, that is, of the heart.*

God desires to express something by His Spirit in our corporate connection together that becomes a letter written by the Spirit of God that others can read. We are still learning from the spiritual letters that were written to the various congregations of the New Testament Church. That was just the beginning! We should expect that God is writing a continual increase of His written letter of purpose and grace in diverse ways in the different expressions of His corporate Body in the earth. This is sometimes hard for those of us from the "western world" to understand. We are so used of having things our own way; we resent anything that resembles being told what to do. We must know that God does command specific things for specific purposes in specific times. Our obedience is necessary to fulfill God's purpose and will. It is the grace of the Spirit of Counsel that will give us the ability to walk in obedience to God's corporate will.

The Scriptures give us countless examples of times when God commanded specific things for specific purposes. It is true both in the Old and New Testaments. If God gave commands in the Old Testament when people could not hear the Holy Spirit in their hearts, what makes us think He won't command specific things at specific times by those who can hear His voice in their hearts? I believe that to think otherwise is presumptuous, irresponsible, rebellious, and defiant of God's corporate purpose and plan. I'm not advocating we impose a government of instruction and rules. I'm advocating that if God gives a corporate instruction to a congregation, then every member of that congregation should position themselves to hear the commands for themselves. They shouldn't position themselves to prove God commanded something, nor should they position themselves to question whether God really did say something. I think this is huge in the Body of Christ!

God will give specific tasks for specific times. Our obedience is necessary to fulfill God's purpose and will. I suggest you study Josh. 5:13-15 and Josh. 6:1-20. The following things can be found as instructions to a corporate people of God. Consider what happened when not everyone was obedient to the command of God. What do you think would have happened if there was further disobedience? If God gave you and your corporate church commands like Joshua, do you think obedience would be necessary? Do you think obedience would fully happen in your local church? These are just some thoughts to consider.

...... "as Commander of the army of the LORD I have now come." And Joshua fell on his face to the earth and worshiped, and said to Him, "What does my LORD say to His servant?"
...... march around the city
...... go all around the city once. This you shall do six days.
...... seven priests shall bear seven trumpets of rams' horns before the ark.
...... the seventh day you shall march around the city seven times,
...... the priests shall blow the trumpets.
...... when they make a long blast with the ram's horn
...... all the people shall shout with a great shout;
...... then the wall of the city will fall down flat.
...... the people shall go up every man straight before him."
...... You shall not shout or make any noise with your voice,
...... nor shall any word proceed out of your mouth,
...... until the day I say to you, 'Shout!'
...... Then you shall shout."
...... by all means keep yourselves from the accursed things,
lest you become accursed when you take of the accursed things,
and make the camp of Israel a curse,
and trouble it.

Let me share with you from my own personal experience as the senior leader of a church congregation. Our church is called "Abundant Life". My son Jonathan is now the senior leader of this ministry, but for twenty years I was the senior leader. God established the foundation of this God-directed ministry for the future generations. He gave the name in a dream and through divine confirmations of that dream. I believe that God was writing, and continues to write, a divinely inspired letter of His Spirit with us as a corporate body. We are a congregation of believers in Christ whom the Lord has called to be an expression of "Abundant Life". As a local church, the foundation of our vision was, "To cause people to see, experience, and walk in the Abundant Life that Jesus came to give!" When I was the senior leader of this ministry, we would begin each year with the leaders of Abundant Life gathering to seek God for the coming year. At this gathering, vision and strategy was set for the year. The leaders looked at the previous year of ministry, as well as the prophecies given to the ministry. They spent a considerable amount of time in prayer and strategy before this meeting so that they had a sense of what they believed God was saying for the coming season. They shared what they sensed and saw for the coming year with one another. They took all of this and submitted it to the prophecies that had been previously given to the church body. They then drafted a vision for the year. This included a strategy to implement that vision. We were also careful to listen for the voice of God through every member of the church body.

The prophecies that had been given in the previous year were judged by the following criteria in order to constitute the direction that God was giving to the congregation. Any prophecies considered met the following criteria:

√ The prophecy had to line up with God's written word.

√ The leadership looked for prophecies that witnessed with their spirits, as God had anointed them with the grace of leadership.

√ More weight was put upon prophecies that came through proven ministries, especially those who had a long-term commitment to and responsibility for the local church.

√ The leaders looked for common themes.

√ The leaders discussed the prophecies together as a leadership team.

√ The leaders submitted their conclusions to their apostolic relationships for a further witness.

In doing these things, we were seeking to submit to the corporate will of Christ's Spirit for our local church. We relied upon the grace of the Spirit of Counsel and the level of relationship foreseen in the "heave offering". We believed in the ministry of the laying on of the hands of Christ. Together we were bringing Christ's light to the darkness around us!

NOTE: Let the Holy Spirit speak to you regarding the importance of true sent authority. Consider God's plan for your life in the setting of the corporate Body of Christ.

Chapter 4.4

The Fourth Eye of Grace

I believe "continuing in the apostles' doctrine" implies first of all that we emulate those who are mature in Christ before us. These are our spiritual fathers who have known Him who is from the beginning (1 Jn. 2:13, 14). These are those who remind us of Christ in His character, nature, way, power, and authority (Heb. 6:12). The apostle Paul gave us good testimony to this thought.

1 Cor. 4:15 For though you might have ten thousand instructors in Christ, yet you do not have many fathers; for in Christ Jesus I have begotten you through the gospel. 16 Therefore I urge you, imitate me. 17 For this reason I have sent Timothy to you, who is my beloved and faithful son in the Lord, who will remind you of my ways in Christ, as I teach everywhere in every church.

1 Cor. 11:1 Imitate me, just as I also imitate Christ. 2 Now I praise you, brethren, that you remember me in all things and keep the traditions as I delivered them to you.

Apostles and sent leaders are a gift to the Church. Let me share just a few things that I have discovered while studying the New Testament Church. I am not saying that you have to adopt this pattern, but I find it interesting. I believe the model can be flexible, but the principles are true for us today. In the New Testament the function of Christ's Body was done by the Headship of Christ, with the function of the apostles, the elders, and the brethren:

Acts 15:22 Then it pleased the apostles and elders, with the whole church, to send chosen men of their own company to Antioch with Paul and Barnabas, namely, Judas who was also named Barsabas, and Silas, leading men among the brethren. 23 They wrote this letter by them: The apostles, the elders, and the brethren, To the brethren who are of the Gentiles in Antioch, Syria, and Cilicia: Greetings.

131

It appears that the physical expression to the leadership of the local church was in the expression of "apostles and elders". This was true with the Church in Jerusalem (Acts 11:30; 15:4; 20:17; 21:18; 1 Tim. 5:17; Jam. 5:14; 1 Pet 5:1). I have found one case where it is presented differently:

Phil. 1:1 Paul and Timothy, servants of Jesus Christ, to all the saints in Christ Jesus who are in Philippi, with the bishops and deacons...

My personal opinion is that "elders" are both "bishops and deacons". Their character is "elder" and their responsibility and gifting of function is either that of a "bishop" or a "deacon". The category is "elder" for the local church, but the function is either in the role of a bishop elder or a deacon elder. I have come to conviction and faith in this thought. For the sake of this book, I am merely presenting that there is diversity in leadership gifts given to the local church. Apostolic ministry is what connects the local church to the Body of Christ at large. Whereas elders (bishops and deacons) are local church leadership functions, the apostolic ministry represents that which joins the local church to the global Church.

I believe the government of God is a Theocracy. Whether it involves the life of an individual Christian, the corporate expression of a family, the corporate expression of the Body of Christ known as a congregation, or any divinely called assembly of believers; a Theocracy is the rule of Christian faith. In a Theocracy, God speaks, and we respond to what He wills. It is a governing by God. The result is always life and peace. The result is the abundance of life He desires for us all to have. The result is a furtherance and advancement of His kingdom in the earth. This sounds simple enough, but we don't hear God well alone. We all have dull ears and blind spots of various kinds to His voice at times and we are therefore dependent upon His grace to help us. His grace is not just given to us as individuals alone, but is also given to us as various expressions of His grace to one another. God has joined us in relationship together and has granted various measures of grace in order for us to articulate what He is saying to us.

We are dependent upon one another in order to be able to hear God clearly. I believe there are several aspects for this to happen in any corporate expression of God's house. God provides a source, a resource, and a means of furthering His generations and purpose in His eternal plan for the Church. He provides a means by which He can appoint the furtherance of His corporate will for the Church. From what has been, God appoints what is and is to be. This is then seen in various corporate expressions of His will. For every father there is a father, and for every mother there is a mother. It is the way of generations.

I believe God also appoints specific prophetic voices to a body of believers. These are not apostolic authorities but they are an objective voice of God to the local body. These voices help the local body hear God's word to their lives. There should be a plurality of prophetic voices to the local church. God appoints prophets and prophetic voices to bring direction to a local body. This is Prophetic Council. These voices help the local church hear God's direction to them corporately.

God always appoints a leader to provide responsible headship accountable to articulate His will for any measure of His house. This God appointed individual is a gift of God's grace sent specifically to a corporate expression of God's family as a leadership gift to them. This is a leader, not a dictator or controller.

Every God-appointed leader must also be relationally joined to other leaders in the dynamic of leadership in order to articulate God's voice through a fuller measure of Christ's leadership to the Church. These leaders are gifts of God's grace sent to the leader and the corporate body in order to fully lead the corporate house.

God also anoints members of the household to hear His voice in order to respond to His will. These are God's individual gifts of diversity within the house to fully articulate His expression of life in and through that house for the work of ministry in Christ.

There are five theological names that describe these means of hearing His voice. The authority to appoint a sent leader to any given expression of God requires a source of sending. Something generational must exist to provide the authority of further generations. This is known as Apostolic Leadership. This is a source and resource to any corporate expression of the Body of Christ. This leadership is plural and diverse. It is diverse to the manifold expression of God to the Church. A plurality of diversity in source provides a fuller resource to the future generations of God's will.

God always sends a leader to lead specific expressions of His will to reveal His increasing glory in the earth. The sending, or appointing, of a leader is known as an Episcopal form of leadership. God simply sends or appoints a leader to lead a body of believers. He puts a special grace upon that individual to be a leader of leaders for the sake of the corporate household.

Another aspect is that of a Presbytery. This is a team of diversely gifted leaders working together to function as one team in leadership. Various levels of grace are given by God within this Presbytery to lead. God bestows different kinds and various measures of grace upon each of these individuals to create a fuller expression of leadership to the household. Some members of this team are graced by God to make decisions of a governmental nature. These individuals exhibit a tangible power of leadership to put new direction from God into motion for the body. They release direction and grace to the body to respond to His will and voice for their lives. Some members have a grace to creatively implement the governmental direction and decisions of function given by God. They themselves did not receive the direction or make the decision, but they have a grace to see to it that works are facilitated in accordance with God's given direction and decision. These individuals have a grace to activate and facilitate works that speak of the faith of the corporate house and its members. Some members of the leadership team have a God-given grace to equip individuals of the house for individual function and faith that leads to the actions of ministry in the house. A plurality of these equipping graces will release a harmonious expression of Christ's function within the church body. Within each of these expressions of leadership there is diversity according to the various measures of grace given by God.

The final aspect of God's rule to the corporate house is found in the lives of individual members of the household. This is an aspect known as Congregational function, where every believer carries the responsibility of hearing the voice of God within the corporate expression. God gives various kinds and measures of grace to individual members to reveal His voice in and through His household. Some are graced to prophesy, some pray, some see God's treasures in others, some draw treasures out of others, and so on. There is an endless supply of diversity in any expression of God's house.

I believe it requires all five of these aspects divinely working together in order to discern and articulate God's will for the corporate house. I believe a true Theocracy requires the submission of each of these aspects of family life in order to make correct conclusions as to the will of God for any corporate expression of the Body of Christ. This is not Apostolic rule, Prophetic rule, Episcopal rule, Presbyterian rule, or Congregational rule. It is these five aspects of body dynamic submitting to God's grace given to each measure in order to clearly hear Him and respond to Him. It is the active function of Theocratic Rule in the Church. A church body needs various apostolic leaders as a source and resource to God's purpose for the corporate house. Those apostolic leaders release the local church to become a further expression of what God is doing generationally in the earth. Each individual apostolic source is a unique individual resource to the corporate expression of the house. Each apostolic source is unique to the grace given them by God to supply life to the local body. I also believe a local church needs various prophetic voices sent to the local house to aid in hearing God's voice of direction. These prophetic councils should be plural and diverse in nature as well. In its local expression, there is a sent leader to the house, there is a team of leaders joined with that leader to fully express leadership to the house, and there are living members of the local house to fully articulate Christ's expression to and through the church body. I believe these five expressions, or equivalent expressions, work together to allow a local church to respond to the Theocratic rule of God. It is not the will of apostolic direction, prophetic council, an episcopal leader, a presbytery team, or congregation members that will accomplish God's will for the corporate body. It is God's voice to the body and that body's corporate response to His voice that will fulfill the will of God for that body.

The following is an example of how my church was led as a team:

1. The team relies upon the input and counsel of those trusted apostolic relationships God has given to them to relay objective insights concerning team function from their arenas of God-given grace. The team sees these apostolic relationships as a source and resource to the local church body.

2. The team also relies upon the council of various prophets sent to the local church by God's divine choosing. These prophets have a 'relationship' with the local church and are not just prophetic voices that come for an event or merely a moment in history. They are fully submitted to the local church authority and the apostolic mission of the ministry.

3. The lead bishop is the leader of the team. This is the ruling elder with the final shepherd's authority in the local house. He is the 'sent leader' of the church and of the leadership team. Don't translate the word bishop to mean any form of hierarchy. It implies responsibility, not position.

4. The bishops (ruling elders), as pastors, articulate what God is saying to the church and the team into practical instruction. Like parents, they are apt to teach (give directional instructions).

5. The deacons are facilitators and administrators who serve as leaders in the church by assisting the congregation in walking out the practical instruction given by the bishops. All of the leaders do this, but the deacons carry this responsibility as their primary role of leadership. Again, the term deacon does not denote position, but a grace and responsibility of function.

6. The equippers train, activate, and facilitate body members into ministry according to each equipper's God-given grace. All of the leaders do this as well (apostles, bishops & deacons), but the equippers carry this responsibility as their primary role of leadership.

7. Team members rely upon the input and counsel of one another in all of these areas to help each member walk out God-given strategy and action for his or her individual areas of responsibility.

8. The team willingly and diligently seeks to hear God's voice through every member of the corporate house. This is often discrete and simply a daily awareness of the leaders to recognize God's voice to the corporate body through every source. This includes paying attention to individual prophecies, dreams, visions, and sense of things. Every member of the congregation has the responsibility of hearing God and sharing what they believe He is saying.

9. Each of the above named aspects of leadership work together to fulfill the full function of leadership.

10. There are times when the set leader meets with the apostles alone for direction and input to lead the team of leadership. There are times when the bishops meet alone to facilitate the input of the voice of God in practical ways of direction as God has spoken through the team, the congregation, and to them personally. There are times when the bishops meet with the deacons alone to coordinate the practical ways of facilitating the instruction given by God through the bishops. There are times where the whole team meets together (including the equippers) for the full expression of leadership as it pertains to the will of God and the congregation. There are times when the leadership calls upon various members of the congregation for their sense of things within their own God-given measure of rule. Various aspects of this leadership dynamic can occur in order to practically facilitate the task of responding to the Theocratic rule of God to the local church.

NOTE: Stop and consider the subject material of this chapter. Once again, let the Holy Spirit minister to you personally throughout this day.

Chapter 4.5

The Fourth Eye of Grace

What is the responsibility of apostolic ministry? Apostolic Ministry is God's sent ministry to individuals and ministries whom God joins in relationship. Apostleship serves to allow those in relationship to be strengthened for "obedience to the faith". I believe God is restoring this grace to the Body of Christ in this present time. God wants to do a global work of life through His Church. He is joining local expressions of the Body of Christ together through apostolic connections. Much of the Body of Christ might not even articulate it as a restoration of "apostolic ministry", but God is doing a work of grace at this time that is causing the faith of the Church to take on a greater corporate expression. I have been a part of a weekly prayer meeting with other pastors in my city. It is an act of God's grace that has gathered us together. We don't come together to define what is "apostolic" or who is an "apostle". Some of the pastors I meet with wouldn't even profess to believe in apostles. There is an "apostolic" work being accomplished, however. We are getting a vision for our city and not just our individual congregations. We are realizing that God has a bigger plan than just our individual ministries. We value our time together and realize we are better off together than we are apart. We hear God's apostolic grace in words like "networking" or "brotherhood". God has a corporate plan for His Church!

Rom. 1:5 ...through whom we have received grace and apostleship for obedience to the faith among all nations for His name...

Apostleship ministry serves to impart "spiritual gifts" to those with whom they have a relationship. I am involved with many churches in different parts of the world. Many of them look to me as an apostle to their lives and ministries. It is very obvious that "gifts" are imparted to individuals and congregations as I come to them as a sent grace to their lives. These churches are becoming stronger because of our relationship with one another. There is fruit in the

137

form of character strength as well as spiritual gifting. Apostles impart gifts!

Rom. 1:11 For I long to see you, that I may impart to you some spiritual gift, so that you may be established—

When God sends an apostolic gift to a congregation, the testimony is obvious. Our local church looks to several individuals as apostles to our congregation. The testimony is obvious as to the activation and impartation they bring. Our church has tremendously changed as a result of these apostolic gifts. I have also tremendously benefited through these apostolic relationships. Apostleship provides God's authority to individuals and congregations. That authority is manifested.

2 Cor. 10:8 For even if I should boast somewhat more about our authority, which the Lord gave us for edification and not for your destruction, I shall not be ashamed—

2 Cor. 11:5 For I consider that I am not at all inferior to the most eminent apostles. 6 Even though I am untrained in speech, yet I am not in knowledge. But we have been thoroughly made manifest among you in all things.

2 Thes. 3:7 For you yourselves know how you ought to follow us, for we were not disorderly among you; 8 nor did we eat anyone's bread free of charge, but worked with labor and toil night and day, that we might not be a burden to any of you, 9 not because we do not have authority, but to make ourselves an example of how you should follow us.

2 Cor. 13:10 Therefore I write these things being absent, lest being present I should use sharpness, according to the authority which the Lord has given me for edification and not for destruction.

2 Cor. 10:13 We, however, will not boast beyond measure, but within the limits of the sphere which God appointed us—a sphere which especially includes you. 14 For we are not extending ourselves beyond our sphere (thus not reaching you), for it was to you that we came with the gospel of Christ; 15 not boasting of things beyond measure, that is, in other men's labors, but having hope, that as your faith is increased, we shall be greatly enlarged by you in our sphere, 16 to preach the gospel in the regions beyond you, and not to boast in another man's sphere of accomplishment.

There must be a confirmed manifested evidence of apostolic ministry. The signs of apostleship must be evident. As a local church we have experienced physical healings, divine revelation, the healing of heart issues, the development of leadership skills, evangelistic inspirations, nurturing impartations, and supernatural breakthroughs as a result of our apostolic connections. We have also learned to endure, which is a huge testimony of apostolic ministry.

2 Cor. 11:12 But what I do, I will also continue to do, that I may cut off the opportunity from those who desire an opportunity to be regarded just as we are in the things of which they boast. 13 For such are false apostles, deceitful workers, transforming themselves into apostles of Christ.

1 Cor. 2:4 And my speech and my preaching were not with persuasive words of human wisdom, but in demonstration of the Spirit and of power, 5 that your faith should not be in the wisdom of men but in the power of God.

Four main things confirm apostolic ministry. They involve the character of Christ, the power of Christ, the authority of Christ, and the fruit of Christ in our lives as a church. These things could be described as:

1) Perseverance (endurance)
2) Signs and wonders
3) Mighty deeds
4) The life of God's Spirit and fruit of that life which writes a letter

2 Cor. 12:12 Truly the signs of an apostle were accomplished among you with all perseverance, in signs and wonders and mighty deeds.

I consider apostolic connections essential. If you are part of a ministry that doesn't acknowledge apostolic ministry, you should still look for the evidence of apostolic ministry in your area of responsibility. You don't have to call it "apostolic", but you need to find those divine relationships that allow you to experience the developing and increasing character of Christ, power of Christ, authority of Christ, and fruit of Christ's ministry. These things may already be taking place in your ministry. You just may not have identified them as "apostolic" connections. Think of the word "apostle". It means, "sent one". What are the divine relationships that have been sent to you that are producing the character, power, authority, and fruit of Christ's ministry? Apostleship provides a flow of spiritual life to a congregation.

> *2 Cor. 3:1 Do we begin again to commend ourselves? Or do we need, as some others, epistles of commendation to you or letters of commendation from you? 2 You are our epistle written in our hearts, known and read by all men; 3 you are manifestly an epistle of Christ, ministered by us, written not with ink but by the Spirit of the living God, not on tablets of stone but on tablets of flesh, that is, of the heart.*

Apostolic relationship serves to help "establish" local churches. We all go through tests and trials. We all face deceptions, things that seek to devour us, and warfare that seeks to bring conflict to us. God has granted a grace that is "outside of" our local responsibilities to help establish us in Christ.

> *Rom. 16:25 Now to Him who is able to establish you according to my gospel and the preaching of Jesus Christ, according to the revelation of the mystery which was kept secret since the world began.*

> *1 Thes. 3:1 Therefore, when we could no longer endure it, we thought it good to be left in Athens alone, 2 and sent Timothy, our brother and minister of God, and our fellow laborer in the gospel of Christ, to establish you and encourage you concerning your faith, 3 that no one should be shaken by these afflictions; for you yourselves know that we are appointed to this.*

Apostolic ministry serves to "build" the house (spiritual house) of God. They help connect us to the "roof" of the house. That roof is our covering. His name is Jesus Christ. He is the only true head of the Church. Apostolic ministry is not sent to lord over us or control us. It is sent to connect us to the "roof" of the house. Apostolic ministry is sent to assure the building material of the house matches the building material of the foundation that is found in Christ. He is the only foundation (1 Cor. 3:11). Apostolic ministry is not the foundation of the Church. It is a grace gift given to assure we are attached to the true foundation. That foundation is Jesus Christ (Heb. 3:1).

> *1 Cor. 3:10 According to the grace of God which was given to me, as*

a wise master builder I have laid the foundation, and another builds on it. But let each one take heed how he builds on it.

2 Cor. 12:19 Again, do you think that we excuse ourselves to you? We speak before God in Christ. But we do all things, beloved, for your edification.

Apostolic ministry will serve to "plant" ministries and to "plant" those things within ministries that will enable them to come to maturity in Christ. God has given us a grace that allows us to see His kingdom influence expand beyond the boundaries of yesterday.

1 Cor. 3:6 I planted, Apollos watered, but God gave the increase.

Apostolic ministry is a "fathering" ministry and therefore serves to provide an example to be imitated and followed in Christ. This is probably one of the greatest benefits of apostolic ministry. Inheritance comes from fathers and apostles are living expressions of our Father in heaven. They cannot replace Him, but they will serve to reveal Him to us.

1 Cor. 4:14 I do not write these things to shame you, but as my beloved children I warn you. 15 For though you might have ten thousand instructors in Christ, yet you do not have many fathers; for in Christ Jesus I have begotten you through the gospel. 16 Therefore I urge you, imitate me.

1 Cor. 11:1 Imitate me, just as I also imitate Christ.

2 Cor. 6:13 Now in return for the same (I speak as to children), you also be open.

Heb. 6:12 ...that you do not become sluggish, but imitate those who through faith and patience inherit the promises.

1 Thes. 1:6 And you became followers of us and of the Lord, having received the word in much affliction, with joy of the Holy Spirit...

Apostolic ministry releases the authority to local sent leaders to appoint church elders or leaders. All authority comes from authority. Apostolic ministry empowers the leadership development of the local church. This has proven to be very true for our local church. I have also experienced this in a great way with churches that receive me as an apostle in their lives. I have helped numerous leaders identify further leaders in their ministries. I have imparted a grace to them to impart to others. It is a wonderful grace. It is a part of the grace of the Spirit of Counsel. It is a part of the ministry of the laying on of hands. It also allows dark places to become light!

> _Titus 1:5 For this reason I left you in Crete, that you should set in order the things that are lacking, and appoint elders in every city as I commanded you—_

What gives apostolic ministry a right? Apostolic ministry is received from the Lord Jesus Christ. It is not something contrived. Apostles will be clearly recognized by those Christ has sent them to. If you have to prove you are an apostle, you are not one. It is about being yourself and allowing God to make His appointments (Acts 9:15, 24; Rom. 1:1; 1 Cor. 1:1; 15:9, 10; 2 Cor. 1:1; Gal. 1:1, 11, 15-17; Eph. 1:1; Col. 1:1; Titus 1:1; 1 Tim. 1:12; 2:7; 2 Tim. 1:1, 2, 11). Apostolic ministry is a grace gift given to the church by God (1 Cor. 12:29). It is only true for those to whom God sends it. It involves a God-given "sphere of influence" or "measure of rule" (Rom. 11:13; 15:16; 1 Cor. 9:2; Eph. 1:1; 3:5). This was true for the apostles of the New Testament:

> _2 Cor. 10:13 We, however, will not boast beyond measure, but within the limits of the sphere which God appointed us—a sphere which especially includes you. 14 For we are not extending ourselves beyond our sphere (thus not reaching you), for it was to you that we came with the gospel of Christ; 15 not boasting of things beyond measure, that is, in other men's labors, but having hope, that as your faith is increased, we shall be greatly enlarged by you in our sphere, 16 to preach the gospel in the regions beyond you, and not to boast in another man's sphere of accomplishment._

Apostleship serves to strengthen those they are in relationship with for "obedience to the faith". It serves to impart "spiritual gifts" to those in relationship with them. It provides God's authority to individuals and congregations. That authority is manifested. There must be a confirmed manifested evidence of apostolic ministry. The signs of apostleship must be evident. It will be marked with: 1) perseverance (endurance); 2) signs and wonders; 3) mighty deeds; and 4) the life of God's Spirit and fruit of that life which writes a letter. Apostleship provides a flow of spiritual life to a congregation. It serves to help "establish" local churches and to "build" the house (spiritual house) of God. Apostolic ministry will serve to "plant" ministries and to "plant" those things within ministries that will enable them to come to maturity in Christ. It is a "fathering" ministry and therefore serves to provide an example to be imitated and followed in Christ. Apostolic ministry releases the authority to local apostolic leaders to appoint elders.

The mark of apostolic relationship is seen in the manifested flow of the spiritual life that happens as a result of the divine sending of apostleship and the divine reception of such.

2 Cor. 3:1 Do we begin again to commend ourselves? Or do we need, as some others, epistles of commendation to you or letters of commendation from you? 2 You are our epistle written in our hearts, known and read by all men; 3 you are manifestly an epistle of Christ, ministered by us, written not with ink but by the Spirit of the living God, not on tablets of stone but on tablets of flesh, that is, of the heart. 4 And my speech and my preaching were not with persuasive words of human wisdom, but in demonstration of the Spirit and of power, 5 that your faith should not be in the wisdom of men but in the power of God.

1 Cor. 9:2 If I am not an apostle to others, yet doubtless I am to you. For you are the seal of my apostleship in the Lord.

NOTE: Consider the leaders who have been sent into your life. How have they been an example of and an inspiration to endurance in the faith, supernatural testimonies of Christ, mighty deeds, and the life of God's Spirit and fruit of that life.

Chapter 4.1 – 4.5 - The Fourth Eye of Grace

Statements and Questions to Consider
For a Group Discussion:

1. The fourth of the *Seven Eyes of Grace* involves the subject of "apostolic teaching" and "submission one to another" in the Body of Christ. Discuss what this means. Define "apostolic teaching".

2. The "laying on of hands" is the grace of the Spirit of Counsel. This is a corporate anointing. Discuss what this means.

3. The hands represent our ability to receive instruction and perform work. The laying on of hands imparts the blessings of the Father. It is by the laying on of hands that someone is sent forth in authority. How do you think these things relate to submission one to another?

4. As the heave offering was taken, lifted up to the Lord, and lowered to become the provision of the priest and his home it was a symbolic statement of; "I submit to you as unto the Lord". This was symbolic of the Spirit of Counsel, a corporate grace of submission one to another in the Body of Christ. This is a "grace", not merely an action. Discuss the difference between a grace and a work.

5. The government of the church must be focused on seeking and maintaining the Lordship and direction of Jesus Christ over His Body. Paul wrote that God had given two gifts for this purpose. These were the gifts of "grace" and "apostleship". Discuss how both of these keep us obedient to the faith.

6. All members of the Body of Christ are responsible for seeing their God-given leadership as a gift to them. Leaders are a source of authority in their lives. They are those to be thought of, considered, followed, and joined to. Leadership is not a control, but a source of activation and life-giving direction. Discuss this.

7. How does the Holy Spirit work in the Body of Christ as the true government of grace?

8. It is the grace of the Holy Spirit within the Body of Christ that gives it the power to live and function. But it is the God sent leadership to the Body of Christ that gives it the proper "restraint" and "focus" to allow it to accomplish the work it was designed to accomplish. How does this happen?

9. Read Eph. 4:7-16 and discuss the functions of five-fold ministry.

10. Continuing steadfastly in the apostles' doctrine (instruction taught them by the apostles) is to keep in God's "sent word" to the corporate Body. Discuss what this means and looks like.

11. "Continuing in the apostles' doctrine" implies first of all that we emulate those who are mature in Christ before us. How do you do this?

12. In a Theocracy, God speaks, and we respond to what He wills. It is a governing by God. The result is always life and peace. Explain a "Theocracy" and give examples in the room as to how their individual lives are governed as a "Theocracy".

13. The author uses five theological names that describe these means of hearing His voice. They are Apostolic rule, Prophetic rule, Episcopal rule, Presbyterian rule, and Congregational rule. Discuss each of these.

14. Discuss the apostolic attributes of:

    1) Perseverance (endurance);

    2) Signs and wonders;

    3) Mighty deeds;

    4) The life of God's Spirit and fruit of that life which writes a letter.

15. Discuss the attributes of apostolic ministry, what it looks like, and how it functions;

    - strengthen for obedience to the faith;
    - impart spiritual gifts;
    - build God's house to be connected to the Roof (Jesus);
    - establish local churches;
    - assure foundational building material;
    - plant ministries;
    - fathering and example;
    - appoint leaders;
    - connect the local church to the kingdom plan;
    - established by Christ;
    - provides authority.

Chapter 5.1

The Fifth Eye of Grace
- The Spirit of Might

We have now come to the fifth grace of the *Seven Eyes of Grace*. This grace relates to the resurrection of the dead and the Spirit of Might. The earth has been cursed with the perpetual pattern of entropy. Apathy and atrophy mark the landscape of the earth. The spiritual realities of the Body of Christ are the opposite. The resurrection life of Christ guarantees increasing glory in the earth! Our fellowship is not with the darkness, death, and decay of the earth. Our fellowship is with Christ in the power of His resurrection.

The fifth step toward living in the blessings of the kingdom of God is the grace of the Spirit of Might. It is a part of God's grace process in the Body of Christ (Heb. 10:5-7). It correlates to "The Spirit of Might" and the level of relationship in the Body known as the "vowed offering".

> *Deut. 12:5 "But you shall seek the place where the LORD your God chooses, out of all your tribes, to put His name for His habitation; and there you shall go. 6 "There you shall take your* [1]*burnt offerings, your* [2]*sacrifices, your* [3]*tithes, the* [4]*heave offerings of your hand, your* [5]*vowed offerings, your* [6]*freewill offerings, and the* [7]*firstlings of your herds and flocks. 7 And there you shall eat before the LORD your God, and you shall rejoice in all to which you have put your hand, you and your households, in which the LORD your God has blessed you."*

The vowed offering of the New Covenant is not what we "vow" to God. It is according to Christ's vow. It is a level of offering that relates to who we are in Christ according to the grace and power of His resurrection. We are a part of His calling and part of the riches of His inheritance (Eph. 1:18). It is not who we think we are that counts. It is who we really are. God has given to each of us a measure of grace to bring a contribution to the fellowship of the Body of Christ.

146

This grace is also seen in the second chapter of Acts. The Church had experienced the Spirit of the Lord to commit their lives to Christ, the Spirit of Wisdom to act in faith toward God, the Spirit of Understanding as a testimony of the life of the Holy Spirit upon their lives, and the Spirit of Counsel to submit one to another as the life-giving Body of Christ to continue steadfast in the increasing glory of God in the earth. This fifth grace is another aspect of the Holy Spirit that was poured out on the Body of Christ on the day of Pentecost. It is also a testimony of a Spirit of jubilee and the liberation experienced in the lives of those who believe in Christ.

Acts 2:42 And they continued steadfastly in the apostles' doctrine (instruction taught them by the apostles) and fellowship, in the breaking of bread, and in prayers.

Here we see that the believers continued steadfastly in "fellowship". This is the fruit of the grace of the Spirit of Might. It is the true fellowship of the Spirit as spiritual members of the living Body of Christ. This grace can also be found in the foundation of Christ known as the "resurrection of the dead" (Heb 6:2). It is the manifestation of 'who He is' and 'who we are in Christ'. The mark of true fellowship in Christ is to be alive in Christ! This is not merely fellowship of a social nature. It is fellowship filled with the resurrection power of Christ. It is fellowship with the manifest presence of God in our lives. It is fellowship with one another around His throne of grace. It is fellowship according to the contribution given by each of us to reveal His manifest presence in our midst. The key to fellowship is Christ in our midst!

Mt. 18:20 "For where two or three are gathered together in My name, I am there in the midst of them."

1 Cor. 1:9 God is faithful, by whom you were called into the fellowship of His Son, Jesus Christ our Lord.

Acts 2:42 And they continued steadfastly in   ...fellowship...

The Greek word for fellowship is the word "koinonia". It means, *"partnership; social intercourse"*. It comes from three root words meaning, *"a sharer"*, *"common"*, and *"union; with; together"*. The idea of true fellowship in Christ is for each one to do his or her part. We each bring a contribution to the fellowship of Christ. True fellowship comes from the resurrection Might of Christ. Fellowship is not possible according to our old destiny in First Adam. We must find our fellowship in the revealing of the Last Adam, Jesus Christ. We are in a "partnership" in the corporate expression of His living Body. We must each do our share to reveal the common purpose of the Body of Christ. It is not what we determine to become. It is a matter of discovering who we are in our part of revealing the mystery of the fellowship of Christ. It is according to the "vow" of Christ that we become who we are.

I remember wrestling with this as a young Christian. My problem was a common problem found in the Church. I wrestled with discovering who I was, because I thought the callings on others were greater than my own. I didn't know how to just allow myself to become me. I remember a time that I observed a man with a revelatory gift of the word of knowledge. He flowed quite strongly in the manifestation of the word of knowledge. I desired to operate in the word of knowledge like he did. I struggled to figure out how to do what he did. It was very common for me to function in the discerning of spirits. Deliverance ministry was very common through me just being myself. I didn't like that as much. It seemed messy to me. I thought working in the word of knowledge like the man I knew would be much better. I spent many days wrestling to be someone I was not. One day I became resigned to the idea that all I had to do was be myself. I quit trying to work in the word of knowledge and just began to be at peace with how God was using me in my own unique way. Pretty soon I found that I was working in word of knowledge in my own way. I didn't even know I was doing it half the time, but Jesus was getting the credit. This is just one example of how the grace of the Spirit of Might works. He comes to reveal who we are in Christ, not who we want to be. Who we are is more than enough to bring glory to the name of Jesus. We must be at peace with who God has made us to be. The key is to seek to magnify Jesus in being ourselves in Him. It is centered on His resurrection might, not who we want to be in Him.

I remember when God called me into the ministry. It was in the mid-70's. I had been a Christian for several years. The Holy Spirit was speaking to me about my destiny in Christ. He spoke to me about being an intercessor. I argued with Him at first. I told Him that was women's work. I asked Him if He had any openings for apostles, prophets, evangelists, pastors, or teachers. He prompted me to read a book on intercession by Derrick Prince. When I concluded the book, I came to the decision that being an intercessor was a wonderful calling. I was a driver for United Parcel Service at the time. It was at about 10:30 in the morning. I remember stepping out from my delivery truck into the morning sun and saying to God, "I'll be an intercessor". When

I did so, I knew it was the highest calling anyone could possibly have in life. I knew that Jesus was at the right hand of the Father doing the same thing. I didn't really understand what He was saying to me at the time. I didn't know that He has myriads of ways of expressing His intercessory calling. I have been a full-time minister for over thirty-five years now and I have to say that intercession is what I do. I am in the gap as an apostle and stood in the gap as a pastor for over twenty years. The one thing that is truer than anything is that He has made me to be me. I cannot compare myself to anyone else. When I am myself, I bring the life of heaven to barren places in the earth. This is a ministry of intercession. It was my perception of the calling of others that made me argue with God in the first place in regard to my calling to intercession. I have found that if I trust Him in what He says, things turn out precisely for who we are in Him.

I can recall another story. I knew a man who had received a prophecy that he would be part of a musical evangelistic calling. He was very obviously evangelistic in his anointing and ability. He immediately understood his calling to be that he would be a lead singer of an evangelistic music ministry. The big problem was, "he couldn't really sing!" He was a fantastic event coordinator. He was awesome at administrating and running a sound system. He was a good guitar player. He could play lead electric guitar, rhythm guitar, and bass guitar. He had plenty of gifting to be a part of what had been prophesied over him. His problem was that he was trying to be someone he wasn't gifted to be. He was thinking as an "individual", rather than considering his "corporate" destiny in the Body of Christ.

Have you ever watched those reality television shows where people from the general population come and audition to become the next great singer? Some of the people who try out are absolutely awful at singing! The problem is, they are deceived into believing they are great singers! Their real problem is that they don't like who they are. God has no doubt given them gifting, but they have considered the gifting of singers or performers to be better than what they have been given in life. It is the same in the Body of Christ. The key to finding our calling in Christ is to seek Him, not our calling. Our life comes from the resurrection life of Christ! We are each given a 'measure' in Christ!

Eph. 4:7 But to each one of us grace was given according to the measure of Christ's gift.

When we don't know who we are, we seek to find who we are in various sources. We look to the circumstances of the world and begin to judge what things are good and what things are bad. We often seek to identify with what we consider to be valuable. We can never find out who we are by merely looking at the examples of others in the world. We can never find out who we are by merely looking at the examples of others in the Body of Christ! We are uniquely ourselves in Christ, but the key to discovering who we are is to look to Christ. For some of us God speaks clearly to us in a moment, for others it is simply a process that evolves to reveal who we are in Him.

Several years ago, I wanted to really know who I was in Christ. I felt it was important for my wife to know as well. I was preparing to go to a place in the mountains, where I would sometimes go to fast and pray. I went to my wife and told her of my plans to go to the mountain and find out who I was. I told her she should pray as well and find out who she was in Him. She, being secure with who she was, told me she didn't desire to find out. I wanted her to pray anyway and to even ask on my behalf as well. I went to the mountain expecting to fast and pray for the whole week before God spoke. I was not at the mountain more than ten minutes and God spoke to me very clearly. He said to me, "You expose the walls of the false and activate the pursuit of truth". He talked to me the entire week and showed me how I had always exposed false walls and activated the pursuit of truth. When working a secular job, I would always look for ways to expedite production. I was never good at assembly line tasks or repetitious patterns. In every situation I would see a way to expand the boundaries and improve things in some way. It wasn't something I had to work at. It was simply who I was. God continued to speak to me and even revealed to me what my wife was gifted to be. He told me, "Bonnie is a keel. She will keep you upright and on course. Like the keel of a ship, she runs deep. She will never be at the forefront of ministry as the one who leads it, but she will under gird everything and keep it upright and on course." He continued to speak, "Son, you are rough water. Bonnie is deep. Rough water or smooth she will always be the same. You will stir things up and she will keep it upright and on course." I knew it to be true. Neither of us has to work at being who we are. We simply are who we are. The more we seek Him and serve Him by serving His Body, the more we become ourselves. It is not something we strive to do. It is simply who we live to be. To testify of the differences in the lives of my wife and I; when I went home, I found that God had told Bonnie what my purpose was, but she didn't ask about herself. She runs deep and didn't need to know.

I have seen church members battle with one another over the massive insecurity issues that reside in the hearts of those who struggle to find out who they are. The key to finding out who we are is not found in the works of the flesh. It is found in the place of the heart. It begins with loving God just as we are. We are more than enough to bring glory to His name.

NOTE: Once again it is time to stop and allow the Holy Spirit to minister to you. Consider the uniqueness of who you are and how you give life to others. Have a conversation with God in regard to your part in bringing life to this world and to the Body of Christ.

Chapter 5.2

The Fifth Eye of Grace

The grace of the Spirit of Might and the mystery of the fellowship not only reveals who we are, but it also gives life to those that God divinely joins us to. This is why it is essential to find the "vowed offering" of Christ in who we are and not merely a testimony of self that exhibits something less than our true destiny. When we find our place in the hope of His calling, we become a life supply to those He joins us to.

Eph. 4:16 Under his direction, the whole body is fitted together perfectly. As each part does its own special work, it helps the other parts grow, so that the whole body is healthy and growing and full of love.

God has given a grace for a union of close joining relationships that raise up His Body. The supply of life to one another is according to a portion of God's resurrection life that He has given as a grace to each one for the other. Fellowship by the Spirit causes each of us to bring a contribution to others that will cause the Body and its parts to come to life within each one's effective sphere of operation. Our vowed offering is to contribute to one another according to the grace given us by God. It is our offering, but according to Christ's vow. We must learn to be ourselves and to carry our load. Each of us must learn who we are according to the grace that has been given to us by God. We must then live to be ourselves and give life to others. The apostle Paul revealed this in his writings.

Rom. 12:3 For I say, through the grace given to me, to everyone who is among you, not to think of himself more highly than he ought to think, but to think soberly, as God has dealt to each one a measure of faith.

In this verse Paul was not telling us that we should not value who we are in Christ. He was simply saying that we should not think beyond the boundaries of who we are. We should not strive to be someone else. To think more highly than we ought to think is to think on things, which aren't real for us. It is not better to be someone else. We must "keep our feet on the ground". We must live within the realm of our God-given abilities. We must learn to be content with who we are and then present our bodies as living sacrifices to the service of God and His Body (Rom. 12:1).

Rom. 12:4 For as we have many members in one body, but all the members do not have the same function...

It is impossible to figure out our function by looking to someone else other than Christ Himself. Others can inspire us; we can be mentored by others, and we can be influenced by others. We can receive benefits from others, but we can only find out who we are in Christ. What is the key to figuring that out?

Rom. 12:5 ...so we, being many, are one body in Christ, and individually members of one another.

The key to figuring out who we are is to serve others in who they are. I'm not talking about joining ourselves to someone else to become like him or her. I'm talking about simply serving in whatever way we can. When we serve in whatever way we can, we soon find out what we can do. What is it that motivates our hearts?

One common thing that I have heard in the Body of Christ is the phrase, "I'll pray about it". I think praying about things is important. We definitely want to do what God wants us to do, but I think there are many things we don't need to pray about. Many consider me to be a successful minister with a successful ministry. I have prayed about the direction that God leads me in everything, but there have been many times where I have seen a need and I simply met it. I knew I could do it; it needed to be done, so I did it! This is not always the right thing to do, but I believe that most of the time it is. I can't tell you how many things I have had to do as a pastor because members of the church had to "pray about it". I saw the need and had to do it! They prayed about it and didn't do anything. Many of them are still praying and wondering why they aren't doing anything. They have even come to me and said, "Pastor, I really want you to help me find out what I'm supposed to do in ministry." I think it would be better to ask the question; "what can I do to serve God and the Body of Christ?"

In most cases, you just need to look at what needs to be done and then ask yourself if you are able to do it. I'm not talking about doing things to find your identity, nor am I talking about doing things simply to impress God or others. I am talking about genuine service in love. As you are faithful to do practical things, God will guide your steps in spiritual things. I still preach the word, lay hands on the sick, cast out devils, mop floors, do construction work, watch children, administer budgets, greet people, set up chairs, or whatever is necessary to fulfill the tasks of any given day. The unique thing is that I do everything I do as me!

Part of our uniqueness is a God-given gift of motivation intrinsically placed within us by God Himself. These are sometimes called a person's motivational gifting. There are different motivational gifts in the Body of Christ.

Rom. 12:6 Having then gifts differing according to the grace that is given to us, let us use them: if prophecy, let us prophesy in proportion to our faith; 7 or ministry, let us use it in our ministering; he who teaches, in teaching; 8 he who exhorts, in exhortation; he who gives, with liberality; he who leads, with diligence; he who shows mercy, with cheerfulness.

Some of us are perceivers, some are servers, some are teachers, some are exhorters, some are givers, some are leaders, and some show mercy when needed. No two individuals are the same, but some are similar. These are not learned gifts; they are motivations of the heart. What is it that motivates us? We must learn to be ourselves. If you ever get an opportunity to take a "motivational gifting test" you should do so. It will help you understand what makes you work. My motivational gifts are administrative, perceiver, server, and exhorter. My wife is an exhorter, mercy gift, and giver. We are great complimentary gifts to one another. Diversity is a gift from God! Our Father in heaven gave our motivational gifts to us when we were formed in our mother's womb. The key to finding the fullness of these gifts is to discover them in the anointing of the Spirit of Might and the fellowship of the Body of Christ.

Not only are there motivational gifts given to us by our Father in our creation, but there is also a mandate to minister to one another by the anointing of Christ in the charisma of who He is in our midst. Our fellowship is with Him and with one another.

1 Cor. 14:26 How is it then, brethren? Whenever you come together, each of you has a psalm, has a teaching, has a tongue, has a revelation, has an interpretation. Let all things be done for edification.

The key in the level of relationship foreseen in the "vowed offering" is that our contribution will bring edification to others in the Body of Christ. These are offerings of fellowship. We don't give a psalm to impress others. We give a psalm to impart the life of the Spirit to others. We don't speak revelation to impress others with our ability to receive revelation. We give revelation to build up others. We do everything to give life to others. This is the mystery of the fellowship. It is an offering of contribution. It is not a taking from another, but rather a giving of life to another. It is hidden in the mystery of the resurrection life that is found in Christ. The earth is bound to apathy and death. If we are earthly minded, we will always think of ways that others can meet our own needs. If we think with heavenly minds, we will look for ways to give life to others. This is the testimony of His resurrection life in our midst! Our needs are met in meeting the needs of others! When we die, we live! When we lose our lives, we find them! This is the secret of fellowship and the vowed offering. It is understood by the grace of the Spirit of Might. To find our own identity is to give of who we are to others. When we know who we are, we submit one to another and we provide life one to another!

> *Eph. 5:18 And do not be drunk with wine, in which is dissipation; but be filled with the Spirit, 19 speaking to one another in psalms and hymns and spiritual songs, singing and making melody in your heart to the Lord, 20 giving thanks always for all things to God the Father in the name of our Lord Jesus Christ, 21 submitting to one another in the fear of God.*

In these verses there are several keys given to finding out who we are in Christ. The first key is to be "filled with the Spirit". In order to understand the grace of the Spirit of Might we must seek to be filled with the Holy Spirit. He is the source of resurrection life and resurrection identity. The second key is to focus on giving life to others. We must first be filled with life, and then we must live to give life to others. The third key is thankfulness to God the Father as a son or daughter in Christ. This is the reason we seek to be spiritual on behalf of others. We do everything as worship to our Father in heaven. It is more important to worship God than it is to strive for identity. When we worship Him, we discover who we are. The final key in these verses is found in our ability to "submit" one to another in the fear of God. We don't submit one to another to worship one another. We don't submit one to another to impress one another. We don't submit one to another in the hope of being noticed and

155

promoted. We submit one to another because we do so as unto the Lord. We live to please Him. He is the source of all of our motivation. We live for Him in His resurrection Might! The real issue is our ability to love God and to love people. We offer who we are for His glory!

As a leader, and someone who helps people find their calling in Christ, I have had many people approach me with a desire to be ministers for Christ. One situation that always gives me a "flag of warning" is when someone comes and says, "I just have to go into the ministry, because I love the anointing". Loving the anointing is a benefit of ministry, but it is not a reason for ministry. The first reason for desiring to minister is that of loving God. The second reason is that you love people. The mystery is that we actually love God by loving people. It is more important to love people than it is to love prophesying, or miracles. If you love miracles more than you love people, you aren't ready for miracles. If you love prophesying more than you love people, you aren't ready to prophesy. We love God by loving people, but we love people by the supernatural evidence of Christ in His resurrection.

I minister to many people. I have prophesied to thousands of people. I have seen many healings and miracles in the lives of people I have ministered to. There is one thing I love more than anything. That is to see the Father love His children and to bring them the freedom that comes to them through His only begotten Son, Jesus Christ. More than the accuracy of word of knowledge, is the accuracy of the intimate touch of the Father and the resurrection power of the Son. That is what makes it all worthwhile! It is then that the thorns and thistles of the earth become overpowered by the holiness of Christ. Rivers are found in desert places and where jackals once lived, there is a highway of holiness in the once desert places of human hearts!

Isa. 35:3 Strengthen the weak hands, and make firm the feeble knees.
4 Say to those who are fearful-hearted, "Be strong, do not fear!
Behold, your God will come with vengeance, with the recompense
of God; He will come and save you." 5 Then the eyes of the blind
shall be opened, and the ears of the deaf shall be unstopped. 6 Then
the lame shall leap like a deer, and the tongue of the dumb sing. For
waters shall burst forth in the wilderness, and streams in the desert.
7 The parched ground shall become a pool, and the thirsty land
springs of water; in the habitation of jackals, where each lay, there
shall be grass with reeds and rushes. 8 A highway shall be there, and
a road, and it shall be called the Highway of Holiness. The unclean

shall not pass over it, but it shall be for others. Whoever walks the road, although a fool, shall not go astray.

NOTE: Stop here and spend some time with the Holy Spirit again. Consider how you love God and people. Contemplate how you can serve God and others through who God uniquely made you to be. Meditate on anything the Holy Spirit quickens in your heart while you read this chapter.

Chapter 5.3

The Fifth Eye of Grace

It is important that we know who we are in Christ. The vowed offering has to do with knowing who we are in the Body of Christ. It is in the Body of Christ that the resurrection power of Christ is found in His fullness. The vowed offering will make us able to experience His resurrection life and power! Thinking we are someone we are not will distract us from the truth and will leave us short of our destiny in Christ. We are uniquely formed in Christ according to His resurrection Might. He has chosen our uniqueness and called us to be a part of Him in our own special gift of grace. We are not the same as one another. We are the same together as the spiritual house of God's habitation, but we are uniquely different in our part of comprising the whole house of God!

Jn. 14:2 "In My Father's house are many mansions; if it were not so, I would have told you. I go to prepare a place for you."

I believe the "mansions" of the Lord are not just in heaven. They are in the Body of Christ. The Father has prepared a place for each of us in Christ. We can contribute to the fellowship. We used to be a part of the old house of Adam that was bound to the thorns and thistles of the earth. The barrenness of the earth held us as captives to lives that were circumstantially motivated. We were crisis managers, not kingdom influencers. We have now become a part of the living house of Christ in the earth and into eternity! We are part of the mystery of the fellowship in Him (1 Cor. 1:9; Eph. 3:9)!

What are some attributes of fellowship? What is the fruit of the testimony of our fellowship one with another in the Body of Christ?

Phil. 2:1 Therefore if there is any consolation in Christ, if any comfort of love, if any fellowship of the Spirit, if any affection and mercy, 2 fulfill my joy by being like-minded, having the same love, being of one accord, of one mind.

Our fellowship is in Christ. Through our fellowship we find the comfort of love and we give the comfort of love to others. This grace of the Spirit of Might reveals the true affection and mercy of the Spirit to one another. It is through accepting diversities together that we can really become empowered to be like-minded toward one another. A lot of people think that unity is everyone doing the same thing. I believe that true unity is everyone doing different things for the same purpose. This is how we can give the same love to one another. We come, as we are, not pretending to be someone else. Through our diversity we have unity. Our common purpose is Christ and to know Him in His resurrection, that is what causes us to be in one accord.

Phil. 3:8 But indeed I also count all things loss for the excellence of the knowledge of Christ Jesus my Lord, for whom I have suffered the loss of all things, and count them as rubbish, that I may gain Christ 9 and be found in Him, not having my own righteousness, which is from the law, but that which is through faith in Christ, the righteousness which is from God by faith; 10 that I may know Him and the power of His resurrection, and the fellowship of His sufferings, being conformed to His death, 11 if, by any means, I may attain to the resurrection from the dead.

It is not the cross that gives us unity. It is the power of Christ's resurrection! The cross was an act of Christ's mercy that justified us to become eligible for His amazing grace. It is not being justified from a life of sin that we seek. It is being justified to be a member of the Body of Christ! We seek to be found in Him. We desire to know Him in His righteousness, not our own. It is the grace of the Spirit of Might that anoints us to know Christ in His living character and power. We have the great hope of resurrection from the dead after we physically expire, but we also have this hope of knowing Him in His manifest presence today. We can know Him in the power of His resurrection.

There has been a real work of the grace of the Spirit of Might in the past few decades. I believe that it began in the 70's when the Holy Spirit inspired the Church to know Christ in the power of His word. It was then that the "word faith" movement came to the forefront. It was then that many teaching ministries were birthed that inspired the members of the Body of Christ to seek to hear God in His word. It became increasingly common to seek Christ in the power of His resurrection. The Body of Christ was inspired with new faith to hear God speak His word to men. This led to the prophetic birthing of the 80's. In the 80's many prophetic ministries emerged like

Bishop Hamon and Christian International Ministries. Numerous prophetic ministries manifested throughout the world. The resurrection power of the prophetic voice of God was restored to the Church in a tremendous way. This led to the 90's when the rivers of renewal began to flow. Laughter was restored to the Church to testify that in the presence of the Lord there is the fullness of joy (Ps. 16:11). Renewal touched the world through places like Toronto and Brownsville. The grace of the Spirit of Might became very evident in the past few decades. These things will continue to progress to more evidence of the increasing grace of the Spirit of Might. Members of the Body of Christ are finding their place in the fellowship of Christ. The value of Christ's manifest presence in Christ's Body is being restored to the Church. Christ's presence and a hunger for His presence will continue to increase in the Body of Christ in the generations to come.

Fellowship with Christ in the power of His resurrection is essential for the Body of Christ to come into the fullness of His stature. We are called to be the light of His presence to the world. Fellowship with Him and one another will cause us to walk in the light!

> *1 Jn. 1:1 That which was from the beginning, which we have heard, which we have seen with our eyes, which we have looked upon, and our hands have handled, concerning the Word of life— 2 the life was manifested, and we have seen, and bear witness, and declare to you that eternal life which was with the Father and was manifested to us— 3 that which we have seen and heard we declare to you, that you also may have fellowship with us; and truly our fellowship is with the Father and with His Son Jesus Christ. 4 And these things we write to you that your joy may be full.*

John was blessed to have known Jesus in the flesh, but He also knew Him in the power of His resurrection. We are blessed to be able to know Christ in the power of His resurrection. We need to hear Him by the grace of the Spirit of Might. We need to see Him and touch Him by that same grace. His life must be manifested to us. We can have fellowship with the Father and with His Son Jesus Christ by the grace of the Spirit of Might. It is in His manifested presence that our joy will be full!

> *1 Jn. 1:5 This is the message which we have heard from Him and declare to you, that God is light and in Him is no darkness at all. 6 If we say that we have fellowship with Him, and walk in darkness, we lie*

160

*and do not practice the truth. 7 But if we walk in the light as He is
in the light, we have fellowship with one another, and the blood of
Jesus Christ His Son cleanses us from all sin.*

When we have fellowship with Christ in His resurrection, we are given
power over the thorns and thistles of the world. The lifeless things that try
to afflict us with the bitterness and wounds of a dead earth do not distract
us. The grace of the Spirit of Might and the resurrection life of Christ will
cause us to be clothed in the holiness of Christ (Rev. 3:4, 5).

In my early years of ministry training, I spent a lot of time fasting and
praying. I spent many hours focusing on the manifest presence of Christ. It was
only part of the equation for me. I have since learned to love people as I love
the presence of Christ. He is manifest in both places. Those years of focusing
on His manifest presence and power have had a huge long-term impact upon
my life. In my early years of ministry, I was amazed with encounters with God
by His Spirit. I have experienced supernatural phenomena that have amazed
me, but I have grown to understand that Christ's presence is not only found in
supernatural encounters with His Spirit but also with His Body. The mystery of
the fellowship is found in the power of His resurrection Might. I have discovered
that Christ's manifest presence is both found in personal experiences with His
Spirit and with the unity of the Spirit with one another. This has come to be
a part of the community in which I live. There is a hunger for more of God's
presence and for fellowship with one another. It is common to hear leaders
of the Church and members of various congregations call out for Christ in
His manifest presence. It is common for Christian leaders and congregation
members to seek to come together for the unity of the faith.

I have been blessed to be a part of a couple of leadership prayer gatherings
for the past several years. I meet regularly with other pastors to pray. We
represent both denominational and nondenominational ministries. There is
one profound commonality in our prayers. There is an ever-increasing desire
to know Christ in the power of His resurrection. It is common to find these
leaders calling out for the manifest presence of God in our community. These
prayers are the result of a restored grace of the Spirit of Might in the Church.

Another common thing among these leaders is that there is a cry for
unity through diversity. We have grown to embrace one another in a common
purpose, and we appreciate one another in each other's differences. I believe
the credit has to go to the Holy Spirit and the grace of the Spirit of Might. We

are being drawn together by the fellowship of the Spirit. We are becoming a greater expression of Christ's Body in our community. We have tried doing things for the sake of unity in the past, but now we are finding unity through a unified effort of seeking God's presence. We are not only finding that there is diversity within the members of our own congregations and ministries, but there is also diversity among our corporate purpose in our community. The basis of our fellowship is the presence of Christ among us. It is not fellowship around common works, but rather fellowship of a common purpose.

There are some common words around the world and in the Church that testify of this restored grace of the Spirit of Might and the mystery of the fellowship. One is the word "networking". This has become common both in the world and in the Church. We are finding that we are better off together than we are apart. Other words are words like "roundtables", "relational covenants", and "prophetic" and "apostolic networks". In the world there are "mergers" and "corporate amalgamations". These are all signs of the grace of the Spirit of Might and the mystery of the fellowship. Whenever God does something in the Church it can also be seen in the counterfeits of the world. It is not because they are copying the Church. It is because God is releasing something in the Spirit. I often find that the "buzz words" of the world are very commonly a twist of the truth God desires to bring to the Church. I also find that it is common for the world to hear it before the Church does. I believe it is because the world is "ice cold" and are on a continual search for something "hot". People in the world are "searching for life". People in the Church often become satisfied with old moves of the past. They were "hot" when they discovered a truth in Christ, but then settled to live with a measure of blessing. They then become "lukewarm" toward any attitudes of new and unexpected things. The "buzz words" of the world often point to a truth God wants to bring to the Church. The mystery of the vowed offering and the mystery of the fellowship is one of those.

NOTE: It is meditation time once again. Consider the subject material of this chapter and let the Holy Spirit fellowship with you today.

Chapter 5.4

The Fifth Eye of Grace

The early Church was faithful to continue steadfastly in the "fellowship" (Acts 2:42). That "fellowship" is the power of the life and light of Christ. It is the evidence of the unity of His resurrection Might. Fellowship in Christ ends the works of the flesh and commences the revealing of the works of the Spirit!

Rom. 13:11 And do this, knowing the time, that now it is high time to awake out of sleep; for now our salvation is nearer than when we first believed. 12 The night is far spent, the day is at hand. Therefore let us cast off the works of darkness, and let us put on the armor of light. 13 Let us walk properly, as in the day, not in revelry and drunkenness, not in licentiousness and lewdness, not in strife and envy. 14 But put on the Lord Jesus Christ, and make no provision for the flesh, to fulfill its lusts.

1 Cor. 3:2 I fed you with milk and not with solid food; for until now you were not able to receive it, and even now you are still not able; 3 for you are still carnal. For where there are envy, strife, and divisions among you, are you not carnal and behaving like mere men?

In order to truly experience the fellowship of the Spirit, we must know the death of the flesh. We cannot live for ourselves, but for Christ and one another. We must live for a corporate purpose and destiny, not for carnal self-seeking agendas. We must live for Christ's resurrection! Our fellowship with the Holy Spirit and with one another by the power of Christ's Spirit will enable us to do works of righteousness as the Body of Christ. As members of Christ's Body, we each contribute to the stature of Christ. It is the Spirit of Might that causes us to live according to the Spirit and not according to the flesh. True righteousness is to be in a right relationship with God and man. This is only possible in Christ. It is according to Christ's gift, not our own abilities. Fellowship is the true source of works of righteousness. All New Covenant Believers have the ability to do works of righteousness.

163

Eph. 2:10 For we are His workmanship, created in Christ Jesus for good works, which God prepared beforehand that we should walk in them.

The key to the fellowship is found in God's workmanship. It is not in who we think we want to be. It is a discovery in Christ. We must each discover who we are in Christ and then we must also discover who others are to us and with us within the Body of Christ. It is for the corporate purpose of God in heaven and earth! It is only in the place that was prepared beforehand that we can truly discover the power of Christ's Might. It is the testimony of the resurrection of the dead (Heb. 6:2). It is there we find the authority of His resurrection life! We are clothed in the resurrection life of Christ that we might bring a testimony of that life to those that God sends us to. We are clothed in Christ's resurrection life! We come in the name of Jesus, because we are sent in the name of Jesus. We are part of the fellowship of His Body! It is according to the confession of Christ before His Father in heaven! As a part of the fellowship, Christ makes a confession of who we are before God our Father and before angels (sent ones), speaking of a "sending forth" by the power of His Might for works of righteousness (destiny).

Rev. 3:5 "He who overcomes shall be clothed in white garments, and I will not blot out his name from the Book of Life; but I will confess his name before My Father and before His angels."

Jesus not only confesses us before His Father, but He also confesses us before the Father's angels. The word "angel" means "sent one". Christ's confession of our names before the Father and His angels is a testimony to our authority in Christ. It is a confession that is given according to the power of Christ in His resurrection. He does not confess all men. He only confesses those who are clothed in the garment of Christ. The Spirit of Might is the corporate expression of works of righteousness and the sending of the Father given to those who are the sent members of the Body of Christ. The testimony of our sending is found in the power of Christ's life given to us by the power of His resurrection Might! In Christ we were made alive to give life to the world to which we have been sent!

Eph. 2:1 And you He made alive, who were dead in trespasses and sins, 2 in which you once walked according to the course of this world, according to the prince of the power of the air, the spirit who now works in the sons of disobedience, 3 among whom also we all once conducted ourselves in the lusts of our flesh, fulfilling the desires of the flesh and of the mind, and were by nature children of wrath, just as the others. 4 But God, who is rich in mercy, because of His great love with which He loved us, 5 even when we were dead in trespasses, made us alive together with Christ (by grace you have been saved), 6 and raised us up together, and made us sit together in the heavenly places in Christ Jesus, 7 that in the ages to come He might show the exceeding riches of His grace in His kindness toward us in Christ Jesus. 8 For by grace you have been saved through faith, and that not of yourselves; it is the gift of God, 9 not of works, lest anyone should boast. 10 For we are His workmanship, created in Christ Jesus for good works, which God prepared beforehand that we should walk in them.

The context of this Scripture reveals that those who are dead are those bound to disobedience and those who have been granted life are those who walk in obedience to the Father as the Body of Christ. Life is not found in the works we do, but in the place we live. If we are members of the Body of Christ, we are also ministers of the life of Christ. We have been made alive together in Christ! We are seated with Him in the power of His resurrection life. Because of His Spirit of Might and our fellowship with Him in the power of His Might, we have been sent to the ages of the world to reveal the riches of Christ's grace. This is the testimony of the fellowship in Christ. It is not merely fellowship of the soul, but fellowship of the Spirit. It is according to the workmanship of God and not the will of our flesh. It is a place of discovery and spiritual sending. We are sent with His manifest presence and authority to be the testimony of His resurrection story!

1 Cor. 1:9 God is faithful, by whom you were called into the fellowship of His Son, Jesus Christ our Lord.

The fellowship of Jesus Christ is a "fellow-ship". We must see ourselves in the same Body as Christ Himself. It is the place where we abide in Him, and He abides in us. It is a testimony that declares that if others see us, they see Him, and if they see Him, they see us. It is a place where we must be aspired to be clothed in Him. It is all about His headship and body ministry in the power of His resurrection Might. Are we those who have had the resurrected hands of Christ laid upon us? If so, are we not then those who can lay hands upon others with the resurrected touch of Christ? This is only true if we remain steadfast in the mystery of the fellowship. We cannot live like the world, fellowship the darkness of the world, and expect to bring the ministry of the life of Christ. We must remain in fellowship with Christ in His headship, and we must live as contributors to the life and light of His Body. This is only made possible by the testimony that comes from His heavenly grace of the Spirit of Might. This testimony was seen in the early Church and must be seen even greater in the Church that culminates Christ's glory in the earth.

To be spiritual can often mean to show our spirituality in ways that are practical. It is a matter of the heart and the testimony of the Spirit, not merely the phenomena of the Spirit. The apostle Paul revealed this when he commended the church of Macedonia in their ability to give of their money to the needs of the saints in Jerusalem. It was a testimony to the Spirit of Might and the mystery of the fellowship. Paul sent Titus to inspire the church of Corinth to do the same. It was important for the saints to minister to the needs of others based upon Christ's grace of Might and not according to their own fears or limitations. Paul called the giving of money a "grace", not merely an action to be taken. He was identifying the source of their giving. The source was Christ and His resurrection Might.

2 Cor. 8:3 For I bear witness that according to their ability, yes, and beyond their ability, they were freely willing, 4 imploring us with much urgency that we would receive the gift and the fellowship of the ministering to the saints. 5 And this they did, not as we had hoped, but first gave themselves to the Lord, and then to us by the will of God. 6 So we urged Titus, that as he had begun, so he would also complete this grace in you as well.

The fellowship of Christ is a mystery. It was pre-existent in Christ. It was hidden, but it can now be revealed by the power of God's resurrection Might. It is the vow of God and our portion within the context of Christ in His Body. It is a place that is above principalities and powers. It is not a theological reality, but a manifest reality in Christ. It is the place of the testimony of the resurrection of the dead in Christ (Heb. 6:2). Our lives are expressed through the works of resurrection life brought about by the functioning Body of Christ. It is a corporate place and a corporate ministry. It is a ministry to reveal Christ, not the works of Christ. It is meant to reveal the love of the Father through the actions of His Church.

Eph. 3:8 To me, who am less than the least of all the saints, this grace was given, that I should preach among the Gentiles the unsearchable riches of Christ, 9 and to make all people see what is the fellowship of the mystery, which from the beginning of the ages has been hidden in

God who created all things through Jesus Christ; 10 to the intent that now the manifold wisdom of God might be made known by the church to the principalities and powers in the heavenly places, 11 according to the eternal purpose which He accomplished in Christ Jesus our Lord. 12 in whom we have boldness and access with confidence through faith in Him.

NOTE: Stop and reflect the subject material of this chapter. Let the Holy Spirit speak to you in regard to the Spirit of Might and the resurrection of the dead. Let the Holy Spirit stir you in His resurrection life.

Chapter 5.5

The Fifth Eye of Grace

We have seen that being a part of the fellowship of Christ means to be a part of the sent Body of Christ. Christ confesses us before the Father and before His angels. To be confessed by Christ before the "sending ones" (angels) of heaven is to be commissioned as the sent Body of Christ. The resurrected One makes a confession of our names before the Father, because we are clothed in the garments of Christ (white garments). We are part of the fellowship found in His resurrected Might. What kinds of things are found in the fellowship of Christ? They are the things that make for life in Christ. Our conduct must be that of the Last Adam and not the former Adam of death (Eph. 4:22). Our priorities must be for a right relationship with God and a right relationship with our fellow members of the Body of Christ. We must live as holy members of a heavenly Body being made known in both heaven and earth (Eph. 1:10; 4:24). We must speak truth to one another, knowing that we are members of one another in Christ (Eph. 4:25). Self-seeking agendas and bitterness of heart must not be found within our lives (Eph. 4:26, 27; Jam. 3:13-18). We must live our lives with the purpose of edifying one another and giving grace to one another in Christ. We are being empowered by the grace of Christ's resurrection Might. We must live for others and not for ourselves. We have been given the ministry of resurrection life in Christ. We have been commissioned to bring life to death and light to darkness. Our purpose is found in the anointing of the Holy Spirit and the grace of the vowed offering in Christ. We are a Body for His will and not our own.

> *Eph. 4:28 Let him who stole steal no longer, but rather let him labor, working with his hands what is good, that he may have something to give him who has need. 29 Let no corrupt communication proceed out of your mouth, but what is good for necessary edification, that it may impart grace to the hearers. 30 And do not grieve the Holy Spirit of God, by whom you were sealed for the day of redemption.*

In my many years as a senior pastor, I saw numerous pointless causes of division in the church. People often tend to focus on a form of godliness and fail to see that the point of Christianity and the heart of God is to bring life to others. I use an example with worship teams. We are not likely to grieve the Holy Spirit with a missed note, a forgotten song line, a choice of a wrong song, or a wrong arrangement of music in some way. It is not the form of worship that God cares about as much as the heart of the worshipper. If we have a bad attitude toward God or toward one another, we are likely to grieve the Holy Spirit every time. If we choose to fellowship with works of darkness, we are likely to grieve the Holy Spirit. God is not disappointed with true attempts of light, but He will withdraw His presence from true attempts of darkness. We must stay in that spiritual place of giving life to one another.

We must live for the unity of the faith and not for any personal agendas of retribution, revenge, retaliation, or demanded restitution (Eph. 4:31). Our actions must be those found in the resurrection life of Christ (Eph. 4:32). We must be willing to lose our lives for the sake of others in order to save them for the sake of Christ. We are the Body of Christ, and it is the grace of the Spirit of Might that grants us the ability to live as life-giving members of Christ. We die to the flesh, but live to His eternal Spirit of life (Eph. 5:1, 2). We must live as holy members of the holy habitation of God's presence. Anything less is a breach in the fellowship.

Eph. 5:3 But fornication and all uncleanness or covetousness, let it not even be named among you, as is fitting for saints; 4 neither filthiness, nor foolish talking, nor coarse jesting, which are not fitting, but rather giving of thanks. 5 For this you know, that no fornicator, unclean person, nor covetous man, who is an idolater, has any inheritance in the kingdom of Christ and God. 6 Let no one deceive you with empty words, for because of these things the wrath of God comes upon the sons of disobedience.

To live according to the desires of the flesh is to live in the flesh. To live in the flesh is to deny the life found in Christ. To live in the garments of the flesh is to reject the garments given by the grace of the Spirit of Might and Christ's life found in the resurrection of the dead. Actions of the flesh not only harm us, they harm the entire Body of Christ. They especially affect the place of our divine joining in the Body of Christ. Remember, the vowed offering is according to God's vow and not our own. To choose fellowship with darkness is to deny fellowship with light. To deny fellowship with light is to deny our place of contribution to the light. It is to deny our place with the testimony and confession of those who are known as the increasing witness of the resurrection of the dead in Christ.

> *Eph. 5:8 For you were once darkness, but now you are light in the Lord. Walk as children of light 9 (for the fruit of the Spirit is in all goodness, righteousness, and truth), 10 proving what is acceptable to the Lord. 11 And have no fellowship with the unfruitful works of darkness, but rather expose them. 12 For it is shameful even to speak of those things which are done by them in secret. 13 But all things that are exposed are made manifest by the light, for whatever makes manifest is light.*

The testimony of the resurrection of the dead is to be "awake" to God in Christ. Jesus referred to death as "sleep" (Jn. 11:11-14). The opposite of "sleeping" is to "be awake". To be "awake" is to be on "watch" (Mt. 26:40-41). To be on "watch" is to remain in the fellowship of the Spirit. The flesh is weak, but the "Spirit is willing". The emphasis cannot be on the weakness of the flesh. It must be upon the willingness of the Spirit! Resurrection life is a grace that is available to all who seek it. The Spirit of Might makes us alive toward God in Christ.

I believe this whole issue has been greatly confused in the Body of Christ. We often focus on the weakness of the flesh and not the willingness of the Spirit. When we do that, we give life to that weakness. The Spirit is willing, so we must stay in fellowship with the Spirit! We must remain "awake" to God in the life of His Spirit. If we are "awake" towards God, we will be dead to sin. The key is His life-giving grace, not our determination to overcome the flesh. He is the one who has the power to bring true strength when we are weak, but we must stay in fellowship with Him in His strength. His saving strength is the same strength that raised Christ from the dead! It is the grace of the Spirit of Might.

The grace of the Spirit of Might was proclaimed at the death of Christ. At the death of first Adam came the testimony of the resurrection life found in Last Adam! When the veil of the temple was rent, the graves of many saints were opened. Those who had died in faith were awakened from their sleep. They were manifestly revealed to be members of the Body of Christ.

> *Mt. 27:51 And behold, the veil of the temple was torn in two from top to bottom; and the earth quaked, and the rocks were split, 52 and the graves were opened; and many bodies of the saints who had fallen asleep were raised; 53 and coming out of the graves after His resurrection, they went into the holy city and appeared to many.*

That must have been some sight when the bodies of the saints walked through the city of Jerusalem to testify of the resurrection of the dead in Christ! It is for that testimony that we must live as members of the Body of Christ according to His resurrection Might. We must live to bring that same testimony to the cities in which we live! We must live to be a testimony of His resurrection Might!

Eph. 5:14 Therefore He says: "Awake, you who sleep, arise from the dead, and Christ will give you light." 15 See then that you walk circumspectly, not as fools but as wise, 16 redeeming the time, because the days are evil. 17 Therefore do not be unwise, but understand what the will of the Lord is.

Being a steadfast member of the fellowship of Christ is the will of God for us all. It is according to God's vow and the power of His resurrection Might. The testimony of His resurrection power is the evidence of His resurrection Spirit. We must be clothed in Christ and filled with His Spirit. We are called by God in Christ to be the life of God one to another.

Eph. 5:18 And do not be drunk with wine, in which is dissipation; but be filled with the Spirit, 19 speaking to one another in psalms and hymns and spiritual songs, singing and making melody in your heart to the Lord, 20 giving thanks always for all things to God the Father in the name of our Lord Jesus Christ, 21 submitting to one another in the fear of God.

The fellowship of the Spirit in the Body of Christ is the one true unshakable place in heaven and earth. It is the place of Christ's resurrection power. His resurrection Might cannot be shaken, but rather shakes the things that can be shaken. When we find the place of Christ's sanctuary, we find the place that is beyond shaking (Ps. 29:8; Heb. 12:22, 23, 27). It is the holy place of the fellowship of His Spirit. It is a place of grace. We must seek to live for the purpose of His Body in all that we do. To live for ourselves will always prove to divide the Body of Christ. We must die to our own wills and live for the will of Christ. We must not live as mere men. We must live as members of the Body of Christ!

1 Cor. 3:3 ... For where there are envy, strife, and divisions among you, are you not carnal and behaving like mere men?

To live as members of the Body of Christ is to live beyond our old lives of flesh. We can neither live according to the flesh, nor can we judge one another

171

according to the flesh. Our perceptions must be made by the Spirit and not by the flesh (Isa.11:3). We must live our lives according to the grace of the Spirit of Might, the resurrection of the dead, and the mystery of the fellowship.

2 Cor. 5:14 For the love of Christ constrains us, because we judge thus: that if One died for all, then all died 15 and He died for all, that those who live should live no longer for themselves, but for Him who died for them and rose again. 16 Therefore, from now on, we regard no one according to the flesh. Even though we have known Christ according to the flesh, yet now we know Him thus no longer.

The context of the book of Jude is very eye opening. Jude writes to the Church concerning the "common salvation" of the Body of Christ (Jude 3). He addresses the problem of those who make judgments of others according to the flesh because of judgments of the flesh. He begins by revealing that the "common salvation" was given like the deliverance of Israel from Egypt, but death was chosen by those who refused to believe (Jude 5). He presents the contrast of unbelievers speaking against believers, fallen angels lusting for the flesh of men (Gen. 6:1-5), and the sexual lust of Sodom and Gomorrah for the flesh of bestiality and homosexuality (Jude 5-7). He compares these acts to those who seek to divide the Body of Christ (Jude 7, 8). These break fellowship by denying the fellowship of the Spirit. Jude gives the ultimate example of a life-giving testimony by revealing that the archangel Michael wouldn't even bring a reviling accusation against a fallen archangel (Lucifer – now Satan), but trusted the Lord with His rebuke (Jude 9). Michael refused to speak evil of his own kind, even when his own kind had fallen from his place of authority and function. I believe Jude was making a point of being careful not to bring dishonor to our own kind. Even an archangel would not speak evil of a fallen archangel, how much more must believers be careful to not speak evil of fellow believers. Jude goes on to reveal that those who seek to destroy the fellowship and deny the "common salvation" of the Body of Christ are those who speak evil of what they "do not know" or even what they "know naturally". They corrupt themselves by their judgments of the members of the Body of Christ. They are breaches in the fellowship and are themselves reserved for darkness having made judgments of darkness.

Jude 10 But these speak evil of whatever they do not know; and whatever they know naturally, like brute beasts, in these things they corrupt themselves. 11 Woe to them! For they have gone in the way of Cain, have run greedily in the error of Balaam for profit, and perished

172

in the rebellion of Korah. 12 These are spots in your love feasts, while they feast with you without fear, serving only themselves; they are clouds without water, carried about by the winds; late autumn trees without fruit, twice dead, pulled up by the roots; 13 raging waves of the sea, foaming up their own shame; wandering stars for whom is reserved the blackness of darkness forever.

Jude gives the key to the mystery of the fellowship for the believer. He challenges the spiritual believer to not respond to the unspiritual acts of those who choose to make judgments according to the flesh. He reveals that those who speak evil due to misunderstandings, or even natural understandings, are not to be responded to by any form of defense or retaliation. The believer is to simply know that those who choose to live outside of the fellowship of Christ will live according to their senses and will cause division in the Body of Christ (Jude 19). The spiritual believer is to stay connected to the fellowship. The source of that fellowship is not based upon natural understanding. It is the connection of the Holy Spirit. Therefore, Jude instructs the believer to build themselves up in their most holy faith by praying in the Holy Spirit. We must stay in the place of love for God and for one another in Christ.

Jude 20 But you, beloved, building yourselves up on your most holy faith, praying in the Holy Spirit, 21 keep yourselves in the love of God, looking for the mercy of our Lord Jesus Christ unto eternal life.

We must seek to remain steadfast in the fellowship of God and of His saints. We are the Body of Christ. We are dependent upon the grace of the Spirit of Might to know who we are as contributing members of Christ's Body of life. We must be empowered by His resurrection power of Might to become all that He has ordained for us to be in Him! We cannot allow the thorns and thistles of life to distract us from being clothed in the garments of Christ. Jesus is confessing our names before the Father and His angels. We are ordained and commissioned to bring the ministry of resurrection life in Christ to the world in which we live.

NOTE: Stop and consider your part in the vowed offering of God and the ministry of resurrection life in Christ. Meditate on what it means to continue steadfastly in the fellowship. Be sensitive to all that the Holy Spirit ministers to you today.

Chapter 5.1 – 5.5 - The Fifth Eye of Grace

Statements and Questions to Consider for a Group Discussion:

1. This fifth grace correlates to "The Spirit of Might" and the level of relationship in the Body known as the "vowed offering". The vowed offering of the New Covenant is not what we "vow" to God. It is according to Christ's vow. Discuss what the vowed offering looks like in the context of function and relationship in the Body of Christ.

2. Our fellowship is according to the contribution given by each of us to reveal His manifest presence in our midst. The key to fellowship is Christ in our midst! How do we reveal His manifest presence in our midst?

3. The key to finding our calling in Christ is to seek Him, not our calling. Our life comes from the resurrection life of Christ! We are each given a 'measure' in Christ! What are some testimonies in the group?

4. The key to finding out who we are is not found in the works of the flesh. It is found in the place of the heart. It begins with loving God just as we are. Give some testimonies of how we love God as we are.

5. When we find our place in the hope of His calling, we become a life supply to those He joins us to. Share testimonies of how others have given life to members of the group.

6. Each of us must learn who we are according to the grace that has been given to us by God. We must live within the realm of our God-given abilities. Are there any brave members in the group who will share an experience of what happened when they tried to be someone else other than him or herself?

7. The key to figuring out who we are is to serve others in who they are. When we serve in whatever way we can, we soon find out what we can do. Discuss practical ways this can happen.

8. As we are faithful to do practical things God will guide our steps in spiritual things. Share testimonies in the group.

9. The idea of true fellowship in Christ is for each one to do his or her part. What does that look like?

10. Read Eph. 5:18-21. Discuss what it means to be filled with the Spirit. What does it mean to focus on giving life to others? How do we live lives of thankfulness to God the Father as a son or daughter in Christ? Discuss what it means to submit one to another in the fear of God.

11. We are uniquely formed in Christ according to His resurrection Might. He has chosen our uniqueness and called us to be a part of Him in our own special gift of grace. It is through accepting diversities together that we can really become empowered to be like-minded toward one another. Discuss how diversity actually reveals unity.

12. The grace of the Spirit of Might and the resurrection life of Christ will cause us to be clothed in the holiness of Christ. What does holiness look like? Read Eph. 5:1-16 and discuss its content. Notice that the center of the chapter is verses 17-21. How do you think this relates to fellowship and the presence of God in our midst?

13. Our fellowship with the Holy Spirit and with one another by the power of Christ's Spirit will enable us to do works of righteousness as the Body of Christ. What do works of righteousness look like?

14. We cannot live like the world, fellowship the darkness of the world, and expect to bring the ministry of the life of Christ. We must remain in fellowship with Christ in His headship, and we must live as contributors to the life and light of His Body.

15. We must live as holy members of a heavenly Body being made known in both heaven and earth.

16. The testimony of the resurrection of the dead is to be "awake" to God in Christ. The flesh is weak, but the "Spirit is willing". Discuss what it means for the Spirit to be willing.

17. To live as members of the Body of Christ is to live beyond our old lives of flesh. We can neither live according to the flesh, nor can we judge one another according to the flesh. Read 2 Cor. 5:14-21 and discuss what it means to not judge anyone according to the flesh.

Chapter 6.1

The Sixth Eye of Grace
- The Spirit of Knowing

Let's begin now by looking at the sixth grace of the *Seven Eyes of Grace*. This sixth grace is the Spirit of Knowing. It is the Spirit of Knowledge (Isa. 11:2). God's knowledge is not like the knowledge of men. Man's knowledge is founded upon information. God's knowledge is founded upon intimacy. God is concerned with relationship, while man is often merely interested in facts. God's knowledge will always join our lives to Him and one another, while the knowledge of men will often separate us from God and one another. God's knowledge leads to humility, while the knowledge of men leads to pride. It all stems from the curse of the fall. Man chose the knowledge of good and evil over intimacy with God and the Tree of Life. He chose to be "informed" and lost the place of "intimacy" with God whereby he could be "transformed". The sixth curse of the fall was that man would eat bread by the sweat of his brow (Gen. 3:19). In the Scriptures, bread speaks of communion and life. It has little to do with the mind, but a lot to do with the heart. However, the mind has a lot to do with communion and the heart. I have found that in the kingdom of God, whatever is in the heart will be made known in the mind. I have also found that in the realm of the world, whatever is in the mind ends up in the heart. The facts of the world will influence the mind with the knowledge that leads to death, but intimacy with God will influence the heart with a knowledge that leads to life. God's kind of knowledge comes from the place of intimacy with God, and it is empowered by the sixth grace of the Spirit of Knowing. This sixth grace of the *Seven Eyes of Grace* is all about communion and God's eternal judgment of eternal life for all who believe in Christ.

In these next chapters I will reveal how God's grace of the Spirit of Knowing relates to "eternal judgment" (Heb. 6:2), the "freewill offering" (Deut. 12:6), and the testimony of "communion with God and His City" (Rev. 3:12). These three things testify of a Body made living in Christ. The eternal judgment of life for all who believe in Christ is an awesome gift of living bread to the nations and the generations of the world. There is no doubt there will one day be a throne of judgment for all wickedness that opposes Christ and His ways, but God desires that all would be saved and come to the knowledge of the truth (1 Tim. 2:4). I am not saying that everyone will be saved. I am simply saying there is no reason for anyone to be lost. Salvation is a gift from God through Christ to all who call upon the name of Jesus (Rom. 10:13). That is an eternal judgment made by God. It is all about the Father's love for all people! The gift of the living bread of Christ was a freewill offering of the Son and it activates all of God's sons and daughters to become freewill offerings for the name of God and the namesake of God among the continuing generations of mankind. Communion with God and His city is nothing short of loving God with all of our hearts, minds, souls, and strength; and loving our neighbors as we love ourselves. This is the grace of the Spirit of Knowing! This grace testifies of the breaking of the bread of life as an exchange of life with God and one another. This grace is given that we might understand and intimately share the life of Christ with God and one another.

I believe this sixth grace is particularly relevant to the present time in history. I believe a lightning flash of Christ's revelation has struck the ground of the earth and the sound of thunder is being resonated in the hearts of men to become empowered to love God and to love one another like never before. It is all about people showing up for their own lives and then giving their lives for the life of God and one another. In September of 2007 I had an opportunity to visit a little plot of ground in the United Kingdom where George Fox preached in 1652. George Fox was the founder of the Quaker Movement, one of numerous expressions of the Christian faith during the Holiness Movement. On this particular plot of ground, George Fox preached to 1000 seekers in June of 1652. The power of God fell as he preached, and the Quaker movement was birthed. As I stood upon the rock that George Fox preached upon, I experienced the power and presence of God. The wind began to blow in my face and the surrounding sheep began to bleat spontaneously. God asked me, "Do you hear those sheep? Those are the ones who are crying out for reformation. They are the seekers." He also turned my attention to a group of silent sheep in front of me. He told me that even those who were not seeking would be blessed because of those who are hungry for His present move of grace. God told me that the present move of God would bring furtherance to the reformation and maturation of the Church. I began to weep with the presence of God. I believe this move to be all about a love for God and a love for people. It is the power of the breaking of bread for the nations. It is the giving of living bread to the families of the world. It is filled with healing, deliverance, and multiplication for the feeding of multitudes. It entails the intimate expressions of the Father's will and love for His people. The hand of God will write history, but I believe this is a time for the breaking of bread, the freewill offering, and the Spirit of Knowing in the earth. The eternal judgment of eternal life for all men will take on new strides and definition in the next ten to twenty years.

This sixth grace is again a part of the blessing of God given to the Body of Christ. It is the sixth step toward living in the blessings of the kingdom of God. It is a part of God's grace process in the Body of Christ. It is not about an act called "communion". It is about an action, an attitude, an attribute, and an attained achievement of intimacy in Christ. Remember, sacrifices and offerings God did not desire. He has always desired a Body; a place of habitation for His manifest glory in the earth.

> *Heb. 10:5 Therefore, when He came into the world, He said: "Sacrifice and offering You did not desire, but a body You have prepared for Me. 6 In burnt offerings and sacrifices for sin you had no pleasure. 7 Then I said, 'Behold, I have come—in the volume of the book it is written of Me—to do Your will, O God.'"*

The sixth grace of the *Seven Eyes of Grace* has to do with the "Spirit of Knowing" and the level of relationship in the Body known as the "freewill offering". This was shadowed in the "freewill offering" of the Old Covenant. This was again one of seven offerings commanded by God to be given in the place of God's choosing for each individual of the tribes of Israel. That place of God's choosing represented God's divine connection for each of us as members of the Body of Christ. Remember, it was a Body He wanted when He commanded the shadows of sacrifices and offerings.

> *Deut. 12:5 "But you shall seek the place where the LORD your God chooses, out of all your tribes, to put His name for His habitation; and there you shall go. 6 "There you shall take your [1]burnt offerings, your [2]sacrifices, your [3]tithes, the [4]heave offerings of your hand, your [5]vowed offerings, your [6]freewill offerings, and the [7]firstlings of your herds and flocks. 7 And there you shall eat before the LORD your God, and you shall rejoice in all to which you have put your hand, you and your households, in which the LORD your God has blessed you."*

Jesus Christ became the Body of God's habitation in the flesh. He came as the freewill offering of life for the eradication of humanity's bondage of death. He came to make a way for us all to become a part of that living Body of Christ. Once the living Body of Jesus Christ ascended to the throne of glory in heaven, He poured out His Spirit upon the Body of Christ gathered in the upper room in Jerusalem. Once again, the pouring out of the Holy Spirit on the day of Pentecost was the giving of the mantle of God's manifold grace upon the Body of Christ (Acts 2:1). Those graces are a part of the Spirit of 'Pentecost'. 'Pentecost' means 50, which is a testimony to the celebration of jubilee. Jubilee was a time for the forgiveness of debts and the restoration of inheritances to men. It was a testimony to the increasing salvation of God given to us in Christ. In the second chapter of Acts, we can find a testimony to this sevenfold grace of God given in the outpouring of His Holy Spirit upon the Church. Each of the attributes of the sevenfold Spirit of God is a jubilee grace given to bring Christ's Body to maturity and the fullness of life.

To understand this sixth grace of the Spirit of Knowing we must look at the sixth evidence of the Holy Spirit's power upon the Church in the second chapter of Acts. This is found in verse 42:

*Acts 2:42 And they continued steadfastly in the apostles' doctrine (instruction taught them by the apostles) and fellowship, in **the breaking of bread**, and in prayers.*

The sixth testimony of the Church was that they continued steadfastly in the "breaking of bread". This is the testimony of "communion". The true testimony of "breaking bread" is to become living bread for others. It is to gather together for the purpose of communing with God and one another around the life of His Spirit. It is not merely the act of eating bread with one another. It is the testimony of becoming bread for one another. That bread is the testimony of the living Body of Christ anointed and led by the life-giving Spirit of God. It is the manifestation of truly 'loving God' and 'loving one another'.

This sixth grace can also be found in the foundation graces of Hebrews, Chapter 6. The sixth foundation is that of "eternal judgment".

Heb. 6:1 Therefore, leaving the discussion of the elementary principles (principality) of Christ, let us go on to perfection, not laying again the foundation of repentance from dead works and of faith toward God ......2 of the doctrine of baptisms, of laying on of

179

*hands, of resurrection of the dead, and of **eternal judgment**.*

We often think of "eternal judgment" as the day of the great white throne, but what about the "eternal judgment" of "eternal life" for all who choose to believe in Jesus Christ (Rom. 10:13; 1 Jn. 5:13)? God made an "eternal judgment" for all men, when He allowed His only begotten Son to die for all of the sins of the world (Rom. 6:10; Heb. 10:10; 1 Pet. 3:18).

Jn. 3:16 "For God so loved the world that He gave His only begotten Son, that whoever believes in Him should not perish but have everlasting life. 17 For God did not send His Son into the world to condemn the world, but that the world through Him might be saved."

God's eternal judgment for humanity was that all men should be saved. Man's judgment was to reject God's gift of love. Man chose his own judgment by loving darkness rather than the light of Christ. Man's judgment was condemnation, while God's judgment was eternal life. The only condition required is to willingly receive the Father's judgment over the judgment of men.

Jn. 3:18 "He who believes in Him is not condemned; but he who does not believe is condemned already, because he has not believed in the name of the only begotten Son of God. 19 And this is the condemnation, that the light has come into the world, and men loved darkness rather than light, because their deeds were evil. 20 For everyone practicing evil hates the light and does not come to the light, lest his deeds should be exposed. 21 But he who does the truth comes to the light, that his deeds may be clearly seen, that they have been done in God."

True communion is all about enforcing God's judgment and renouncing judgments made according to the flesh by men. It is about embracing the bread of life sent down from heaven! It is about becoming the living bread of heaven for the earth! As we look at this sixth grace of the Spirit of Knowing, we should be stirred in our hearts to embrace all that God has done, is doing, and is about to do in the earth!

NOTE: Stop and contemplate the gift of eternal life. Eternal life is to know God and Jesus Christ whom He has sent (Jn. 17:3). Consider Christ's death for you and the judgment He made in forgiving your sins. Let the Holy Spirit quicken any thoughts or further thoughts on this chapter.

Chapter 6.2

The Sixth Eye of Grace

Let's look at the evidence of the grace of the Spirit of Knowing as seen in the sevenfold Holy Spirit of God poured out upon the Church. I believe the sixth testimony of the power of God's grace found in the second chapter of Acts, was seen as the Church continuing steadfast in the "breaking of bread" (Acts 2:42). I believe this specifically attests to the grace of the Spirit of Knowing (Isa. 11:2). Again, it is another one of the *Seven Eyes of Grace* that confirms the love of God in heaven and on the earth. It reveals God's eternal judgment. It testifies to God's eternal judgment to wickedness and His victory over the flesh. It also testifies of God's eternal judgment of eternal life for all who believe in Christ Jesus. It has to do with the life of the Spirit and testimony of the word made flesh. It has to do with our lives becoming life-giving bread for the lives of others. It is a testimony of "communion".

What is communion? Webster's Dictionary defines communion as: "A sharing, an intimate relationship with deep understanding." Communion is not merely the ceremonial act of breaking bread and drinking juice or wine. Huge debates, conflicts, judgments, and divisions have come about over the dispute of the details of the elements of the "communion table". We must be missing something! Communion must be more than the elements of "bread" and the "fruit of the grape". How can we share and come to an intimate relationship with deep understanding simply by taking the elements of the "communion table"? Maybe if we find the true elements of communion, we will automatically find the true "communion table"?

We are so easily distracted by things, events, and moments of tangible evidence. I believe we have deviated from the true reality of communion by viewing it as a thing we do. We have seen it as an "event". We have left churches because the "event" wasn't often enough; or the "event" was with the wrong "elements". For the sake of a debate on what we have called "communion" we have chosen separation, isolation, and even division. Have we missed something here? We have had great theological debates over wine and juice. The improper choice of bread has caused some to depart from the sharing of their lives with the congregation of saints they thought was their home. I have seen this dozens of times in various congregations around the world.

I believe in many cases communion has become nothing less than a thing of judgment. It has become a "Nehushtan". Do you recall the story? The children of Israel on their journey in the wilderness had become discouraged against God and against Moses (Num. 21:1-9). The Lord sent fiery serpents among the people as a result of their murmuring and complaint; those serpents bit them and many of the people died. The people came repentant to Moses, begging that they might be forgiven of their sin. God instructed Moses to make a fiery serpent of brass and lift it up on a pole among the people. All who looked to the bronze serpent on the pole were healed of the serpent bites. It was a wonderful picture of Jesus Christ being lifted up upon our cross for our deception and sin. When we look to Jesus Christ as the sacrifice for our sin, we are healed of the bite of sin in our lives. Moses' obedience to craft the bronze serpent was a response to a God-given instruction. However, there remained a problem. The children of Israel kept that bronze serpent around for hundreds of years and even began to include it with the articles of worship upon their high place. The very God-given thing became an abomination of idolatry. It became a place of judgment, rather than a place of blessing. King Hezekiah, a righteous king of Judah, broke in pieces the bronze serpent that Moses made, for the people burned incense to it and called it Nehushtan (2 Kin. 18:4). The name Nehushtan means, "brass thing". Brass is often symbolic of judgment in the Scriptures. The thing of blessing had become a thing of judgment, because the people chose to worship it. I believe the elements of communion have often become like that. We have chosen to worship the table upon which the elements of communion reside instead of worshipping the God in which everyone abides. We have worshipped the elements of communion and missed the true intimacy of communion. We have failed to honor the Body that contains the presence of the Bread of Christ and the life of the Spirit of Christ. I believe the true communion table is the coming together of the Body of Christ. I believe the true elements of the bread of that table are the members of the Body of Christ. I believe the true cup of the communion table is the life of the Spirit within each and every member of the Body of Christ. We eat that bread when we lay our lives down for the lives of one another. We drink that cup when we choose the life of the Spirit over the life of the flesh.

Have you ever been in one of those condemnation services where the minister challenges you to examine the works of the flesh in your life around the elements of bread and juice? Truly there is a truth presented in the act, but many times the act ends up being a tool of condemnation in the hands of men in their ministry. Many people become condemned at what they believe to be the "communion table", but fail to consider the other times they gather together as the Body of Christ. They fail to see the importance of living their daily lives for the purposes of God and one another. They may practice religiously the partaking of the bread and the drinking of wine as symbols upon a sacred tray, but they are spiritually, emotionally, and physically cursed for despising the true bread of the Body of Christ and for rejecting the cup of being led by the Spirit.

Communion can be described in the act of "breaking bread", but communion itself is also an act of truly "breaking bread". It is not just the natural bread of communion, but rather the spiritual bread of life that each of us represents as members of the living Body of Christ. I believe this is what was testified of in the practices of the early Church.

*Acts 2:42 And they continued steadfastly in the apostles' doctrine and fellowship, **in the breaking of bread,** and in prayers.*

True communion was initiated in the fulfillment of Passover. Jesus became the true Passover Lamb, who took away the sins of the world. In preparation of that sacrifice, Jesus ate the Passover meal with His disciples. He had eaten that meal with them before. He had most likely eaten the bread of Passover and drank the cup at least twice before with His men. He had experienced the physical elements of bread and wine at numerous settings of his $33^{1/2}$ years of human life. As the Word of God, He had observed the Passover meal hundreds and hundreds of times from the realm of heaven. However, this meal was different. This is the one Passover meal that He had longed to see. This was the one that would fulfill all of the previous meals leading up to that moment. This is why Jesus said, "With fervent desire I have desired to eat this Passover with you before I suffer" (Lk. 22:15). This was the one that would reveal the truth of the Passover meal. At that meal there was the Passover bread and the cups of the Passover wine.

The first cup of the Passover meal was a cup of Thanksgiving (Kiddush), for bringing the children of Israel out of Egypt. This cup is sometimes referred to as the cup of Sanctification. The second cup of the Passover meal was a cup of Telling or Testimony (Maggid), for stories of deliverance from Egyptian slavery. The third cup was the Cup of Redemption or Blessing (Birkat

Hamazon), to demonstrate God's redemption power for all who believe in Him. It testified of the death of the flesh of Egyptian inheritance and the protection unto new life for the believer in Israel. The fourth cup was the cup of Praise (Hallel) to testify that God had acquired His people as a Holy nation unto Himself (Ex. 6:6, 7). Jesus had come to the world as the Word made flesh. He was born as flesh to proclaim that all flesh could be born-again in Him. We can be thankful that He lived a natural life for 30 years that we might all live our everyday lives as new creations in Christ (2 Cor. 5:17) He Himself had fled to Egypt to free all who were bound to the bondage of sin. He was born as the cup of Thanksgiving to God. He lived his life as the cup of Telling. When He was baptized by John the Spirit of God came upon Him in full measure and He went about demonstrating the deliverance power of God in Israel. He healed the sick, cast out devils, multiplied bread, and even raised the dead as a testimony of deliverance for all people. His life in the flesh set precedence for all who would follow Him to become the living testimonies of God's story in the earth. The time had now finally come for Jesus to take the unleavened bread of the Passover and the third cup of Passover wine (the cup of Blessing or the cup of Redemption). Jesus finished its symbolism in the presence of His disciples. He proclaimed to them that He was about to give His life as a ransom for all men. The cup to follow the cup of Redemption would be the cup of Praise.

Jesus has become the resurrection life within the Body of Christ that we might drink the Cup of Praise anew with Him (Mt. 26:29). That cup is not a cup of earthly wine. It is a cup of heavenly wine! It is the cup of resurrection life given to all who believe in Jesus Christ. It is the cup that testifies that the cup of Redemption and Blessing has been drunk once for all men through the shedding of the Blood of the Lamb, Jesus Christ. To drink that cup of resurrection life one must first be a partaker of the Bread of Life. By drinking the Cup of Praise, we proclaim the fulfillment of the Cup of Redemption for all mankind. We proclaim that Jesus was the testimony of the cup of Thanksgiving, the cup of Testimony (Deliverance), and the cup of Redemption for all men. In sharing the cup of the Spirit, we experience the intimacy of the Body of Christ. In experiencing the intimacy of the Body of Christ we proclaim the death of Jesus Christ for all men.

The hour had come for the life of the flesh to be exchanged for the life of the Spirit for all of mankind. Jesus had come to complete the death of the old Adam and initiate the birth of a new human race through the seed of His flesh as the Last Adam. His life would be sown in corruption, but raised to incorruption (1 Cor. 15:42). He would endure the cross once for all, but for the sake of the joy set before Him He would embrace its suffering (Heb. 12:2). He would prove to be the beginning of the true bread and cup of life for all men (Jn. 6:35, 48). The Body of Christ would become a new creation in the earth (2 Cor. 5:17). The elements of the Passover meal would be revealed in the flesh of the Body of Christ and the cup of the Holy Spirit that flows within Her being. The Bible teaches that the life of the flesh is in the blood (Lev. 17:11). Without the shedding of blood there can be no remission of sins (Mt. 26:28; Heb. 9:22), thus Jesus shed His blood once for all. The cup of Redemption's Blessing for the believer was drunk once for all by Jesus Christ. It was His willingness and obedience that shed His blood once for us all. We need not drink that cup ever again. He has given to us the cup of Praise. He has given to us the cup of the Spirit. In drinking the Cup of the Spirit, we proclaim the death of Jesus Christ. For unless One had drunk the cup of Blessing, we could not drink the cup of Praise. God has not called us to drink the cup of Blessing. He has made a way for us to drink the cup of Praise! He has the authority to bring all men out of sin as the cup of Thanksgiving. He set precedence for the testimony of all men as the cup of Telling (Deliverance). He has fulfilled the death of the flesh for all men as the cup of Redemption and Blessing. He is now calling all men to drink of the cup of Praise, proclaiming we are a Holy nation unto God our Father. Is this not the cup of the New Covenant table?

1 Cor. 12:13 For by one Spirit we were all baptized into one body— whether Jews or Greeks, whether slaves or free—and have all been made to drink into one Spirit.

The communion of the blood of Christ gave us the communion of the Spirit of Christ. The sacrifice of the body of Jesus Christ made us members of the Body of Christ.

1 Cor. 10:16 The cup of blessing which we bless, is it not the communion of the blood of Christ? The bread which we break, is it not the communion of the body of Christ?

We are part of the inheritance of God as members of the Body of Christ. The Passover bread has been fulfilled in the kingdom of God (Lk. 22:15). The cup of Redemption and Blessing has been made complete and all that remains is to become members of the living Body of Christ and to drink of the cup of the Body of Christ. That cup is the cup of Praise. It is the cup of the Resurrection Life of the Holy Spirit. It is the cup that identifies us as His Holy nation. We are members of His calling and contributors to His inheritance throughout the ages.

> *Eph. 1:18 ...the eyes of your understanding being enlightened; that you may know what is the hope of His calling, what are the riches of the glory of His inheritance in the saints...*

NOTE: It is time again to stop and let the Holy Spirit quicken your thoughts in considering this chapter. Consider each of the four cups of communion and what they mean to you in Christ.

Chapter 6.3

The Sixth Eye of Grace

In this chapter we will look at the beginning of the communion meal. To find the beginning of the communion meal, we have to understand the completion of the Passover meal of the Old Covenant. It was the fulfillment of the bread and wine of the Old Covenant that made the way for us to partake of the true bread and wine of the New Covenant. Let's examine the true elements of the communion table. An account of what Jesus did for presenting communion can be found in Luke 22:14-20 and Matthew 26:26-29:

Mt. 26:26 And as they were eating, Jesus took bread, blessed it and broke it, and gave it to the disciples and said, "Take, eat; this is My body." Then He took the cup, and gave thanks, and gave it to them, saying, "Drink from it, all of you. 28 For this is My blood of the new covenant, which is shed for many for the remission of sins. 29 But I say to you, I will not drink of this fruit of the vine from now on until that day when I drink it new with you in My Father's kingdom."

Lk. 22:15 Then He said to them, "With fervent desire I have desired to eat this Passover with you before I suffer; 16 for I say to you, I will no longer eat of it until it is fulfilled in the kingdom of God." 17 Then He took the cup, and gave thanks, and said, "Take this and divide it among yourselves; 18 for I say to you, I will not drink of the fruit of the vine until the kingdom of God comes." 19 And He took bread, gave thanks and broke it, and gave it to them, saying, "This is My body which is given for you; do this in remembrance of Me." 20 Likewise He also took the cup after supper, saying, "This cup is the new covenant in My blood, which is shed for you."

The setting of the communion table was one of friendship, fellowship, and life! Jesus and His disciples were not just eating a meal. They had come together to partake of a spiritual fulfillment. This particular meal was to testify of the fulfillment of the Passover meal, once for all. It marked the crucifixion of Christ to become the Lamb slain for all the sins of the world. It also marked the beginning of the increase of the Body of Christ. It was the fulfillment of the testimony of God's life for the entire world! The disciples didn't know this, but Jesus was well aware of the significance of this time together. The bread at the table was not just any bread. It was the unleavened bread of the Passover meal. It was like every portion of bread made for every Passover meal to that date in time. It was made in the same way, and it looked the same as every previous illustration. However, Jesus saw this bread in its reality. He took it, blessed it, broke it, and gave it to the disciples. As He did, He said some profound words: "Take, eat; this is My body." The bread before them was a shadow of the true Body who stood in their midst. The bread of the Passover meal was only a shadow, but the Man standing in their midst was the real thing! He was the Man of heaven who cast a shadow into the past to reveal that He was the Lamb slain from the foundations of the world (Rev. 13:8). I believe Jesus' statement was an invitation. I believe Jesus was saying: "Do you know what this bread really is? It has been sitting at this meal hundreds of times! Did you know that it is not just bread baked with a particular recipe? It is bread that has specifically and precisely represented Me. It is a shadow on the ground of My reality in heaven, but I have good news for you! Here I am! This bread is My body, but here I stand in bodily form. Receive My gift, take Me into your heart, become part of Me. Let's transition the bread from picture form to flesh and bone reality! Come, be a part of My living Body." This was the meal that Jesus fervently longed for. This was the final meal of the shadow and the beginning of reality for the Bread of Life sent down from heaven! The completion of this meal would be the suffering of Christ and it would lead to full communion of the Body of Christ.

Jesus took the cup. It was likely the third cup of the Passover celebration. It was the cup of Redemption and Blessing. It was the type and shadow of His shed blood for the redemption of all men. It represented the life of the flesh, as the life of the flesh is in the blood (Lev. 17:11). Jesus was ready to give the fullness of His sinless life for the fullness of the sinful flesh of the world. The qualifier of this transaction was not the goodness of mankind. It was the goodness and love of the Man Jesus Christ. He took the cup, gave thanks, and gave it to his disciples saying, "Drink from it, all of you" (Mt. 26:27). Luke's account says that Jesus told them to "divide it among themselves". This was the once for all cup of Redemption for all men. Jesus revealed that this cup was not the wine that they supposed. The cup of Redemption was the shed blood of Jesus Christ. In His death, all men can find the fulfillment of their death. It was the completion of the wages of sin, for the wage of sin is death (Rom. 6:23). Jesus drank the fullness of that cup by shedding His blood upon the cross. This Passover meal was the final meal of its kind. It was the last of the shadow meals. Jesus became the real deal when He was wounded for our transgressions and bruised for our iniquities. He became our Peace through His death upon the cross. The stripes upon His back attained healing for each and every member of the Body of Christ (Isa. 53:5). Jesus told them all to drink this cup. He was saying, "I am about to complete this cup, once for all. It is for you, Judas! It's for you Peter! It's for all of you guys who will wrestle with being faithful to Me! It is a demonstration of My faithfulness to you. I am going to complete this. I have identified with you in your meal, now I am going to make a way for you to identify with Me in My meal. The next time we drink this cup, it will be fulfilled in the kingdom of God (Lk. 22:18). We will never again drink it like this. The next time we drink it, it will be new in the kingdom of My Father (Mt. 26:29). I am making a way for you to drink the true cup of Praise (the completion of the earthly cups of the Passover meal). I am making a way for us to drink the cup of the Spirit together. I am going to willingly drink the cup of Redemption by My shed blood for you, so that we can drink the cup of Resurrection Life together. It will be the cup of Praise. When you drink the cup of Resurrection, I will drink it with you. By drinking the cup of Resurrection, you will proclaim My death. By partaking of the Bread of the Body of Christ and drinking the cup of the Holy Spirit's life among you, you will release the authority of My fulfillment of the flesh for you. You will live together as the Body of Christ, not the flesh of Adam. You will be in Me and in the Father and the Father in you and Me in you!"

The elements of the New Covenant communion table are revealed in verses 19 and 20 of Luke, Chapter 22. He told them to do this in remembrance of Him. It was not the cup of verse 17 that he told them to drink. It was the cup of verse 20. The cup of verse 17 was the cup of Redemption that Jesus drank for all men when He shed His blood. The fourth cup of verse 20 was the cup of Praise. It represents the life of the Spirit! It is the cup of Resurrection. It is not the death of Jesus Christ that guarantees our resurrection. It is the resurrection of Christ that guarantees our resurrection! It is the partaking of life that guarantees the fullness of life! The death of Jesus gave all men the right to drink of the cup of resurrection through faith in Him. When we receive the life of the Holy Spirit, we are guaranteed the full resurrection! It is the cup that Jesus drinks new with us in the kingdom of His Father. It is not a cup to be drunk in heaven. The fourth cup was the cup of Praise, a cup to be drunk upon the earth. It is the testimony of His resurrection life that guarantees the fullness of the resurrection to come. It guarantees the resurrection of heaven, because the members of the living Body of Christ are drinking the cup of resurrection of heaven upon the earth.

> *Lk. 22:17 Then He took the cup, and gave thanks, and said, "Take this and divide it among yourselves; 18 for I say to you, I will not drink of the fruit of the vine until the kingdom of God comes." 19 And He took bread, gave thanks and broke it, and gave it to them, saying, "This is My body which is given for you; do this in remembrance of Me." 20 Likewise He also took the cup after supper, saying, "This cup is the new covenant in My blood, which is shed for you."*

The cup of Christ's blood for the New Covenant believer is not the third cup. It is the fourth cup! By drinking of the cup of Praise (Resurrection) with God by His Spirit, we proclaim that Jesus Christ has drunk the third cup of Redemption for all of mankind! The communion table of the New Covenant is not set with the third cup of Redemption. It is set with the cup of Praise. When we drink of His resurrection life together as living members of the Body of Christ, we truly experience the communion table of the New Covenant. We do this in remembrance of Him! Communion is not coming together to drink the third cup of the Passover again. It is coming to drink the cup that followed the supper. It is the cup that was meant to be drunk after the lamb had been eaten. It is not the shadow cup of Praise, but the real cup of Praise! We are called to receive one another as the living members of the Body of Christ and then drink the cup of His resurrection together as the Body of Christ! The true Lamb of God is to be received (eaten) for the death of all mankind and true life (the cup of the Spirit) is to be received by all men.

On one of my many ministry journeys to Eastern Europe, one church asked me to minister on communion. They have a very strong traditional view on communion in Eastern Europe as a whole. I understood that as I went to share on the truth of communion. I was very careful to honor the tradition of the communion elements used in the church I was ministering at. I laid out the principles of true communion as I see them and presented them in the context of using the elements of communion bread and wine. Many people in the room were responding to the life of the Holy Spirit as I shared that true communion was the bread of the Body of Christ and the cup of the living Spirit of God. I saw understanding begin to come to the hearts of many as they listened to the voice of the Holy Spirit within them. I noticed one man in particular among the congregation. He was a former Muslim man who had recently been converted to the Christian faith. He appeared to hang on every word of my message. At the conclusion of my message, the congregation partook of the elements of bread and wine to present a picture of the communion of the Body and of the Spirit. When it came time for the sharing of the communion elements, I saw an astounding display of religious bondage! This man was so eager to partake of the elements of communion. As he reached out for the bread, a lady in front of him stopped him quickly! I found out later that this man had not yet been baptized in water and therefore, she refused to let him touch the bread or wine. When I observed this anti-communion demonstration, I was grieved in my spirit. When the meeting concluded I went straight for that man and gave him my touch and the life of the Spirit within me. I wanted him to experience the bread of life and the Spirit of life contained within me. He may not have taken the elements of bread and wine, but he was one of few in the room who truly experienced communion that day. He hung on every word I spoke with hunger, and He drank of the Holy Spirit's living presence. He had experienced true communion already. I wanted to be sure to go specifically to him to receive the bread that I saw him to be and to share in the cup of the Spirit with him. The cup we drank was the cup of Praise and the bread we ate was a sharing of the Body of Christ. We celebrated the resurrection of Jesus Christ, while many others mourned the death of Jesus Christ. In mourning the death, they partook of death. Even their religious acts and attitudes demonstrated a spirit of death, and not life. It was not so for that man and me. Religious rules and legalistic rituals didn't stop us from experiencing an exchange of the life of Christ. I have no doubt that true communion was happening in the room in many places, but true death was also attempting to bring division to the Body of Christ. I don't believe the true communion was the taking of the bread and wine. I believe the true communion was sharing in the bread of the Body of Christ and the cup of the Spirit. There was a furtherance to intimacy with a deeper understanding of God and one another. It wasn't the elements of bread and wine that made for a communion service. It was a receiving of the Holy Spirit and the Body of Christ!

I want to propose that the "breaking of bread" of the early church was not meant to be a ritual of bread and wine. It was meant to be the daily celebration of the gathering together of the Body of Christ. It can include the elements of food, but in its greater reality it reveals the food of the Body of Christ and the life of the resurrection Spirit in the Body of Christ. It is a celebration of human brethren living together according to the Spirit of Christ. It is void of judgments according to the flesh. It is a testimony of a love for God as their

191

The Seven Eyes of Grace

Father and a love for one another as members of God's city; His community of sons and daughters in His kingdom.

> *2 Cor. 5:14 For the love of Christ constrains us, because we judge thus: that if One died for all, then all died; 15 and He died for all, that those who live should live no longer for themselves, but for Him who died for them and rose again. 16 Therefore, from now on, we regard no one according to the flesh. Even though we have known Christ according to the flesh, yet now we know Him thus no longer. 17 Therefore, if anyone is in Christ, he is a new creation; old things have passed away; behold, all things have become new. 18 Now all things are of God, who has reconciled us to Himself through Jesus Christ, and has given us the ministry of reconciliation, 19 that is, that God was in Christ reconciling the world to Himself, not imputing their trespasses to them, and has committed to us the word of reconciliation. 20 Therefore we are ambassadors for Christ, as though God were pleading through us: we implore you on Christ's behalf, be reconciled to God. 21 For He made Him who knew no sin to be sin for us, that we might become the righteousness of God in Him.*

NOTE: Stop and consider the subject matter of this chapter. Consider the cup of the Spirit and the life-giving expression when our flesh is transformed to become an expression of God's word (living bread) to others.

Chapter 6.4

The Sixth Eye of Grace

That which was "shadow" in the Old Covenant, has now become "complete"! Passover has been made "complete" in Christ. The writer of Hebrews reveals this clearly.

Heb. 10:5 Therefore, when He came into the world, He said: "Sacrifice and offering You did not desire, but a body You have prepared for Me. 6 In burnt offerings and sacrifices for sin you had no pleasure. 7 Then I said, 'Behold, I have come—in the volume of the book it is written of Me—to do Your will, O God.' "

Jesus didn't come to invoke more sacrifices. He didn't come to exchange the ritual of the Old Covenant for a ritual of New Covenant ceremony. He came to establish the Body of Christ upon the earth. Jesus became the completion of the Passover meal in order to establish the true bread of the Body of Christ and the true life of the cup of Praise in human form! We have been sanctified to God, not for further ceremonies and sacrifices, but to be the Body of Christ.

Heb. 10:8 Previously saying, "Sacrifice and offering, burnt offerings, and offerings for sin You did not desire, nor had pleasure in them" (which are offered according to the law), 9 then He said, "Behold, I have come to do Your will, O God." He takes away the first that He may establish the second. 10 By that will we have been sanctified through the offering of the body of Jesus Christ once for all.

The obedience of Jesus to His Father fulfilled all of the requirements concealed in the Passover meal. He was the Lamb slain for our deliverance from sin. He was the fulfillment of the bread of Adam to give us the bread of Christ. His life was given for the bitter herbs of slavery and suffering in the bondage of sin. He identified with us that we might identify with Him. Jesus shed tears of sorrow for the captivity of all men, as was portrayed in the green herbs dipped in salt water. He exchanged the mortar of the kingdoms of men for the relationship of the kingdom of God, as seen in the "charoset" set at the table to represent the mortar used by Israel to build the palaces and pyramids of Egypt. He was born as the cup of Thanksgiving, lived as the cup of Telling, died as the cup of Redemption, and forever lives as the cup of Praise for all who receive Him in the power of His resurrection. All of these He drank in the "common bowl" of human flesh! He completed Passover and is seated at the right hand of God offering us the bread and wine of true communion!

> *Heb. 10:12 But this Man, after He had offered one sacrifice for sins forever, sat down at the right hand of God, 13 from that time waiting till His enemies are made His footstool. 14 For by one offering He has perfected forever those who are being sanctified. 15 And the Holy Spirit also witnesses to us; for after He had said before, 16 "This is the covenant that I will make with them after those days, says the Lord: I will put My laws into their hearts, and in their minds I will write them," 17 then He adds, "Their sins and their lawless deeds I will remember no more."*

The testimony of the communion that Jesus offers us is a change in our lives together as the Body of Christ. We have experienced His resurrection life in that we love God with all of our hearts, souls, and strength. We have partaken of the life of His living bread, in that we love one another as we love ourselves (His city). We are free from condemnation and shame (Rom. 8:1)! We must judge no one according to the flesh (2 Cor. 5:14-16)!

> *Heb. 10:18 Now where there is remission of these, there is no longer an offering for sin. 19 Therefore, brethren, having boldness to enter the Holiest by the blood of Jesus, 20 by a new and living way which He consecrated for us, through the veil, that is, His flesh...*

The veil that Jesus rent was not merely the shadow veil of an earthly temple. It was the skin of the real temple! It was the opening up of the Body of Christ for all to come in! It is a holy of holy place! It is a corporate place! It is filled with many members. It is filled with broken pieces of living bread. When those pieces come together, there is a fullness of the bread of the Body of Christ! We are bread with feet! It is our responsibility to come together to drink the cup of Praise. In doing this, we proclaim the death of Christ and the life of Christ! We enforce His victory and subdue His enemies beneath the feet of the Body of Christ!

It is for the sake of the living testimony of the Body of Christ that we seek to find our divine placement in the house of God. We are the temple of His Holy Spirit and together we express the fullness of His habitation. He is the High Priest over the house of God, and we are the house of God. This is why we seek to come together. This is why we seek to build one another up in the faith. We live to stir one another up to love and good works as members of the Body of Christ.

> *Heb. 10:21 ...and having a High Priest over the house of God, 22 let us draw near with a true heart in full assurance of faith, having our hearts sprinkled from an evil conscience and our bodies washed with pure water. 23 Let us hold fast the confession of our hope without wavering, for He who promised is faithful. 24 And let us consider one another in order to stir up love and good works, 25 not forsaking the assembling of ourselves together, as is the manner of some, but exhorting one another, and so much the more as you see the Day approaching.*

The very essence of true communion is to draw near with a true heart. It is to seek to come together, knowing that our bodies are living sacrifices one for another (Rom.12:1). We don't just hold fast to the confession of our hope for ourselves, we hold fast for the sake of one another. Our aim is to consider one another, and our goal is to stir one another up to love and good works. Our communion is to love God and to love one another. The more we see of His coming, the more we come together to give one another the life of His presence. Our lifeblood is found in exhorting one another. We love God and we love people! When we choose to live together by the life of His Spirit, we confirm that we no longer live according to the flesh. We seek to live according to the Spirit. The cup is a sharing of His blood and Spirit. The bread is a sharing of His Body.

> *1 Cor. 10:16 The cup of blessing which we bless, is it not the communion of the blood of Christ? The bread which we break, is it not the communion of the body of Christ? 17 For we, being many, are one bread and one body; for we all partake of that one bread. 18 Observe Israel after the flesh: Are not those who eat of the sacrifices partakers of the altar?*

The bread of Christ is not the bread upon the communion table. It is the bread of the communion table, called the Body of Christ. "The bread which we break is the communion of the Body of Christ!" We are the "one bread" that Jesus put into reality through the mercy given by His death and the grace

195

given by His resurrection. We must live for one another and not for the life of our own flesh. When we fellowship darkness, we defile the table of the Lord. We do so because we are members of one another. If we seek darkness, we also seek to defile the bread of Christ. We are not properly discerning the Body of Christ.

> _1 Cor. 10:21 You cannot drink the cup of the Lord and the cup of demons;_
> _you cannot partake of the Lord's table and of the table of demons._

The "cup of blessing" mentioned in 1 Corinthians, Chapter 10 is the life of God's Spirit among us as believers. The blood covenant that Christ made at Calvary enables all human beings to come into a personal relationship with God by His Spirit. True communion is to drink of the cup of God's Spirit as members of a new flesh known as the Body of Christ. In Christ we have the life of His Spirit within us, and our bodies are members of His Body that we might serve one another with a living sacrifice of life (Rom.12:1). This was made possible through the blood sacrifice of Jesus Christ. The wages of sin is death and Jesus paid the wage of our sin that we might find life in Him. The life of the flesh is in the blood (Lev. 17:11), and Jesus poured out the life of His sinless flesh to become atonement for the sins of our sinful flesh. His sacrifice has opened a door for us to commune with God and one another through the "cup of blessing" as living members of the Body of Christ. Our cup of blessing is the cup of Praise. It is the cup of His resurrection life made possible by His partaking of the cup of Redemption on our behalf. He died for us that we might live in Him! Because we are members of the Body of Christ, we must seek to drink the cup of the Spirit, the cup of blessing, that we might fulfill the desires of God's will and not the desires of our flesh. The cup of the Lord is the life of God's Spirit that edifies one another (1 Cor. 10:23, 24).

We live for God and one another and to fulfill God's purposes in the earth. We are the Body of Christ. We must be seekers of God and not seekers of self. If we live self-seeking lives, we despise our place as a member of the Body of Christ and we provoke the Lord to jealousy. There is one Body and one Spirit, and we are partakers of and contributors to both.

> _1 Cor. 12:13 For by one Spirit we were all baptized into one body—_
> _whether Jews or Greeks, whether slaves or free—and have all been_
> _made to drink into one Spirit._

> _2 Cor. 13:14 The grace of the Lord Jesus Christ, and the love of_

God, and the communion of the Holy Spirit be with you all. Amen.

True "communion" is "an intimate relationship with God through His Holy Spirit, with deep understanding." It is also "an intimate relationship with one another with deep understanding." How is this possible? Jesus is the living bread that makes us all "living bread".

Jn. 6:33 "For the bread of God is He who comes down from heaven and gives life to the world." 34 Then they said to Him, "Lord, give us this bread always." 35 And Jesus said to them, "I am the bread of life. He who comes to Me shall never hunger, and he who believes in Me shall never thirst."

Jesus took the bread and blessed it. The true bread is His Body TODAY. He broke the bread so it could be shared. We are each a piece of the bread of Christ. We each share in the ability to "freely give" of our lives as He "freely gave" His life for us. We are the reality of the "freewill offering" in the New Covenant. Jesus made a way for us to freely share in His gift of love. It was an eternal judgment on our behalf called eternal life for all who join themselves to Him and His house. It is the key to victory over sickness, disease, and death. Healing is the children's bread (Mt. 15:26, 27). When we discern that we are ourselves pieces of the one bread of Christ and that our brother or sister in Christ is also a piece of that same bread, we experience the healing power of Christ. We need each other for this very purpose. It is for the life of the Body of Christ! He didn't give to us the full loaf. He gave each of us a part. It is not about Jesus and us alone. It is about us with Jesus as our Head and one another as members of His Body. He was broken, as the law had been broken to reveal that GRACE saves us! He is united as we share Christ in one another. We must eat of His flesh and to do so is to no longer regard one another or ourselves according to the flesh.

NOTE: Contemplate the subject of communion. Consider what it means to be a part of the Body of Christ. Invite the Holy Spirit to reveal to you the cup of life in Him to be shared with Jesus your head and joining members in the Body of Christ.

Chapter 6.5
The Sixth Eye of Grace

I want to now look at a chapter in the Bible that is very well known as a source for teaching on communion. We will find this in the 11th Chapter of 1 Corinthians. Historically, the church of Corinth had a tradition. They would gather together weekly to have a meal as an act of "communion". This was not necessarily a practice of other churches at the time, but it was a custom in the church of Corinth. It was one form of "breaking bread" in the church. It was a physical act that was meant to depict the spiritual truth of communion in the Church. I do not believe it was the hard fast, set model for "communion" in the Church. This meal was a tradition of that particular church. Paul addressed the problem in their "act" of communion. Paul was not addressing their meal, but rather their attitudes and actions as a church. If you study the entire book of 1 Corinthians, you will find that this church had problems of insecurity, division, promiscuity, and selfishness. Some members sought to associate themselves with "important" men of God. They wanted to be a part of the "exclusive club". There were problems of immorality in this church. Some members were taking other members to court with lawsuits against them. The leadership of this church was failing to accept the responsibility of leading with correction. This church was using the gifts of the Spirit for their own personal agendas. The core value of this church was to live for themselves and not for one another. This core flaw was also causing their form of "communion" to take on the same characteristics. Some were eating more than others. Some were getting drunk. Their communion "feast" was just another expression of their carnal problems. Paul wrote to address this problem.

Paul knew that true communion is to happen whenever the saints come together. The true bread is the bread of the Body of Christ.

1 Cor. 12:12 For as the body is one and has many members, but all the members of that one body, being many, are one body, so also is Christ.

Paul confirmed what true communion is. In his letter to the church of Corinth, he revealed how communion should operate whenever members of the Body of Christ come together. He took the one thing that the church of Corinth thought of as communion and revealed to them that it was not. It was merely an ACT of communion. It was nothing more than another carnal expression of their lives. This church should have been living in communion in everything, but instead they had created a feast they called a "communion meal" and hoped it would be sufficient to fulfill Christ's command. There was nothing wrong with their tradition of having a meal together each week, but it was not fulfilling the condition of communion. Let's examine Paul's instruction:

1 Cor. 11:17 Now in giving these instructions I do not praise you, since you come together not for the better but for the worse. 18 For first of all, when you come together as a church, I hear that there are divisions among you, and in part I believe it. 19 For there must also be factions among you, that those who are approved may be recognized among you. 20 Therefore when you come together in one place, it is not to eat the Lord's Supper. 21 For in eating, each one takes his own supper ahead of others; and one is hungry and another is drunk. 22 What! Do you not have houses to eat and drink in? Or do you despise the church of God and shame those who have nothing? What shall I say to you? Shall I praise you in this? I do not praise you.

Paul's rebuke was not just about their communion meal. It was in regard to their lack of communion in all of their life practices. They were filled with divisions and factions. They thought this one meal would make up for their carnality, but even in that meal there were divisions and factions. Some were eating more than others. Those who had much were not sharing with those who had little. Some were drinking their own wine to drunkenness. There was not a spirit of sharing among them. Paul clearly says that their communion feast was not communion at all. He told them it had nothing to do with the Lord's Supper.

1 Cor. 11:20 Therefore when you come together in one place, it is not to eat the Lord's Supper.

The eating of natural bread and the drinking of natural wine was no substitute for the sharing of the Body of Christ and communion of the Spirit. Their feast was not even a good copy. Even in their tradition, they were exhibiting the same carnal attitude that was in the church. They thought they were keeping the Lord's Supper, but Paul said that their feast had nothing to do with the Lord's Supper. Paul went on to explain:

1 Cor. 11:23 For I received from the Lord that which I also delivered to you: that the Lord Jesus on the same night in which He was betrayed took bread...

Paul revealed that Jesus shared His life with His disciples equally and without judgment. He even knew they would betray Him, deny Him, and scatter from Him; yet He freely gave them the bread so they could be part with Him. That bread was not the Old Covenant bread of the Passover table, but rather the New Covenant bread of Christ represented upon the Old Covenant table. Jesus gave it to all of His disciples. He freely gave His life for all men!

1 Cor. 11:24 ...and when He had given thanks, He broke it and said, "Take, eat; this is My body which is broken for you; do this in remembrance of Me."

Jesus picked up the "word picture" and said, "This is My body". The shadow was really His body. It was not the true bread of life, but rather a shadow of the bread of life. Jesus was saying, "Do you know what this is? Hundreds of times it has sat upon this table, but today it is being fulfilled. This is My body freely given to be shared with you. I am making an eternal judgment on your behalf. I am inviting you into eternal life. I have come as a freewill offering unto My Father, and I am making a way for you to be the same. I am inviting you into a New Adam. I am going to make you a new creation. I am inviting you to become a part of the living habitation of the Spirit of God."

1 Cor. 11:25 In the same manner He also took the cup after supper, saying, "This cup is the new covenant in My blood. This do, as often as you drink it, in remembrance of Me."

The cup that Paul was referring to was not the Passover cup of Blessing or Redemption. It was the cup of Praise. Remember, the account of the Lord's Supper found in the book of Luke revealed that it was the cup after the supper that Jesus called the cup of the New Covenant (Lk. 22:20). It was the cup after the lamb had been eaten. This is the cup He told them to drink in remembrance of Him. It was the cup of resurrection life. It was the cup of eternal life. It was the cup that proclaims that Jesus has pronounced the eternal judgment of eternal life for all who believe in Him. This was the mystery of the true "holy grail" that many men have sought.

1 Cor. 11:26 For as often as you eat this bread and drink this cup, you proclaim the Lord's death till He comes.

Paul was not talking about the bread of the Corinthian feast. He wasn't talking about the bread of the Old Covenant Passover table. He was talking about the bread of the Body of Christ (1 Cor. 12:12). He was not talking about the wine of the Corinthian feast. He wasn't talking about the old cup of Praise that followed the Old Covenant Passover meal. He was talking about the cup of Praise made NEW in the kingdom of His Father (Mt. 26:29). He was referring to the cup of the Spirit that we are to drink together in intimacy with our Father and one another.

1 Cor. 11:27 Therefore whoever eats this bread or drinks this cup of the Lord in an unworthy manner will be guilty of the body and blood of the Lord. 28 But let a man examine himself, and so let him eat of that bread and drink of that cup. 29 For he who eats and drinks in an unworthy manner eats and drinks judgment to himself, not discerning the Lord's body. 30 For this reason many are weak and sick among you, and many sleep.

Paul was not saying that whoever drank or ate of the Corinthian feast in an unworthy manner would be guilty of the body and blood of the Lord. He was pointing out that they had defiled the Lord's Supper in everything they were doing. He was letting them know that their pretense of communion was not working. They had not examined themselves properly. They had not recognized that they themselves were each a piece of the Bread of Christ. They were not living with a spirit of sharing and intimacy with God and one another. This was bringing judgment upon themselves. It was for this reason that many were weak, sick, and asleep. They were not living according to the eternal judgment of eternal life found in Christ. They were living as though the Old Adam had not died. They were living with carnal motivations, carnal agendas, and carnal actions.

1 Cor. 11:31 For if we would judge ourselves, we would not be judged.

The examination and proper judgment of ourselves is not to find what is wrong with our flesh. It is to decide to live according to the Spirit. Christ is within us (2 Cor. 13:5). We are members of Christ and of the Body of Christ! We must live our lives as living bread and vessels of His presence. It is our responsibility to give life to others, not to take life from others. We all died in Christ when He drank the third cup of the Passover meal, the cup of Redemption. We all live in Christ when we drink the fourth cup of the Passover meal, the cup of Praise; the testimony of His resurrection. We are not judged according to the flesh anymore (2 Cor. 5:15-17).

> *1 Cor. 11:32 But when we are judged, we are chastened by the Lord, that we may not be condemned with the world. 33 Therefore, my brethren, when you come together to eat, wait for one another. 34 But if anyone is hungry, let him eat at home, lest you come together for judgment. And the rest I will set in order when I come.*

Paul was neither condoning nor condemning their traditional meal together. He was simply revealing how to make that meal true communion. There must be times that we eat together; spirit, soul, and body! In all that we do we must prefer one another, wait on one another, and partake together. This is the testimony of our communion together. Paul was not addressing the "form" of communion. He was bringing correction to the "spirit" of communion in the Church.

Your church may have a weekly practice of bread and wine, crackers and juice, or maybe a meal like the church of Corinth. You may have none of these. You may gather in homes to share fellowship of spirit, conversation, and food. You may do this weekly. You may do this monthly. You may do this every now and then. None of these things are the point of communion. The point of communion is to come together whenever you can to share the bread of the Body of Christ and drink the cup of the Spirit. It may or may not include the elements of natural bread and wine, but it must ALWAYS contain the substance of living bread and the cup of the Spirit. In doing this you proclaim the Lord's death, and you will experience the fullness of His resurrection life from heaven.

We live for God and one another and to fulfill God's purposes in the earth. We are the Body of Christ. We must be seekers of God and not seekers of self. If we live self-seeking lives, we despise our place as a member of the Body of Christ and we provoke the Lord to jealousy.

Summary:

Communion is a sharing, "an intimate relationship with deep understanding" (Webster's Dictionary). It is much more than what can be symbolized in bread and wine. It is the reality of being a living member of the Body of Christ and a participant of the life of God's Spirit. Communion was practiced in the early Church (Acts 2:42). True communion was initiated in the fulfillment of Passover. Communion is not just a matter of "intimacy"; it is a matter of "inheritance" (Eph. 1:18; Lk. 22:14-20). True communion is to be an active member of the living Body of Christ. We are part of the inheritance of Christ and a part of His calling. That which was a "shadow" in the Old Testament, has now become "complete". Passover has been made "complete" in Christ (Heb. 10:5-7;11-25). It was not sacrifices and offerings that God desired. He wanted a Body that He could dwell in by His Spirit. Communion is the reality of living as God's dwelling place together for the purpose of fulfilling His will in the earth. The cup is a sharing of His Spirit made possible through the shedding of His blood. His death was the entrance to our life in Christ. To drink of the life of His Spirit is to proclaim His death. The bread is a sharing of His Body and the giving of ourselves for the purpose of His will together as the Body of Christ (1 Cor. 10:16-18, 21).

There is one Body and one Spirit (1 Cor. 12:13; 2 Cor. 13:14). True "communion" is "an intimate relationship with God through His Holy Spirit, with deep understanding." It is also "an intimate relationship with one another with deep understanding." How is this possible? Jesus is the Living Bread that makes us all "living bread" (Jn. 6:33, 34). He came as a fulfillment of all that was revealed as a shadow in the Old Testament. The Passover meal, with the bread and wine, was a symbol of the true Bread of Christ and the Life of His Spirit. Jesus fulfilled the 'word picture' on the very night He was betrayed. He took the bread and blessed it. The bread that he took was a 'word picture' of the true Bread that He was. He was about to be broken for the sins of the old Adam, that all might enter into a Living Last Adam. He was opening the door for all to become a part of the Body of Christ. That true bread is His Body TODAY! He broke the bread so it could be shared. He was broken, as the law had been broken, so that all who had broken the law could be made one in Him as the living Body of Christ. His broken Body is united as we share Christ in one another. We must eat of His flesh and to eat His flesh is to judge no one according to the flesh (2 Cor. 5:16, 17). We must recognize that we are members of the Body of Christ. We must also recognize that others are members to be received as contributing elements of the life of Christ together. A proper examination is to recognize that Christ lives in each of us (2 Cor. 13:5).

The apostle Paul confirmed communion for what it truly is (1 Cor. 11:23-26). The custom of the church in Corinth was to come together for a meal as they gathered in the name of the Lord. In their custom, they were dishonoring one another. Paul was not addressing the form of their custom. He was not promoting a right or a wrong way to perform the 'word picture' of communion. He was addressing an attitude and a relationship problem among the believers of Corinth.

COMMUNION is WHENEVER WE COME TOGETHER (1 Cor. 12:12). True communion is not the breaking of bread and the drinking of wine. It is an intimate sharing with God and one another as members of the Body of Christ and participants of His Spirit of life. We are all members of the one Body of Christ. How does communion operate when we come together? It is an active participation of giving life to one another and intimately sharing who we are in Christ with one another. It is an intimate sharing of the substance of Christ and life of His Holy Spirit with our fellow members of the Body of Christ. It is a freewill offering of life. Paul was not calling their corporate meal communion. He was addressing their attitude in their corporate feast as being a violation of communion that should take place every time we come together (1 Cor. 11:17-34). It is not about natural bread and wine. It is about an intimate sharing of our lives and the life of God's Spirit with one another. We are to prefer one another, wait on one another, and partake together (1 Cor. 11:33-34). This should be a life-style!_

All members of the Body of Christ should experience communion whenever they come together. We must examine ourselves whenever we come together (1 Cor. 11:28). That examination is one that recognizes that we are a part of Christ's Body and those we commune with are the same (2 Cor. 5:14-17; 13:5). It is our responsibility to properly discern the Lord's Body whenever we come together (1 Cor. 11:29). Discerning the Lord's Body means we recognize that Christ's sacrifice for sin was once for all (Heb. 9:26). His Body is His Church here on earth (Col. 1:18; 1 Cor. 12:27). Jesus is the Head of every member and all members together (Eph. 1:20). Together we are brethren, members of the Body of Christ (1 Cor. 12:20-27). This must be our attitude and our action whenever we come together and for whatever reason we come together. By this we will all be awake and healthy members of Christ's Body. We will experience God's grace in one another's lives, and we will drink of the portion of the cup of the life of His Spirit that we each contribute to in our sharing. There will be no judgments of the flesh among us and together we will experience the "cup of blessing," the life of Christ's Spirit among us.

Paul was not addressing the form of communion practiced by the church in Corinth. He was addressing their attitude in relationship with one another in their feast. Whenever we come together it should be to share Christ with one another in the fellowship of the Spirit. This is true communion. Each time we do this, we proclaim the Lord's death and confirm that the "cup of Blessing" has come to us through the once for all sacrifice of Jesus Christ. The confirmation is our ability to drink of the "cup of Praise" together. That is the cup of His resurrection life. He is our Passover Lamb and because of Him we are now living members of the place of His dwelling, the Body of Christ. All are welcome in this place, even as Jesus gave His life a ransom for all! When we drink the cup of Praise (resurrection life in Christ), we drink all the cups of the Passover meal.

NOTE: Stop again and consider the subject material of this chapter. Allow the Holy Spirit to let you experience the cup of Praise and the communion of the Spirit. Consider all four cups of the communion meal as you experience the life of the Spirit today.

Chapter 6.1 – 6.5 - The Sixth Eye of Grace

Statements and Questions to Consider
For a Group Discussion:

1. God's knowledge will always join our lives to Him and one another, while the knowledge of men will often separate us from God and one another. How does God's knowledge join us and what are some ways the knowledge of men separates us?

2. There is no doubt there will one day be a throne of judgment for all wickedness that opposes Christ and His ways, but God desires that all would be saved and come to the knowledge of the truth. Do you suppose that the things that breach our fellowship with God in the Spirit now threaten a breach between Him and us eternally? Read 1 Cor. 6:6-20 and discuss how its content affects true communion now and eternally. Is it possible to despise God's loving judgment of eternal life for all who believe in Him - Read Jn. 3:16-21 also?

3. The sixth grace of the Seven Eyes of Grace has to do with the "Spirit of Knowing" and the level of relationship in the Body known as the "freewill offering". Why has the author connected communion and the Spirit of Knowing? Why is communion like the freewill offering?

4. Communion is "a sharing, an intimate relationship with deep understanding." What is the difference between sharing in God's Spirit and human sharing without God? What is the difference between intimacy by the Spirit and mere social intimacy?

5. Discuss the four cups of the Passover meal. - Thanksgiving, for making us new creations, though we were common sinful people - Telling or Testimony, for stories of deliverance from Egyptian slavery (slavery of darkness) - Redemption or Blessing, to demonstrate God's redemption power for all who believe in Him - Praise to testify that God had acquired His people as a Holy nation unto Himself.

6. The communion of the blood of Christ gave us the communion of the Spirit of Christ. The sacrifice of the body of Jesus Christ made us members of the Body of Christ. Read Lk. 22:14-20 & Isa. 52:13-15; 53:4-6 and discuss the once for all price of Jesus Christ to give to us the gift of being members of the Body of Christ.

7. The cup of Redemption was the shed blood of Jesus Christ. In His death, all men can find the fulfillment of their death. It was the completion of the wages of sin, for the wages of sin is death. The death of Jesus gave all men the right to drink of the cup of resurrection through faith in Him. The fourth cup was the cup of Praise, a cup to be drunk upon the earth. It is the testimony of His resurrection life that guarantees the fullness of the resurrection to come. What do you think drinking this cup looks like?

8. The author proposes that the "breaking of bread" of the early church was not meant to be a ritual of bread and wine. It was meant to be the daily celebration of the gathering together of the Body of Christ. It can include the elements of food, but in its greater reality it reveals the food of the Body of Christ and the life of the resurrection Spirit in the Body of Christ. Discuss ways of experiencing communion, both with bread and as the bread of the Body of Christ.

9. We have experienced Christ's resurrection life in that we love God with all of our hearts, minds, souls, and strength. We have partaken of the life of His living bread; in that we love one another as we love ourselves (His city). What kind of diversity would you find in a city? What kinds of function are there in a city? Could diversity be a challenge to communion? How can we embrace communion with the city of God?

10. We live to stir one another up to love and good works as members of the Body of Christ. What is the difference between stirring someone up to be noticed yourself and stirring someone up so that they find more life?

11. When we choose to live together by the life of His Spirit, we confirm that we no longer live according to the flesh. We seek to live according to the Spirit. The cup is a sharing of His blood and Spirit. The bread is a sharing of His Body. How is living together a choice?

12. We each share in the ability to "freely give" of our lives as He "freely gave" His life for us. We are the reality of the "freewill offering" in the New Covenant. How do we freely give our lives?

13. In Paul's writing to the Corinthian church, he was not saying that whoever drank and ate of the Corinthian feast in an unworthy manner would be guilty of the body and blood of the Lord. He was pointing out that they had defiled the Lord's Supper in everything they were doing. He was letting them know that their pretense of communion was not working. How would we be guilty of eating or drinking in an unworthy manner?

14. We all died in Christ when He drank the third cup of the Passover meal, the cup of Redemption. We all live in Christ when we drink the fourth cup of the Passover meal, the cup of Praise; the testimony of His resurrection. We are not judged according to the flesh anymore. Discuss this.

15. We must recognize that we are members of the Body of Christ. We must also recognize that others are members to be received as contributing elements of the life of Christ together. What are some practical ways of doing this?

Chapter 7.1

The Seventh Eye of Grace
- The Spirit of the Fear of the Lord

We have finally come to the *Seventh Eye of Grace*. That grace has to do with the Spirit of the Fear of the Lord and the power of prayer. This is a "ruling" and "reigning" grace. It is the power of "perfections" in the Church (Heb. 6:1). I believe the Church has a measure of this grace, but there is yet a time to come when the full measure of this grace will be released upon the earth. I don't believe this thunder has been fully released into the earth yet. Time will tell, but I believe there is a day coming when the power of prayer will take on world transformation power! In these next chapters, we will look at the foundation and characteristics of this grace.

I believe prayer relates directly to the Spirit of the Fear of the Lord (Isa. 11:2). This is not the fear of circumstances. It is the "AWE" of God in His manifested presence! It is not merely the power of supplications and petitions spoken to God. It is an audience with the King! It is an encounter with the authority of all the universes and realms of creation. It is a knowing of God at a level of "AWE"! Now, I believe prayer is real today and that God answers prayer. There is already a degree of the "AWE" of God in the Church. There is no doubt a progressive motivation toward the fullness of the grace of prayer. God is bringing to pass His testimony of the power of prayer in the Church.

I believe prayer should be the same as prophecy and that increasing realities of this truth are happening in our lives and in the earth, but I believe the fullness of this grace is yet to come. To understand what I am talking about, I want us to look at the letter to the church of Laodicea found in the book of Revelation.

Rev. 3:14 "And to the angel of the church of the Laodiceans write, 'These things says the Amen, the Faithful and True Witness, the Beginning of the creation of God' "...

208

Jesus is revealed in this letter as the "Amen", the "Faithful", the "True Witness", the "Beginning of the creation of God". These are all key elements of the grace of the Spirit of the Fear of the Lord and the substance of prayer. They are terms for the One, who made all things, sustains all things, and by whom and for whom all things were made (Col. 1:16, 18).

Rev. 3:15 "I know your works, that you are neither cold nor hot. I could wish you were cold or hot."

This lukewarm condition is the opposite of testimony of the grace of the Spirit of the Fear of the Lord. There was no "AWE" of God in the church of Laodicea. Even historically, the city of Laodicea was located between hot springs and cold springs. It was common to find a drink of "warm water" in the region. The symbolism here is that there was no passionate sound of God in the people of Laodicea. They were apathetic. Apathy is one step away from atrophy. Apathy means, "I won't" and atrophy means, "I can't". The works of Laodicea were like that.

Rev. 3:16 "So then, because you are lukewarm, and neither cold nor hot, I will spew you out of My mouth."

The term "I will spew you out of My mouth" is part of the curse for breaking covenant with God. It is specific terminology for living like the nations of the world. Where there is a lack of the "AWE" of God there is a compromising to the ways of the world.

Lev. 18:24 'Do not defile yourselves with any of these things; for by all these the nations are defiled, which I am casting out before you. 25 For the land is defiled; therefore I visit the punishment of its iniquity upon it, and the land vomits out its inhabitants. 26 You shall therefore keep My statutes and My judgments, and shall not commit any of these abominations, either any of your own nation or any stranger who sojourns among you 27 (for all these abominations the men of the land have done, who were before you, and thus the land is defiled), 28 lest the land vomit you out also when you defile it, as it vomited out the nations that were before you.'

True prayer is what transforms our lives in the presence of God. Without the power and passion of prayer, there will always be a compromising to the ways of the world. Without a good prayer life with God, we simply learn to adapt to the lukewarm conditions of our lives. This is revealed in this letter to the church of Laodicea. Prayer is an honor and an awe of God. When mankind honors God, the earth honors man. When there is a lack of awe of man to God, the earth is bound from honoring man. This condition causes the earth to vomit out its inhabitants. It is part of the laws of creation.

Rev. 3:17 "Because you say, 'I am rich, have become wealthy, and have need of nothing'—and do not know that you are wretched, miserable, poor, blind, and naked—"

This is the description of apostasy. It is the absence of faith. It is nothing more than a form of godliness without the power of God. It's no different than the Pharisaic system of the first century (Lk. 18:9-14). A fallen condition in our lives as believers will disqualify us from ministry. The only true qualification of ministry is the power of the presence of the One of whom we minister. Our qualifier is Jesus Christ! Without Him we are bound to our defective conditions of sin. We may think that we are forgiven of our sins, but we are not truly experiencing the transforming testimony of His presence that changes our lives.

Lev. 21:18 'For any man who has a defect shall not approach: a man blind or lame, who has a marred face or any limb too long, 19 a man who has a broken foot or broken hand, 20 or is a hunchback or a dwarf, or a man who has a defect in his eye, or eczema or scab, or is a eunuch. 21 No man of the descendants of Aaron the priest, who has a defect, shall come near to offer the offerings made by fire to the LORD. He has a defect; he shall not come near to offer the bread of his God.'

We cannot live with merely the natural testimony of human flesh. We must find God's transforming grace of His Spirit! Without Him we are bound to natural blindness and ignorance to His glory.

Deut. 29:4 "Yet the LORD has not given you a heart to perceive and eyes to see and ears to hear, to this very day."

Mt. 13:13 "Therefore I speak to them in parables, because seeing they do not see, and hearing they do not hear, nor do they understand. 14 And in them the prophecy of Isaiah is fulfilled, which says: 'Hearing you will hear and shall not understand, and seeing you will see and not perceive; 15 for the heart of this people has grown dull. Their _ears are hard of hearing, and their eyes they have closed, lest they should see with their eyes and hear with their ears, lest they should understand with their heart and turn, so that I should heal them.'"_

2 Cor. 4:3 But even if our gospel is veiled, it is veiled to those who are perishing, 4 whose minds the god of this age has blinded, who do not believe, lest the light of the gospel of the glory of Christ, who is the image of God, should shine on them.

1 Jn. 2:11 But he who hates his brother is in darkness and walks in darkness, and does not know where he is going, because the darkness has blinded his eyes.

These Scriptures give us a hint to the condition of the Laodicean church. This is our condition when we lack the grace of the Spirit of the Fear of the Lord. It is the condition of human lives that are void of an "AWE" of God. What is the antidote for this condition of apathy? The letter to Laodicea reveals the mystery.

Rev. 3:18 "I counsel you to buy from Me gold refined in the fire, that you may be rich; and white garments, that you may be clothed, that the shame of your nakedness may not be revealed; and anoint your eyes with eye salve, that you may see."

Gold refined in the fire represents purity, holiness, and faithfulness to God. God was telling this church to find the place of holiness before God. He was telling them to find the "AWE" of His presence. His glory would heal their apathy! He was telling them to become faithful to Him! Gold is the substance of God Himself, and they were charged to find the substance of God within them.

1 Pet. 1:5 ...who are kept by the power of God through faith for salvation ready to be revealed in the last time. 6 In this you greatly rejoice, though now for a little while, if need be, you have been grieved by various trials, 7 that the genuineness of your faith, being much more precious than gold that perishes, though it is tested by fire, may be found to praise, honor, and glory at the revelation of Jesus Christ...

The "genuineness of our faith" is the true gold of heaven. It comes by testing and only in the presence of God can we find the grace to stand in the day of testing. We don't want to be merely "saved". We have been called and commissioned by God to save the world! We have been sent as His ministers of fire (Ps. 104:4) to reveal those things that testify of His glory! Our testimony must be that of one God in us.

> *1 Cor. 3:12 Now if anyone builds on this foundation with gold, silver, precious stones, wood, hay, straw, 13 each one's work will become manifest; for the Day will declare it, because it will be revealed by fire; and the fire will test each one's work, of what sort it is. 14 If anyone's work which he has built on it endures, he will receive a reward. 15 If anyone's work is burned, he will suffer loss; but he himself will be saved, yet so as through fire.*

The church of Laodicea was instructed to buy "garments of white". I believe those garments are the wedding attire of the Bride of Christ. They are the works of the Father made known by the righteous acts of His house (Eph. 2:10). This church was to put on wedding attire or be replaced (Mt. 22:11-14). They were to take their place as the coheir of Christ that His rule and reign might be known in the earth. These garments of white testify of the grace of the Spirit of the Fear of the Lord that clothes us with the presence of His righteousness. It is prayer that puts us in the right place of authority in His house. Through being a house of relationship with Him we become a house of His power. His righteousness is a right relationship with Him! It is through a right relationship with Him that our mouths will be opened to release the power of His grace to change the world in which we live. His presence empowers the acts that determine blessings upon our future generations in the world. It is like the firstling offering of the Old Covenant (Deut. 12:6).We must be clothed in the garments of righteousness by dedicating all of our earthly lives to Him.

> *Mt. 22:11 "But when the king came in to see the guests, he saw a man there who did not have on a wedding garment. 12 So he said to him, 'Friend, how did you come in here without a wedding garment?' And he was speechless. 13 Then the king said to the servants, 'Bind him hand and foot, take him away, and cast him into outer darkness; there will be weeping and gnashing of teeth.' 14 For many are called, but few are chosen."*

The church of Laodicea was to buy eye salve that they might see. That seeing is not a natural sight that leads to blindness. It is the ability to see by the Spirit of God. Those who see in the natural don't really see at all. It is only through the grace of the Spirit of the Fear of the Lord and prayer that we can truly see with the eyes of the Spirit. Jesus came to open the eyes of the blind and to give us the eyes of the seeing (Isa. 61:1-3; Lk. 4:18; Acts 26:18)! Our authority to rule and reign with Christ does not come by what we can naturally see or discern. It comes by the authority and life of His Spirit (Isa. 11:1-5).

Isa. 11:3 His delight is in the fear of the LORD, and He shall not judge by the sight of His eyes, nor decide by the hearing of His ears; 4 but with righteousness He shall judge the poor, and decide with equity for the meek of the earth; He shall strike the earth with the rod of His mouth, and with the breath of His lips He shall slay the wicked. 5 Righteousness shall be the belt of His loins, and faithfulness the belt of His waist.

1 Cor. 2:14 But the natural man does not receive the things of the Spirit of God, for they are foolishness to him; nor can he know them, because they are spiritually discerned. 15 But he who is spiritual judges all things, yet he himself is rightly judged by no one.

The Spirit of the Fear of the Lord anoints us to be those who are led by His Spirit (Rom. 8:14). It is the grace that empowers us to become the manifested sons of God in the earth (Rom. 8:19-21). It is the grace by which God treats us as sons and inheritors of all that is His.

Rev. 3:19 "As many as I love, I rebuke and chasten. Therefore be zealous and repent."

Heb. 12:6 "For whom the Lord loves He chastens, and scourges every son whom He receives." 7 If you endure chastening, God deals with you as with sons; for what son is there whom a father does not chasten? 8 But if you are without chastening, of which all have become partakers, then you are illegitimate and not sons.

It is the grace of the Spirit of the Fear of the Lord that reveals us as the legitimate sons of God. We become empowered to exercise His rule through the power of prayer. By the "AWE" of Him we can exercise the rule of His grace in the earth!

Prayer is an invitation to sit with Him. It is an invitation to rule with

213

Him. It is an invitation to know Him in His glory!

> *Rev. 3:20 "Behold, I stand at the door and knock. If anyone hears My voice and opens the door, I will come in to him and dine with him, and he with Me. 21 To him who overcomes I will grant to sit with Me on My throne, as I also overcame and sat down with My Father on His throne."*

This is the entrance into the fullness of the New Covenant. It is a place of intimacy and prophetic power. It is a place of faithfulness, righteousness, and glory. It is an invitation to exercise dominion with Christ. Prayer is the guarantee of the unfolding demonstration of Christ's life in the earth!

> *Eph. 1:20 ...which He worked in Christ when He raised Him from the dead and seated Him at His right hand in the heavenly places, 21 far above all principality and power and might and dominion, and every name that is named, not only in this age but also in that which is to come. 22 And He put all things under His feet, and gave Him to be head over all things to the church...*

> *Eph. 2:6 ... and raised us up together, and made us sit together in the heavenly places in Christ Jesus...*

> *Rev. 1:6 ...and has made us kings and priests to His God and Father, to Him be glory and dominion forever and ever. Amen.*

Jesus rules, and will continue to rule, until His kingdom becomes a great mountain and fills the earth (Dan. 2:35, 45). Christ has entered His kingdom already (Col.1:13) with His kings and priests (Rev.1:6). He has defeated the enemy already (Col. 2:15). He reigns now (Acts 2:29-36; Eph. 1:20-22; Mt. 28:18-20). He is engaged now in putting His enemy under His feet (1 Cor. 15:25). It is by the grace of the Spirit of the Fear of the Lord that we can take our place with Him in His kingdom authority. It is in this place of zeal and passion that we will live our lives fully dedicated to Him and all of His purposes in the earth. We will subdue the enemy and reveal the glory of the Father in the world in which we live! We will know His "perfections" in the earth (Heb. 6:1). I believe these things are true now, but there is a day coming when this grace will be released to the Church with a lightning bolt of revelation from heaven and a thunderclap of grace as the earth receives that heavenly sound of the grace of the Spirit of the Fear of the Lord.

The seventh curse of the fall left mankind bound to the dust of the earth. It is from dust we came and dust we return (Gen. 3:19). It is the grace of the Spirit of the Fear of the Lord that restores our dominion over the earth in Christ. I believe this present, coming, and increasing grace from heaven will establish Christ's kingdom throne in the midst of His Church! Christ's perfections will one day culminate in the resurrection of the dead, but I believe the grace of the Spirit of the Fear of the Lord will increasingly exercise His reign and rule to that day!

NOTE: Stop and let the Holy Spirit help you consider the subject matter of this chapter. Spend time in prayer today. Pray in the Spirit!

Chapter 7.2

The Seventh Eye of Grace

Prayer is the seventh step toward living in the blessings of the kingdom of God. It is a part of God's grace process in the Body of Christ. Once again, it was not sacrifices and offerings that God desired. Even though He did not want them, He did command them. He commanded them because they were types and shadows of levels of relationship found in the living administration of the Body of Christ. This seventh grace relates in the same way as the previous six I have already presented in this book. The *Seventh Eye of Grace* is the grace of the Spirit of the Fear of the Lord. It is a level of relationship found in the Holy Spirit's administration of the Body of Christ.

> *Heb. 10:5 Therefore, when He came into the world, He said: "Sacrifice and offering You did not desire, but a body You have prepared for Me. 6 In burnt offerings and sacrifices for sin you had no pleasure. 7 Then I said, 'Behold, I have come—in the volume of the book it is written of Me—to do Your will, O God.'"*

This seventh grace correlates to "the Spirit of the Fear of the Lord" and the level of relationship in the Body known as the "firstling offering".

> *Deut. 12:5 "But you shall seek the place where the LORD your God chooses, out of all your tribes, to put His name for His habitation; and there you shall go. 6 "There you shall take your 1)burnt offerings, your 2)sacrifices, your 3)tithes, the 4)heave offerings of your hand, your 5)vowed offerings, your 6)freewill offerings, and the 7)firstlings of your herds and flocks. 7 And there you shall eat before the LORD your God, and you shall rejoice in all to which you have put your hand, you and your households, in which the LORD your God has blessed you."*

The firstling of our flocks and the firstling of our herds is the key to the rule and reign of Christ in our earthly domain. The firstlings of our herds and flocks represent a principle of first things, or firstfruits. It is the principle of earthly first things. First things are not the same as tithe. Tithe represents the first of heavenly things. Firstfruits represent the first of earthly things made heavenly. It is the evidence of a face-to-face relationship with God in the awe of Him. It is an expression of the grace of the Fear of the Lord and represents the power of prayer. It is the dedication of the first to bring God into all of our earthly responsibilities and destinies. We have been called, appointed, and anointed to change the world we live in. This level of relationship has more to do with our children and our children's children, than simply our few short natural days on the planet. Through the demonstration of the dedication of the first earthly things in our lives, we guarantee the inheritance of heaven in all of our earthly destinies. It is a demonstration of the "AWE" of God, and it is prophetic with the power to change the world in which we live. The firstling of the flock is a type of firstfruits. It is an act of honoring God. It is not an act of obedience to His command, but rather an expression of honor to the "AWE" of His name. The giving of the 'first' brings blessing to all the earthly barns and vats of our inheritance.

Pr. 3:9 Honor the LORD with your possessions, and with the firstfruits of all your increase; 10 so your barns will be filled with plenty, and your vats will overflow with new wine.

Once again, the testimony of this grace can be found in the 2nd Chapter of the book of Acts. It is part of the jubilee Spirit poured out upon the Church that granted the Body of Christ the full substance of the sevenfold Spirit of God. This grace was seen in the fact the Church continued steadfastly in "prayer". It is the evidence of the power of Christ's "perfections" in the Church.

*Acts 2:42 And they continued steadfastly in the apostles' doctrine (instruction taught them by the apostles) and fellowship, in the breaking of bread, and **in prayers**.*

*Heb 6:1 Therefore, leaving the discussion of the elementary principles (principality) of Christ, **let us go on to perfection**, not laying again the foundation of repentance from dead works and of faith toward God ... 2 of the doctrine of baptisms, of laying on of hands, of resurrection of the dead, and of eternal judgment.*

This seventh testimony of the Church was that they continued steadfastly in "prayer". This grace is the manifestation of the 'Fear of the Lord' and the fruit of all things dedicated to Him! A true grace for prayer dedicates our lives, and everything about our lives to God and His purposes in the earth. Prayer is not merely about bringing our needs to God, as though He was the great supermarket of provision sent to meet our needs. Prayer is about finding out what God's needs are and then decreeing them in the earth. Prayer is the professing of our dedication to God and His purposes. It is filled with prophetic power and declaration! The mark of Prayer is an "AWE" of Him and the revealing of His Glory in the earth! Prayer increases the knowledge of the Glory of God in the earth!

What is prayer? Prayer is living before the face of God! It was practiced in the early Church (Acts 2:42). Through Prayer we manifest the glory of God! Through the prayers of the apostle Paul, the church of Corinth became a letter written by the Spirit of God to reveal the glorious testimony of Christ. That testimony was not mere actions of obedience; it was the expression of the "ink of the Spirit" in the hearts and minds of the members of the Church.

> *2 Cor. 3:2 You are our epistle written in our hearts, known and read by all men; 3 you are manifestly an epistle of Christ, ministered by us, written not with ink but by the Spirit of the living God, not on tablets of stone but on tablets of flesh, that is, of the heart.*

The testimony of the letter being written in Corinth was not the power of human might. It was the testimony of the sufficiency of God. The written letter of the Spirit in this church was not the testimony of Paul's work, but of Christ's work through the ministry of Paul.

> *2 Cor. 3:4 And we have such trust through Christ toward God. 5 Not that we are sufficient of ourselves to think of anything as being from ourselves, but our sufficiency is from God, 6 who also made us sufficient as ministers of the new covenant, not of the letter but of the Spirit; for the letter kills, but the Spirit gives life.*

Paul not only acknowledged that the church in Corinth was a testimony of the Spirit on His behalf, he also revealed the key for each of us to find that transforming power of grace. God wants for us all to live in a face-to-face relationship with Him. He wants us to experience the life-changing ministry of His Spirit on a consistent basis. It is not like the ministry of the Old Covenant that brought the perfect knowledge of good. The Spirit brings the perfect power of God's grace to transform our lives to become good. It is not a fading glory, but an increasing one!

2 Cor. 3:7 But if the ministry of death, written and engraved on stones, was glorious, so that the children of Israel could not look steadily at the face of Moses because of the glory of his countenance, which glory was passing away, 8 how will the ministry of the Spirit not be more glorious? 9 For if the ministry of condemnation had glory, the ministry of righteousness exceeds much more in glory.

The glory that comes by the Spirit of God is a far surpassing glory than that which merely comes through the testimony of the Prophets and Law. It is the testimony of Christ within us (Col. 1:27). It is the glory that comes with the demonstration of God's transforming power to perfect our lives in Christ. It is the power to change the world in which we live.

2 Cor. 3:10 For even what was made glorious had no glory in this respect, because of the glory that excels. 11 For if what is passing away was glorious, what remains is much more glorious. 12 Therefore, since we have such hope, we use great boldness of speech— 13 unlike Moses, who put a veil over his face so that the children of Israel could not look steadily at the end of what was passing away.

The veil that denied us the presence of God is removed in Christ. When we turn to the Lord the veil is taken away. Where the Spirit of the Lord is there is liberty. This happens in true prayer. It happens when we discover the "AWE" of God and dedicate our lives afresh to Him again. It is a continual, daily encounter with the Lord of Life!

2 Cor. 3:16 Nevertheless when one turns to the Lord, the veil is taken away. 17 Now the Lord is the Spirit; and where the Spirit of the Lord is, there is liberty. 18 But we all, with unveiled face, beholding as in a mirror the glory of the Lord, are being transformed into the same image from glory to glory, just as by the Spirit of the Lord.

When we encounter God in His manifested presence, we become transformed by His manifested presence. It is in that place that we come alive in Him. It is not merely for the sake of liberty. It is for the sake of His Lordship. Many believers think that where the Spirit is there is liberty, but that is not true. The Scripture says that where the Spirit of the "Lord" is there is liberty. True liberty comes from His Lordship. True dominion comes when the desires of our hearts become one with the desires of God. True dominion is a change of our 'want to', not merely obligations to a command of 'what to do'. True transformation comes from the place of His dominion. It is a testimony of the grace of the Spirit of the Fear of the Lord and the power of His perfections. It is a revealing of the testimony of true prayer. We are dedicated to Him, therefore, we become fruitful to the testimony of Him. It is not just true for our lives. It becomes true for the posterity of our lives. It affects our children and our children's children. It is a "firstling" testimony.

I have found that a face-to-face relationship with God is the key to bringing about His purposes in my life. I used to think that hearing God had to do with being able to know what to do. I have found that hearing God has more to do with knowing who He is. I find that by knowing who He is I become empowered to know what to do by a change of desire within my heart. A relationship with Him is not about receiving information from Him. It is about receiving Him and then being transformed by Him. Sometimes I go to a secluded place to fast and pray before God's presence. I don't go to get answers, although I might be facing many situations in which I need answers. I go to seek God, to love God, and to worship Him. I will often take my guitar with me, and I will sing songs to Him that only He has heard. They are not songs to be sung to anyone but Him. I walk in the mountains to talk with Him and experience His presence. On one such time, I had a particular situation in which I needed an answer as to "what to do". On my first day away with Him I asked Him my question. I felt that He was hesitant and even resistant to answer me. It is like a friend. Sometimes you know when your friend doesn't want to talk about something. I felt that with God. I spent the next five days just loving Him and not asking Him the question again. I wanted Him more than I wanted an answer to my question. I had a wonderful time in His presence. At the end of those five days, I went home and went to sleep. In the middle of my sleep God gave me a dream and gave me the answer to my question. He wanted to give me the answer to my question all the time, but He wanted me to desire His presence more than the answer to my question. I found not only the grace for the answer to my question, but also the grace for further transformation in my life. God is so good!

NOTE: It is time to meditate the subject of a spiritual letter, the Spirit of the fear of the Lord, and the power of prayer through a transformed heart.

Chapter 7.3

The Seventh Eye of Grace

Prayer is being seated with Christ where we manifest the fullness of Him. It is being one with Him. It is not about receiving instruction from Him. It is about becoming a carrier and facilitator of His presence. In prayer we find the spirit of wisdom and revelation in the knowing of Him. Our hearts are opened up to see what He sees. We become who He has called us to be in Christ. It is through prayer that we experience the exceeding greatness of His power.

> *Eph. 1:17 ...that the God of our Lord Jesus Christ, the Father of glory, may give to you the spirit of wisdom and revelation in the knowledge of Him, 18 the eyes of your understanding being enlightened; that you may know what is the hope of His calling, what are the riches of the glory of His inheritance in the saints, 19 and what is the exceeding greatness of His power toward us who believe, according to the working of His mighty power 20 which He worked in Christ when He raised Him from the dead and seated Him at His right hand in the heavenly places, 21 far above all principality and power and might and dominion, and every name that is named, not only in this age but also in that which is to come.*

Through prayer we find the authority of Christ over every principality, power, might, dominion, and name. It is in that place of intimacy with God that we experience the authority over every name that is named. The key to dominion is the grace of the Spirit of the Fear of the Lord. It is an "AWE" of God that releases the power of His name! When we experience this face-to-face reality of God's presence we become the life-empowered Body of Christ that exercises the authority of Christ over all things in the earth. It is in that place that we activate the fullness of Christ within us.

> *Eph. 1:22 And He put all things under His feet, and gave Him to*

be head over all things to the church, 23 which is His body, the
fullness of Him who fills all in all.

Prayer that comes from the realm of heaven's throne of grace is prayer that
is empowered by the Spirit of the Fear of the Lord. It exercises the Fear of the
Lord over all that resists Christ's glory. It is a prophetic power of prayer. This
place of prayer gives us the authority of Christ to see His enemies beneath our
feet. Prophetic prayer is the exercising of Christ's authority to reign in the earth!

1 Cor. 15:25 For He must reign till He has put all enemies under
His feet.

God is a prophetic God and therefore His people are a people filled with
His prophetic character, nature, way, power, and authority. In these recent
years the Church has been experiencing the knowledge and the power of His
prophetic nature in an increasing reality in the saints. We must understand
that along with the liberty of prophetic ministry comes the responsibility of
adequately functioning within God's prophetic parameters. Proper prophetic
ministry is rooted in our ability to behold God's face. In order to understand
the prophetic power of prayer we must look at the New Testament account
of the ministry of the prophet Elijah.

Jam. 5:16 Confess your trespasses to one another, and pray for one
another, that you may be healed. The effective, fervent prayer of a
righteous man avails much. 17 Elijah was a man with a nature like ours,
and he prayed earnestly that it would not rain; and it did not rain on
the land for three years and six months. 18 And he prayed again, and
the heaven gave rain, and the earth produced its fruit. 19 Brethren,
if anyone among you wanders from the truth, and someone turns him
back, 20 let him know that he who turns a sinner from the error of his
way will save a soul from death and cover a multitude of sins.

In this New Testament account of the ministry of Elijah we find that Elijah
is not described as a prophet, but as one who prayed. This Scripture portrays
an account that establishes the anointing of Elijah as being one of a prayer
ministry and not what we would perhaps term as a prophetic ministry. What
is it that causes the New Testament writer to credit Elijah with a ministry of
prayer and not one of being the ministry of a prophet?

The first requirement that we see for an "Elijah prayer ministry" is to be a righteous man (male or female). We receive our righteousness through faith in Christ and the confession of sin (1 Jn. 1:9). Elijah's righteousness was found in his faith in God through the order of God's Law. Just as the Law pointed to our need for Christ, our righteousness is in Christ and is not found in ourselves (Rom. 4:5; 5:17; 10:3, 4, 10; 2 Cor. 5:21). If we have received Christ into our hearts, we qualify for an Elijah ministry of effective prayer and power. God wants our prayers to be those of an effective, fervent, righteous man or woman. This can only happen when we have confessed our sins and received the righteousness that is only found in Christ.

Let's continue on in our look at this New Testament account of the prophet Elijah's ministry.

Jam. 5:17 Elijah was a man with a nature like ours, and he prayed earnestly that it would not rain; and it did not rain on the land for three years and six months.

This Scripture says that Elijah prayed a fervent prayer. A fervent prayer is a "forceful prayer". It is a prayer that is "powerful". In verse 17 it says that he was a man like any one of us, and he prayed earnestly to God that it would not rain. In the Greek these words "prayed earnestly" literally means that he "prayed", "prayed". This phrase is a combination of two words. The first word is the Greek word *proseuchomai* and it means, "to pray to God". It comes from a word that means, "to go forward" or "toward". This word comes from a word meaning, "to wish" and it is derived from another word, which means "in front of". The second word is the Greek word *proseuche* and it means "prayer". It comes from all of the previously mentioned words. Thus, this action implies that Elijah took a determined stance toward God, got in front of Him, and made his heart known to Him. We are to do the same. We are to actually get in God's face! Our purpose is not for selfish gain. Our purpose is to let our hearts become as His. We are not trying to change God's mind, but we are positioning ourselves to receive His mind. We are positioning ourselves in such a spiritual position that would bring heaven to earth. We are expecting the will of God to become the will of our hearts. We are expecting the ways of God to become the cry of our hearts.

As believers in Christ, we have been given the awesome privilege of coming before God's throne of grace with boldness and with full confidence that we are His children and His voice to the earth. There is nothing holding us back from coming into the presence of God (Eph. 2:18; 3:10-12; Col. 1:20). We are not just casually sending a few letters or a couple of post cards to God. When we offer right intercession to God, we decide to move toward God and position ourselves in His presence. We have taken steps toward Him in order to let Him know the God-ordained burden of our hearts. We are "before His face" making our hearts open to Him. We have approached God, are approaching God, and will continue to do so with all persistence and earnestness. We are not going to leave this position until our hearts become as His heart. We are not going to leave this position until we have received His heart's response to our approach. We have not just come to make a request, leave, and return again tomorrow. We have positioned ourselves to stay right there until we see the result of our travail.

Elijah was a man with passions like each of us. He had all the temptations and weaknesses that we do. He was a normal man as we are, but he positioned himself in a place where, as a righteous man, he could offer up effective, fervent prayer. He prayed earnestly that it would not rain and then "he prayed again".

Jam. 5:18 And he prayed again, and the heaven gave rain, and the earth produced its fruit.

Elijah didn't offer up vain repetitions. When it came time to complete the task that he had originally started he was still as fervent and fresh as when he began. As he had wrestled at first, he also wrestled to the end, and at the end he wrestled again. The word of faith was as new and as real at the end of his task as it was when he began.

Elijah's goal in praying was not to stop rain. His goal was to turn the hearts of God's people back to their God. The process involved stopping rain as well as returning rain. His faith for the goal was the same throughout the entire process. When it came time to complete the task of his intercession he went before God and "wrestled anew". He wasn't wrestling over a word that he had a long time ago. The word of the task was still fresh within his heart, and he was able to accomplish the task of the day because there was a brand-new wrestling going on inside of him. The word of faith was still new within him (Rom. 10:8-9).

When I think of Elijah, I immediately think of the ministry of the "prophet". I think of Elijah as the father of prophets. Yet in the context of the task described here in James he is not described as the "prophet". He is described in the task of "intercession". Although Elijah is famous for being a prophet, the New Testament description of him here is that of intercession before God!

"He prayed again, and the earth yielded its fruit." There were results to what Elijah proclaimed because he was a righteous man who relentlessly offered up earnest prayer on behalf of seeing God's people turn back to their God. The prayers that Elijah prayed were fruitful ones. God wants to give us the keys to fruitful prayer and intercession before Him. We are a generation who must make a difference in the earth in bringing about the purposes of our God!

The Bible says that the spirit of Elijah was upon John the Baptist (Mt. 11:14; 17:12; Lk. 1:17). That prophetic spirit was not only upon John the Baptist in the time that Jesus came in the flesh to die for our sins, but that prophetic spirit is upon the Church today to see the living realities of Jesus in the restoration of all things (Acts 3:21; Eph. 3:10). It is not a prophetic spirit with a purpose or intent of releasing right knowledge to the Church. This spirit is one to release the righteous work of God in the earth. God desires to release the earth from the curse. He has poured out His prophetic Spirit upon all flesh that He might turn the hearts of the fathers to the children and the children to the fathers. God desires His covenant family upon the earth.

Mal. 4:5 Behold, I will send you Elijah the prophet before the coming of the great and dreadful day of the LORD. 6 And he will turn the hearts of the fathers to the children, and the hearts of the children to their fathers, lest I come and strike the earth with a curse.

The prophetic Spirit of God is none other than the true heart of the Father. God has given to us His Spirit that we might walk on earth as His sons (male and female - Gal. 3:28). If God is the one true Father, then surely His Spirit that has made us sons is also one to raise us up as fathers of a generation yet bound. God is calling us into the realms of prophetic intercession to set the nations free in Christ! The "AWE" of God and the grace of the Spirit of the Fear of the Lord will cause every earthly thing of our lives to become dedicated to Him and His dominion of life. We can expect to see our children and our children's children honoring His name in the earth!

NOTE: Stop and pray. Let God speak to you today. Pray, then pray again and then pray "anew" again!

Chapter 7.4

The Seventh Eye of Grace

The ministry of prayer is a prophetic expression of the groaning that is locked up within the bound-up earth. Before God releases the earth from its bondage of corruption, He will loose a Spirit of intercession upon His prophetic saints. The key to the release of that Spirit is the grace of the Spirit of the Fear of the Lord. It comes as a result of the "AWE" of His presence. It is the testimony of true sons of God.

Rom. 8:22 For we know that the whole creation groans and labors with birth pangs together until now. 23 Not only that, but we also who have the firstfruits of the Spirit, even we ourselves groan within ourselves, eagerly waiting for the adoption, the redemption of our body. 24 For we were saved in this hope, but hope that is seen is not hope; for why does one still hope for what he sees? 25 But if we hope for what we do not see, then we eagerly wait for it with perseverance.

The power of the prophetic Spirit of God within His sons is not a power of what is seen. It is a power of what is not seen. It is the power to release what is in heaven to the earth. The key to this power is not the intercessor. It is the Spirit within the intercessor.

Rom. 8:26 Likewise the Spirit also helps in our weaknesses. For we do not know what we should pray for as we ought, but the Spirit Himself makes intercession for us with groanings which cannot be uttered. 27 Now He who searches the hearts knows what the mind of the Spirit is, because He makes intercession for the saints according to the will of God.

A true intercessor of God is acting in the role of a son of God. God is raising up His sons in this hour. He wants the working of His name to bring about the eternal purposes of His goodness in the earth. We must answer

226

the call of prophetic intercession in order to see His purpose accomplished in the earth!

Rom. 8:28 And we know that all things work together for good to those who love God, to those who are the called according to His purpose.

There is a working process involved in bringing about the will of God in the earth. God has given us His Spirit by whom we can know all things. There is an intercession of the Spirit of Christ within us that is essential to come forth in this hour in order to see the working of the Lord.

In order to understand the full revelation of this New Testament description of the ministry of intercession, we are going to have to look further at the Old Testament account of the ministry of Elijah referred to by the writer of James.

In 1 Kings Chapter 16, we find that Ahab had become the king of Israel. He was a wicked king. He had allowed Jezebel to become his wife and sit in the seat of the queen mother of Israel. Jezebel, as the queen, had taken over the religious worship of Israel. She, as her name implies, had operated as a non-submissive, uncovered woman. She had propagated Baal worship and had set up the wooden Asherah poles in the kingdom of Israel. It was during that time that God sent Elijah to speak the prophetic word of the Lord to the kingdom of Israel.

1 Kin. 17:1 And Elijah the Tishbite, of the inhabitants of Gilead, said to Ahab, "As the LORD God of Israel lives, before whom I stand, there shall not be dew nor rain these years, except at my word."

Let's extract some key principles from this chapter concerning the prophetic ministry and the function of prophetic prayer. Understand that first of all Elijah was a prophet, even as we are called by God to be a prophetic people (Acts 2:17, 18). As Elijah is described in the New Testament, in regard to 1 Kings Chapter 17, he is not described as a prophet. He is described as an intercessor. In order to accomplish the prophetic work he was sent to do, Elijah functioned in the role of an intercessor. We should be very interested in knowing what the actions were that made Elijah as an intercessor. What caused the work of the Lord to be accomplished was not the fact that Elijah had a word. It wasn't the fact that Elijah heard right knowledge and then spoke a word according to the knowledge he had received. The very first thing that I see in 1 Kings 17:1 is that Elijah was found as one who stood "before the Lord".

> *1 Kin. 17:1 And Elijah the Tishbite, of the inhabitants of Gilead, said to Ahab, "As the LORD God of Israel lives, before whom I stand, there shall not be dew nor rain these years, except at my word."*

We saw in the book of James that the prayer Elijah prayed was one of going toward God, coming before His face, and finding His heart. He stood there and refused to leave that place. The reason that God could send Elijah to deal with Ahab and the situation in Israel was because Elijah was standing before God. If we are going to be key prophetic ministers, key prayer warriors, the first requirement is going to be that we "Stand Before The Lord!"

In verse 1 the Hebrew word "before" has to do with "the face". We are not to reluctantly back into God's presence. We are to boldly enter into His presence looking to find His face.

Elijah spoke a word that there would be no dew or rain. In the Bible dew and rain speak of heaven's blessing upon the earth. The Scripture that says the rain falls on the just and the unjust is not talking about curses. It is talking about blessings (Mt. 5:45). The Bible says that when the righteous flourish the city rejoices (Pr. 11:10). It is a blessing for rain to fall. Rain and dew bring forth the fruit of the earth. It is not Biblical to say that curses fall on the just and the unjust alike. God has not intended curses for His people. It is God's desire to bless all men. Blessings fall on the just and the unjust alike. You can know that when God blesses His people the result will be blessing in the city.

In this Scripture we see Elijah cutting off the blessing of God on the earth, by the word of the Lord he spoke. It is in the ministry of a prophetic intercessor that Elijah cut off the blessing of God on the earth. The word that he spoke, and the action that he took, cut off the abundant blessing from the Lord. This didn't take away the covenant protection of God's people, however. But it did cut off the abundant blessing.

> *1 Kin. 17:2 Then the word of the LORD came to him, saying, 3 "Get away from here and turn eastward, and hide by the Brook Cherith, which flows into the Jordan. 4 And it will be that you shall drink from the brook, and I have commanded the ravens to feed you there."*

228

The second thing that we need to learn concerning the area of prophetic intercession is that "The First Step Will Lead To The Next Step". Elijah didn't have a clear word from God as to what was going to happen. He only knew to speak that there would be no rain or dew. He was simply standing before the Lord and he received an unction, a stirring of the Lord, to go and stop rain and dew.

As we step out in faith to function as prophetic intercessors we are not to try and figure out what comes next. We must simply obey step one. When we obey step one, we will receive the next step. We won't get the next step unless we obey the first step.

God didn't sit down with Elijah and say: "Elijah, because you're my servant, because you're a righteous man and stand before me, here is what's going to happen; You're going to go and speak that there won't be any rain or dew. Then I'm going to take you into a place of hiding. It won't rain for $3^{1/2}$ years. When I take you into hiding, I'll take you to the Brook Cherith until it runs dry. Ravens will feed you. After that you'll go to a widow's house, and she'll take care of you. I'm eventually going to bring you out of hiding and you will challenge the prophets of Baal on Mt. Carmel. Baal's prophets will call out to their gods, but they won't answer. Then you will set up an altar and call on Me. I'll answer with fire! You'll kill the prophets of Baal and begin to intercede on the top of the hill. A rain cloud will appear, and you'll outrun Ahab's chariot as rain returns to the land."

It didn't happen that way and it doesn't happen that way for us either. How many times do we want God to be that detailed before we even think about being obedient to step one? We want to know what's going to happen if we obey step one before we consider taking it. We must remember a simple principle - "Until We Obey The First Step We Won't Get The Next Step!"

Faith requires us to respond by taking steps in a forward direction when we cannot see (2 Cor. 5:7). The issue is one of simple obedience. As prophetic intercessors, we must first of all stand before God. God will then tell us what to do and then we are to be obedient even if it doesn't make sense. Once we are obedient to the first step, God will give us the next step.

God told Elijah to get away from there. He was to go to the Brook Cherith. Cherith means "to cut" or "has to do with covenant". God was telling Elijah to go to the "covenant brook". God was saying, "although the blessing has been cut off from the earth, I am with you Elijah." "I will take care of you!" A third principle that we can extract from this is that "Directions From God Will Remain In Covenant".

God is a covenant God, and He will not violate His own covenant nature. Let's look at this in a practical way. Let's say that we believe that God has spoken to us as an intercessor or a prophet. We take step one, and we receive a word that we believe is the next step. We must always ask ourselves these questions: Will taking this next step be a covenant response? Will it allow us to keep our covenants, or will it violate them? If it isn't a covenant response it wasn't the voice of the Lord. God keeps His covenants, and He expects us to keep ours as well. God will not tell us to do something that will break covenant or is not a covenant requirement or response.

1 Kin. 17:5 So he went and did according to the word of the LORD, for he went and stayed by the Brook Cherith, which flows inro the Jordan.

Elijah was in a place of hiding but he was not without the presence of the Lord. Although the earth was bound to dryness, Elijah was not in a dry season. He was by the Brook Cherith, which flowed to the river Jordan. The name Jordan means "descender" and it speaks of the presence of the Holy Spirit in our lives. Just as Jesus came up out of the water in the River Jordan full of the Holy Spirit (Jn. 1:29-34) at His baptism by John, Elijah was not without the presence of the Holy Spirit while waiting to receive further instructions from God. The instruction of the Lord can come when we are in a place of receiving the life of the Holy Spirit. As intercessors it is as important to get into the presence of the Lord after we speak the word of God, as it is to get into His presence before we speak His word. Once we speak the word of the Lord it is important that we get back into the presence of the Lord to brood over the word that we have spoken in order to see the work for which the word was sent accomplished. "We Must Remain In The Presence Of The Holy Spirit."

1 Kin. 17:8 Then the word of the LORD came to him, saying, 9 "Arise, go to Zarephath, which belongs to Sidon, and dwell there. See, I have commanded a widow there to provide for you."

Once the brook had dried up in the place where Elijah was, once the covenant reason for him to be in that place had been fulfilled, Elijah received a word of where to go next. He received the next step. Elijah had been in hiding. Ahab had been searching for him with the intent of taking his life. By the instruction of the queen mother Jezebel, Ahab had been executing all of the prophets of God in the land. There was no open worship of God allowed. Any open worship of God resulted in an execution of death at the order of Jezebel. They were killing the prophets because they were looking for Elijah. The hideous vengeance of blood upon the heads of the prophets was a direct assault on the one man, Elijah, who had spoken the word of the Lord to bind up the blessing of God upon the earth. Picture this; the reason that Elijah was in hiding was because the king of Israel was hunting for him with the sole purpose of killing Him. The word of the Lord came to Elijah saying - "go to Zerephath". Zerephath means "ambush of the month". "Go to the "ambush of the month" which belongs to "Sidon" (Sidon means "hunting"). This is like saying; "Elijah, they've been hunting for you, so here's the word of the Lord; go to the place called hunting - to the ambush of the month."

We can learn another important point of instruction concerning the ministry of prophetic intercession from this portion of Scripture. As we are laboring before the Lord to see His work accomplished, the wisdom of the Lord that comes to us (the things that God tells us to do) will not make natural sense nor will it protect the personal motives of our lives. God's wisdom doesn't make natural sense. God's wisdom is not for our own agendas. "Wisdom From Above Will Test Our Natural Understanding." The wisdom of the Lord will often give the appearance of costing us our reputation or our individual identities. People might not even know that we are interceding. It's one thing to die a martyr, but what about when people don't even know that we've died? What if no one knows?

We can give someone a word and we can still keep our personal identities. But if we want to move into the next level of doing a work it could cost us our identities. It will at least appear to us that we're losing our identities. We really won't lose our identities, because the Bible says if we lose our lives, we'll save them; if we lay them down, they will be found. We must find our identities in Him! By natural appearances however, our mind may say of the wisdom of the Lord - "This is not for my good". Intercession doesn't necessarily gain us popularity. Anyone involved in intercession will lose his or her identity for a season. The work is not usually accomplished instantly with the word. There is a process and in that process we lose our identities and we see the identity of Christ rise to the situation.

Not only did God tell Elijah to go to the place of "hunting" and the "ambush of the month", He also told him to "dwell there". God even went

231

a step beyond the sensible when He told Elijah that a widow woman would provide for Him. That's about as bad as it can get in the kingdom of Israel! They were in the midst of a drought. There was a famine, and God wanted Elijah to go to the ambush of the month where they were hunting for him; and a widow was going to take care of him!

> *1 Kin. 17:10 So he arose and went to Zarephath. And when he came to the gate of the city, indeed a widow was there gathering sticks. And he called to her and said, "Please bring me a little water in a cup, that I may drink."*

As we continue to follow the progression of this story of Elijah, we find another point that all prophetic intercessors must come to know. God will "Always Bring You Into The Provision Legally". We don't have to get anxious. We don't have to try and take shortcuts if we are walking in obedience to the will of the Lord. He will bring us to "the gate of the city" where the provision is. We won't have to compromise our integrity at any cost. God will bring us into His perfect will through the legal door of life!

> *1 Kin. 17:11 And as she was going to get it, he called to her and said, "Please bring me a morsel of bread in your hand." 12 Then she said, "As the LORD your God lives, I do not have bread, only a handful of flour in a bin, and a little oil in a jar; and see, I am gathering a couple of sticks that I may go in and prepare it for myself and my son, that we may eat it, and die."*

Another principle can be found in Elijah's insistence that the widow not only gave him water, but she also made him a cake with all that she had. The word of the Lord is not limited to human compassion. Often the word and the action of the Lord are very difficult for the human compassion minded individual to understand. Elijah had come to a widow's house in a time of famine and drought, and he asked her to give him water and food. God sent Elijah there not for Elijah's sake only. God sent Elijah there for the widow's sake as well. When Elijah commanded the woman, he had to know in his spirit that God was there as a provider for the widow and that her provision was not in Elijah, but in the God of Elijah. Therefore, Elijah needed to move in obedience; not trying to protect what he could see naturally. Most of us would not have delivered the word if we knew it would require a widow and her son's last meal. We would go before God and say surely there is another way. We might not have the revelation that Elijah did as to how big his

God was. We might not have an understanding of how faithful God is to the responsible. There is a lack of the fear of the Lord in the house of the Lord. Elijah was operating here according to the "Fear of the Lord".

"We Must Walk According To The Fear Of The Lord." Don't try to figure out how God is going to work out the final end of the situation. He will send us to do His work, but we don't have to do the work for Him. He's probably going to tell us to do some things that won't make sense in the natural and won't make sense to human compassion. Our human compassion will say, "let's see the answer now". God has a plan, a process, and a procurement that is much greater than we can reasonably understand.

NOTE: Stop and consider the first eight steps of intercession as they have been described in this chapter:

- "Stand Before The Lord"
- "The First Step Will Lead To The Next Step."
- "Until We Obey The First Step, We Won't Get The Next Step."
- "Direction From God Will Remain In Covenant."
- "We Must Remain In The Presence Of The Holy Spirit."
- "Wisdom From Above Will Test Our Natural Understanding."
- "God Will Always Bring Us Into The Provision Legally."
- "We Must Walk According To The Fear Of The Lord."

Chapter 7.5

The Seventh Eye of Grace

We have looked at some principles of prophetic intercession as seen through the life example of the prophet Elijah. So far, we have seen these valuable keys to prayer that we must receive and take to heart:

- "Stand Before The Lord"
- "The First Step Will Lead To The Next Step."
- "Until We Obey The First Step, We Won't Get The Next Step."
- "Direction From God Will Remain In Covenant."
- "We Must Remain In The Presence Of The Holy Spirit."
- "Wisdom From Above Will Test Our Natural Understanding."
- "God Will Always Bring Us Into The Provision Legally."
- "We Must Walk According To The Fear Of The Lord."

Now let's continue on with our study of the life example of the prophet Elijah.

1 Kin. 17:13 And Elijah said to her, "Do not fear; go and do as you have said, but make me a small cake from it first, and bring it to me; and afterward make some for yourself and your son."

"The Fear Of The Lord Comes From Understanding God Given Responsibility." When we are laboring through something in the process of intercession, we have to take a stand. There will even be believers who will point their finger at us and say that we are wrong, but we must understand that there is something that is more important than us, and that is the responsibility that God has given to us. We have to fear God and know that all authority in heaven and on earth comes from Him. If God has given us a task, He has also given us the authority to accomplish that task. We cannot fear the faces of men. We cannot fear circumstances. We have to carry the thing through, fearing God in the responsibility given to us.

Elijah didn't require the first of the widow provision in order to be mean. Elijah knew that the Lord had required it of him in the position that he was in as the prophet to Israel. The position required that her response was unto the Lord and not himself. He feared God in the position he was in, so he stood his ground in the responsibility of that position.

We must recognize that there are certain responsibilities that come with the task of intercession. We can only let go of a responsibility when God releases us from it. Whether we see the answer yet, or understand how it is to come about, we have to fear God in the responsibility of the task that we are carrying as a prophetic intercessor. We must carry it until God releases us. When God releases us, the task is complete. The completion of the task doesn't come when we see the thing complete. "The Completion Of The Task Comes When God Releases Us From The Task."

1 Kin. 17:14 "For thus says the LORD God of Israel: 'The bin of flour shall not be used up, nor shall the jar of oil run dry, until the day the LORD sends rain on the earth.'"

"Failure To Compromise Will Lead To Life." More specifically - it will lead to the word of the Lord, which leads to life. If we refuse to compromise in what God has told us to do the result will be provision that won't run out.

The story goes on. The widow and her son continued in the provision. After a while the widow's son died. The widow was upset with the prophet and said that they would have been better off if they had just died. She was upset that the prophet brought a hope but now her son was dead.

1 Kin. 17:19 And he said to her, "Give me your son." So he took him out of her arms and carried him to the upper room where he was staying, and laid him on his own bed.

"The Prophetic Word Of The Lord Cannot Be Separated From The Act Of Intercession." Elijah once again acted in the role of the intercessor. The heart of an intercessor is not to accomplish a word. It is to see life! Elijah didn't want a word to stop rain. He wanted to turn the hearts of the people to God. His heart was to see fruit come in the land. He wanted to see the Kingdom of God come. He was in the widow's house and all he wanted was to see life come. As a prophetic intercessor, he didn't have a heart for ministry. He had a heart to minister. If our hearts are for ministry,

God doesn't need us to intercede for others. If our hearts are to minister, God wants and will use us. An intercessor wants to do whatever it takes to bring forth life!

Elijah was stretched out over the body of the boy. He was calling for life! His heart was to minister.

> *1 Kin. 17:21 And he stretched himself out on the child three times, and cried out to the LORD and said, "O LORD my God, I pray, let this child's soul come back to him."*

"Intercession Is A Sacrifice Of Self." It will cause us to stretch. It might cause us to lose some sleep. Notice that the stretching was at the will of the prophet. He was the one who stretched himself. He could have stopped! During this intercession process he could have stopped, but he chose to stretch himself. He stretched himself three times. The number three is a divine number. Anytime we see the number three in Scripture it is talking about the empowerment of God. Elijah stretched himself until the power of God came into the situation. He stretched himself until God's presence and power was a reality.

> *1 Kin. 17:22 Then the LORD heard the voice of Elijah; and the soul of the child came back to him, and he revived. 23 And Elijah took the child and brought him down from the upper room into the house, and gave him to his mother. And Elijah said, "See, your son lives!" 24 Then the woman said to Elijah, "Now by this I know that you are a man of God, and that the word of the LORD in your mouth is the truth."*

Elijah had a heart to love and not a heart to minister. The widow knew that Elijah was a man of God because his heart was to love, not to minister. What made the widow know that Elijah was a man of God was the fact that he wouldn't let go until there was life! He had a heart to love. The love that comes is a flow that comes from God, but it doesn't start out that way. It starts with the stretching of the minister in the act of intercession. "We Must Have A Heart To Love Others!"

> *1 Kin. 18:1 Now it came to pass after many days that the word of the LORD came to Elijah, in the third year, saying, "Go, present yourself to Ahab, and I will send rain on the earth."*

It is through faith and patience that we inherit the promises of God. Elijah was in a process of waiting in faith on the promise of God. We see in this Scripture that it came to pass after many days. I don't even think we have to imagine what that is all about, do we? It's through faith and patience that we inherit the promise of God (Heb. 6:12). "Faith + Patience = The Promise."

We can also see another important part of the intercession process in this first verse of Chapter Eighteen. "God Will Bring Us To The Place Where We Stand And Face The Problem." There comes a time where there is a "face-off" with the problem. In this story of Elijah, we see that $3^{1/2}$ years had passed, but the manifested problem of Jezebel, Ahab, and the godless system in Israel had not changed. Ahab was no different than he was $3^{1/2}$ years earlier. God's plan was working a process in Elijah, but the initial problem of Ahab had not changed. Whatever the process, whatever the length of time might be that we are kept in intercession, God will eventually bring us to the place where we will have a "face-off" with the problem. The problem won't be dealt with just because we spoke the word. The problem will be dealt with because we spoke the word, and we were faithful in the process of interceding over the word that was spoken, and we have become a testimony of the word to finally come face-to-face with the problem and command the change.

According to this account of Scripture, Elijah had only spoken one word in $3^{1/2}$ years. He had spent $3^{1/2}$ years in intercession. Throughout all of the dealings and the process of these $3^{1/2}$ years, the word of the Lord hadn't changed. The word of the Lord was that there would not be rain or dew but by Elijah's mouth.

While in the process of intercession, we cannot measure the success of the prophetic word or intercession by an apparent unchanged condition of the original circumstance. It has nothing to do with how close we are to the victory or not. When Elijah spoke the word, he was $3^{1/2}$ years from the deliverance. When God brought him before Ahab this second time, he was only a matter of days away from the victory. The situation had not changed in any way for what seemed any better. As a matter of fact, the situation looked worse to the natural understanding than it did $3^{1/2}$ years earlier. In the natural it looked like there hadn't been any progress, but because of the prophetic word and the intercession of the Holy Spirit in Elijah's life; because of the work of God during that time he was only a matter of days away from the victory and it still looked the same in the natural. There was not a seemingly progressive improvement. Prophets were losing their heads! Drought and famine were in the land! There was no open worship of the one true God of Israel!

237

If we recall the account of the book of James concerning this event, we will remember that it said that "at the end" Elijah prayed again. We saw that meant he "wrestled anew". Although the natural condition looked worse at the end of $3^{1/2}$ years, Elijah still had faith and a fresh word. He "wrestled anew". He wasn't gritting his teeth and hoping that the word of $3^{1/2}$ years earlier would come to pass. He still believed the word of the Lord. He knew that the word spoken was just part of a process in bringing about God's work. He was full of faith. If we evaluate the spiritual condition of a situation by what we see in the natural, we will have a hard time remaining full of faith. We cannot look at the natural and determine how successful our intercession has been. The natural is not a measuring rod. "We Must Remain Full Of Faith Regardless Of What We See."

As we continue in this story of Elijah, we see that Elijah went before the prophet Obadiah and told him that Ahab was to come to him. Obadiah was reluctant to take the word to Ahab for fear that Elijah would receive new directions from God and would not be there when Ahab arrived and thus result in the death of Obadiah.

1 Kin. 18:11 "And now you say, 'Go, tell your master, "Elijah is here"'! 12 "And it shall come to pass, as soon as I am gone from you, that the Spirit of the LORD will carry you to a place I do not know; so when I go and tell Ahab, and he cannot find you, he will kill me. But I your servant have feared the LORD from my youth."

Elijah aligned his integrity with the integrity of God and His word. Elijah knew that God didn't have a plan "B" in the process. We must be more interested in the situation glorifying God than in ourselves looking good by moving in the gifts of the Spirit. We must be more interested in God being glorified than in us moving in accurate prophecies and good prayer times. We must be concerned with the overall long-term work of the Lord. We must know that the thing that we have covenanted with God to do has no plan "B". God is not going to change His plan of work from what He said He was going to do. When God says He will do something, He will! God doesn't have an alternate plan. God has never deviated from His original plan throughout all of history. We must line up with His word because He is the one who does not change. We can't constantly change our word and expect God to agree with us. We must remain in agreement with Him and His word. We must be relentless to not change.

"Our Integrity Must Become As His Is!" Obadiah delivered the message to Ahab and Ahab found Elijah in the place that he said he would be. Elijah told Ahab to gather the four hundred and fifty prophets of Baal, and the four hundred prophets of Asherah, and all of Israel at Mount Carmel.

> *1 Kin. 18:20 So Ahab sent for all the children of Israel, and gathered the prophets together on Mount Carmel. 21 And Elijah came to all the people, and said, "How long will you falter between two opinions? If the LORD is God, follow Him; but if Baal, then follow him." But the people answered him not a word.*

The focus of the word of the Lord is to draw all to honor God. The purpose of the work of God is to draw all to Himself. The reason we want to see people set free is because first of all we must love people and second, we want that person and everyone around them to be drawn to God.

"The Works Of Christ Testify Of Him." The false prophets and all of Israel gathered on Mount Carmel. The false prophets offered their sacrifice and called upon their god but there was no answer. Elijah then mocked them openly.

> *1 Kin. 18:27 And so it was, at noon, that Elijah mocked them and said, "Cry aloud, for he is a god; either he is meditating, or he is busy, or he is on a journey, or perhaps he is sleeping and must be awakened."*

Elijah didn't fear failure or opposition. Prophetic prayer doesn't mean that we have to go out and mock the devil or mock what the enemy is doing. The point is that we can't fear the opposition. Elijah didn't fear the opposition at Mount Carmel. He knew that there was no competition with God. He didn't fear failure. Failure was not an option. "We Cannot Fear Failure Or Opposition."

> *1 Kin. 18:30 Then Elijah said to all the people, "Come near to me." So all the people came near to him. And he repaired the altar of the LORD that was broken down.*

We must know that "Before The Breakthrough Can Come, There Must Be A Loosing That Takes Place." For $3^{1/2}$ years the earth had been bound. It was bound from receiving the blessing of God. Binding and loosing are not things that we do with our mouths. They are actions that we must do with our lives.

This basic principle of binding and loosing is the key issue in regard to the ministry of intercession. Before we address this issue of binding and loosing, let's review what we have learned thus far. These are valuable truths that we must apply in our process of prophetic Intercession:

"Stand Before The Lord."

"The First Step Will Lead To The Next Step."

"Until We Obey The First Step We Won't Get The Next Step."

"Directions From God Will Remain In Covenant."

"We Must Remain In The Presence Of The Holy Spirit."

"Wisdom From Above Will Test Our Natural Understanding."

"God Will Always Bring Us Into The Provision Legally."

"We Must Walk According To The Fear Of The Lord."

"The Fear Of The Lord Comes From Understanding God Given Responsibility."

"The Completion Of The Task Comes When God Releases Us From The Task."

"Failure To Compromise Will Lead To Life."

"The Prophetic Word Of The Lord Cannot Be Separated From The Act Of Intercession."

"Intercession Is A Sacrifice Of Self."

"We Must Have A Heart To Love Others!"

"Faith + Patience = The Promise."

"God Will Bring Us To The Place Where We Stand And Face The Problem."

"We Must Remain Full Of Faith Regardless Of What We See."

"Our Integrity Must Become As His Is!"

"The Works Of Christ Testify Of Him."

"We Cannot Fear Failure Or Opposition."

"Before The Breakthrough Can Come There Must Be A Loosing That Takes Place."

NOTE: Stop and prayerfully consider these thoughts!

Chapter 7.6

The Seventh Eye of Grace

Now let's continue our look at the principles of binding and loosing as we find them in the story of Elijah. The blessing of rain had been bound in the earth and Elijah was getting ready to release the blessing. The principle is: "Whatever You Bind On Earth Is Bound In Heaven". Earlier Elijah had "bound" the blessing of the Lord. In order to seal and prove the binding, Elijah went into hiding. In other words, the word of the Lord was nowhere to be found. No word of the Lord was heard for $3^{1/2}$ years. It was bound in the earth. Since there was no word of the Lord to be found in the earth there was no blessing to be released from the heavens.

Elijah was about to reverse the process of the binding he had spoken in the earth at the beginning of his journey. In order to do the reverse process Elijah had to first do a loosing on earth before there could be a loosing in heaven. The physical evidence of the blessing of the Lord being bound was that of drought. There was no rain, therefore there had to be a loosing of rain in the earth to release the blessing of heaven. If we understand the process of rain, we will know that rain doesn't begin in heaven. There is an established order in the heavens that releases rain when the right conditions are met, but rain begins in the earth. Rain is initiated when water evaporates from the earth, rises to the upper atmosphere where it goes through a change in pressure as well as temperature where water condenses, and is released back to the earth as rain.

The principle is like this: If we are bound in unforgiveness we must be willing to forgive in order to loose the blessing of forgiveness from heaven. A blessing for forgiveness already exists in the heavens, because of the precious sprinkled blood of Jesus upon the mercy seat of God's throne, but that blessing is bound until a loosing of forgiveness is initiated in the earth. If we are found in a sin it is important that we confess that sin and be released from the binding that has taken place in our own personal life. Until we can confess, the blessing of heaven cannot be released to us; no matter how much

God wants to bless us. That is why it is our responsibility to go to a brother who is found in sin and seek to restore him through confession, repentance, and forgiveness (Mt.18:15-18). The principle is "Whatever Is Bound On Earth Is Bound In Heaven. Whatever Is Loosed On Earth Is Loosed In Heaven."

1 Kin. 18:31 And Elijah took twelve stones, according to the number of the tribes of the sons of Jacob, to whom the word of the LORD had come, saying, "Israel shall be your name."

The first thing that Elijah did was to establish the worship of God. He put God first. He established an altar and he put God first. In order for us to loose what has been bound, we must also put God first. If we are bound up in unforgiveness we must humble ourselves and put God first. This destroys our self-seeking attitude that has us bound in unforgiveness. We must put God first in order to be loosed from our bondage. If we are bound up in poverty or financial debt, the only way that we can be loosed from our bondage is to put God first. We must become faithful in our tithe and offerings. If we are bound up in sickness, we must put God first before God can release our blessing of healing. We must first of all rejoice in God regardless of our sickness.

The second thing that Elijah did was to see himself as a representative of the whole. He made the altar of twelve stones, according to the number of the tribes of the sons of Jacob. Elijah saw that his offering for loosing was for the whole. He was not acting on behalf of himself. We must claim the responsibility of the whole in order to see a loosing of the whole. Whatever it is that God has placed upon us for the purpose of intercession must become a task that we see as our own, but not for our own purpose.

The third thing that Elijah did was to build the altar God's way. He built the altar in the name of the Lord. He was willing to do it God's way and not his own. He was willing to give the credit and the glory to God and not claim it for himself. In order to loose we must follow God's plan of instruction. We must be God-seeking in our motive for loosing and not self-seeking.

The fourth thing that he did was to dig a trench around the altar that was large enough to hold two seahs of seed.

1 Kin. 18:32 Then with the stones he built an altar in the name of the LORD; and he made a trench around the altar large enough to hold two seahs of seed.

In order to succeed in the process of loosing we must be willing to sow. The Bible says that we will reap whatever we sow and that we will reap in due season if we do not loose heart (Gal. 6:7-9). Elijah's altar of loosing was an altar of sowing.

1 Kin. 18:33 And he put the wood in order, cut the bull in pieces, and laid it on the wood, and said, "Fill four waterpots with water, and pour it on the burnt sacrifice and on the wood." 34 Then he said, "Do it a second time," and they did it a second time; and he said, "Do it a third time," and they did it a third time. 35 So the water ran all around the altar; and he also filled the trench with water.

Elijah poured out what he needed. He needed rain. The land had just gone through $3^{1/2}$ years of drought and Elijah was there to loose rain. Elijah didn't put water on the sacrifice and the altar just to make it wet. He was loosing rain! The sacrifice was water! The sowing on the altar was one of water. Elijah poured out the most expensive commodity of the nation Israel. He poured out what they didn't have. They didn't have water, so he poured out water. In order to loose we must give away what we need.

In order to loose heaven's blessing to the earth, we must give away the very thing that we do not have. The principle is to give away the thing that we need. If we are bound up in our finances, we must sow finances or we will not see a loosing of a financial blessing. If we are bound in unforgiveness, we must sow forgiveness. We must sow the thing that we don't have in order to see a loosing in the heavens. If we don't, we will be limited to the source on the earth. If the source of the earth is in lack, then the resource to draw from is in lack. We have to pour out a generous measure of little in order to see a generous measure of much. If we don't loose the thing that we need we cannot see a release of what we need from the storehouse of heaven.

1 Kin. 18:36 And it came to pass, at the time of the offering of the evening sacrifice, that Elijah the prophet came near and said, "LORD God of Abraham, Isaac, and Israel, let it be known this day that You are God in Israel, and that I am Your servant, and that I have done all these things at Your word."

Elijah was persistent to the end. It wasn't until the time of the evening sacrifice that God answered. At the time when it would seem too late, at the time when it seemed that God had been delaying, the answer from heaven was released. The fire of the Lord fell, and the water was taken to heaven. The loosing on the earth was received as a loosing in heaven. The result was a destruction of the false prophets. The source of the binding on the earth was not the word of Elijah. Elijah had only spoken the word of binding $3^{1/2}$ years earlier because of the condition of Israel. The source of the binding on earth was the false worship of false gods by the nation of Israel. The condition had now changed in heaven because of the loosing sacrifice on the earth. Destruction of the fruit of darkness was at hand.

1 Kin. 18:41 Then Elijah said to Ahab, "Go up, eat and drink; for there is the sound of abundance of rain."

There is another important truth that we must see here in regard to the application of true intercession. Elijah continued in faith! He heard the sound of rain! He heard the sound of rain not because he saw the blessing of heaven released. He heard the sound of rain because it was loosed on earth! Loosing is done in faith! "We Must Continue In Faith!"

1 Kin. 18:42 So Ahab went up to eat and drink. And Elijah went up to the top of Carmel; then he bowed down on the ground, and put his face between his knees...

Elijah didn't make meetings and gifts his goal. There was a great meeting on Mount Carmel, but Elijah didn't stand in awe of the awesome meeting that he had just had. He was found in the continued process of intercession. He wasn't looking for a great meeting. He was looking for a completed work. He remained steadfast to the continued process of birthing the release of the blessing from heaven. "We Must Make The Completed Work Of God Our Goal."

1 Kin. 18:43 ...and said to his servant, "Go up now, look toward the sea." So he went up and looked, and said, "There is nothing." And seven times he said, "Go again." 44 Then it came to pass the seventh time, that he said, "There is a cloud, as small as a man's hand, rising out of the sea!" So he said, "Go up, say to Ahab, 'Prepare your chariot, and go down before the rain stops you.' "

Elijah remained in intercession until he saw the end. His faith was not wavered by what he could see naturally yet he knew that there had to also come about a reality of heaven's blessing in the natural. He remained faithful to the task of the Spirit until he saw the release in the natural. "We Must

244

Remain Faithful In The Spirit Until We See It In The Natural."

1 Kin. 18:45 Now it happened in the meantime that the sky became black with clouds and wind, and there was a heavy rain. So Ahab rode away and went to Jezreel. 46 Then the hand of the LORD came upon Elijah; and he girded up his loins and ran ahead of Ahab to the entrance of Jezreel.

The anointing for the next appointment came upon Elijah when the first task was complete. God will be there with His presence when we are faithful to give Him ours. If we are faithful to see the process of intercession through its full course, God will anoint us to run for another day. "The Anointing For The Next Task Will Come When We Have Accomplished The First."

We cannot separate prophetic ministry from the ministry of intercession. If we are called to the ministry of the prophetic, then we are called to the ministry of intercession. May God grant us the grace to run and not be weary, walk and not faint, but most of all - to wait upon Him in His presence.

Let's take a moment to review these key points of bringing loosing for the blessing of heaven to come to the earth. We know that what is bound on earth is also bound in heaven:

"There Must Therefore Be A Loosing Upon The Earth Before There Can Be A Loosing In Heaven."

"We Must Put God First In Order To Be Loosed From Our Bondage."

"We Must Claim The Responsibility Of The Whole In Order To See A Loosing Of The Whole."

"We Must Be God-Seeking In Our Motive For Loosing And Not Self-Seeking."

"In Order To Succeed In The Process of Loosing We Must Be Willing To Sow."

"In Order To Loose We Must Give Away What We Need."

Let's stand to be the prophetic life of God to the earth in a time where intercession is so essential to our earth. We must see His kingdom come and His will be done here on earth as it is in heaven! We can stand to see the blessings of the Lord come to nations of the earth. The earth will be covered with the knowledge of the Lord as the waters cover the sea (Isa. 11:9; Hab. 2:14)!

A Prayer LIFE is filled with the testimony of "LIFE Giving Prayers"! The foundation for prayer and fasting is life, not abstinence. Prayer in the Old Covenant was all about abstaining from the flesh. Prayer in the New Covenant is all about indulging in that which feeds the Spirit. We are called to indulge of the presence of God! The power of prayer in the Old Covenant was centered on one's ability to abstain from that which feeds the flesh. It was filled with sackcloth and ashes. Jesus changed everything through His living in the presence of His Father. The testimony of the New Covenant is to indulge in that which produces spiritual life energy, stimulates life growth, and maintains the life of the Spirit. Prayer flows out from the life of the Spirit!

Mt. 26:41 "Watch and pray, lest you enter into temptation. The spirit indeed is willing, but the flesh is weak."

Rom. 8:26 Likewise the Spirit also helps in our weaknesses. For we do not know what we should pray for as we ought, but the Spirit Himself makes intercession for us with groanings which cannot be uttered. 27 Now He who searches the hearts knows what the mind of the Spirit is, because He makes intercession for the saints according to the will of God. 28 And we know that all things work together for good to those who love God, to those who are the called according to His purpose.

1 Cor. 14:14 For if I pray in a tongue, my spirit prays, but my understanding is unfruitful. 15 What is the result then? I will pray with the spirit, and I will also pray with the understanding. I will sing with the spirit, and I will also sing with the understanding. 16 Otherwise, if you bless with the spirit, how will he who occupies the place of the uninformed say "Amen" at your giving of thanks, since he does not understand what you say? 17 For you indeed give thanks well, but the other is not edified. 18 I thank my God I speak with tongues more than you all; 19 yet in the church I would rather speak five words with my understanding, that I may teach others also, than ten thousand words in a tongue.

We often focus on the weakness of the flesh, but we fail to see that the Spirit is willing. The flesh is weak, but Jesus made a way for us to have the power of the Spirit. He helps us in our weakness. He causes all things to work for good. We have been given the ability to pray in the Spirit. We have been given the power of Christ within us. It is the power of God's life within

246

us! New Covenant prayer releases the increasing life of things NEW, that is things that are made ALIVE! We find a great example of the difference between Old Covenant and New Covenant prayer given by Jesus in the book of Luke. The Pharisees questioned Jesus in regard to fasting and prayer.

> *Lk. 5:33 Then they said to Him, "Why do the disciples of John fast often and make prayers, and likewise those of the Pharisees, but Yours eat and drink?" 34 And He said to them, "Can you make the friends of the bridegroom fast while the bridegroom is with them? 35 But the days will come when the bridegroom will be taken away from them; then they will fast in those days." 36 Then He spoke a parable to them: "No one puts a piece from a new garment on an old one; otherwise the new makes a tear, and also the piece that was taken out of the new does not match the old. 37 And no one puts new wine into old wineskins; or else the new wine will burst the wineskins and be spilled, and the wineskins will be ruined. 38 But new wine must be put into new wineskins, and both are preserved. 39 And no one, having drunk old wine, immediately desires new; for he says, 'The old is better.'"(Mt. 9:14-17; Mk. 2:18-22)*

These Pharisees were trying to trap Jesus in their statements. By the standards of the Old Covenant, Jesus and His disciples were flunking the testimony of prayer and fasting. Jesus revealed to them the greater power of intimacy. He declared that His disciples did not fast because the Bridegroom was present with them. The presence of Jesus was fulfilling the testimony of prayer and fasting in their lives. The point of fasting and prayer is to be in the presence of the Lord, these disciples were living with the presence of the Lord. Jesus went on to say that the time would come when His disciples would fast again. However, He gave a parable that revealed that prayer and fasting for those in the New Covenant would never be the same as it was in the Old Covenant. He compared it to a new garment and a new wineskin.

> *Lk. 5:36 Then He spoke a parable to them: "No one puts a piece from a new garment on an old one; otherwise the new makes a tear, and also the piece that was taken out of the new does not match the old 37 And no one puts new wine into old wineskins; or else the new wine will burst the wineskins and be spilled, and the wineskins will be ruined. 38 But new wine must be put into new wineskins, and both are preserved. 39 And no one, having drunk old wine, immediately desires new; for he says, 'The old is better.'"*

247

The old garment was the Law. The new garment is the testimony of Grace. Jesus was saying that His disciples would again fast and pray, but it would not be according to the old garment. It would not be prayer according to the Law. It would be prayer according to the power of grace. The old wine skin was the container of the covenant. In the Old Covenant it was the constant written code of the Law. In the New Covenant it is the increasing life-giving power of grace. It contains the expanding new wine of the Spirit. The difference was in the access to the throne-room of God. The power of GRACE comes from a face-to-face relationship with God in Christ. It is the power of the Spirit and the testimony of indulging in the Spirit of LIFE! It is not based upon ridged obedience to a written code, but upon a heart moving activation of the "AWE" of God's presence.

Let me give you a key to a successful prayer life. God's general will, will always leads you to His specific will. Do you know what God's way is in the matter? What are nine elements of prayer?

1 Thes. 5:16-25:

1) Rejoice always.

2) Pray without ceasing.

3) In everything give thanks.

4) Don't quench the Spirit / LET THE SPIRT FLOW / LIVE ACCORDING TO THE SPIRIT.

5) Don't despise prophecies – Therefore, PROPHESY!

6) Hold fast what is good.

7) Always remain one with God in your spirit, soul, and body – KNOW HIS PEACE.

8) Depend on His faithfulness.

9) Pray for those in authority and pray for others.

New Covenant prayer is a manifestation of a face-to-face relationship with Jesus Christ. We have been given access to the throne-room of His grace! Let us find the place of the "AWE" of His presence and let us exercise His rule in the earth through His prophetic Spirit of Life!

NOTE: Stop, consider, and practice the elements of a successful prayer life!

Chapter 7.1 – 7.6 - The Seventh Eye of Grace

Statements and Questions to Consider
For a Group Discussion:

1. The grace of the Spirit of the Fear of the Lord is about prayer. It has to do with "ruling" and "reigning" in Christ and the power of His "perfections" in the Church. Discuss this. What are some things the Holy Spirit has been speaking to the group members?

2. A lukewarm condition is the opposite of the testimony of the grace of the Spirit of the Fear of the Lord. True prayer is what transforms our lives in the presence of God. Without the power and passion of prayer, there will always be a compromising to the ways of the world. Discuss how this is true.

3. Read Revelation 3:14-22 and discuss what it means to buy gold refined in fire, white garments, and eye salve. What is the overcoming promise of this letter and how does one receive it?

4. What is the difference between the Fear of the Lord and the fear of circumstances?

5. The testimony of the letter being written in Corinth was not the power of human might. It was the testimony of the sufficiency of God. How is a spiritual letter being written in the lives of members of the group or in the corporate testimony of their church?

6. Read 2 Cor. 3:16-18. What is the difference between liberty and the liberty that comes by the Spirit of the Lord?

7. Prayer is being a place of intimacy with God that we experience the authority over every name that is named. The key to dominion is the grace of the Spirit of the Fear of the Lord. It is an "AWE" of God that releases the power of His name! Discuss this.

8. Prophetic prayer is the exercising of Christ's authority to reign in the earth and proper prophetic ministry is rooted in our ability to behold God's face. Discuss how prayer is prophetic.

9. Read 1 Kin. 17 and discuss the keys of being a prophetic intercessor as given in the story of Elijah:

    "Stand Before The Lord."

    "The First Step Will Lead To The Next Step."

    "Until We Obey The First Step We Won't Get The Next Step."

    "Directions From God Will Remain In Covenant."

    "We Must Remain In The Presence Of The Holy Spirit."

    "Wisdom From Above Will Test Our Natural Understanding."

"God Will Always Bring Us Into The Provision Legally."

"We Must Walk According To The Fear Of The Lord."

"The Fear Of The Lord Comes From Understanding God Given Responsibility."

"The Completion Of The Task Comes When God Releases Us From The Task."

"Failure To Compromise Will Lead To Life."

"The Prophetic Word Of The Lord Cannot Be Separated From The Act Of Intercession."

"Intercession Is A Sacrifice Of Self."

"We Must Have A Heart To Love Others!"

"Faith + Patience = The Promise."

"God Will Bring Us To The Place Where We Stand And Face The Problem."

"We Must Remain Full Of Faith Regardless Of What We See."

"Our Integrity Must Become As His Is!"

"The Works Of Christ Testify Of Him."

"We Cannot Fear Failure Or Opposition."

"A Loosing That Takes Place For The Breakthrough To Come:"

- "There Must Therefore Be A Loosing Upon The Earth Before There Can Be A Loosing In Heaven."

- "We Must Put God First In Order To Be Loosed From Our Bondage."

- "We Must Claim The Responsibility Of The Whole In Order To See A Loosing Of The Whole."

- "We Must Be God-Seeking In Our Motive For Loosing And Not Self-Seeking."

- "In Order To Succeed In The Process of Loosing We Must Be Willing To Sow."

- "In Order To Loose We Must Give Away What We Need."

10. Prayer in the New Covenant is all about indulging in that which feeds the Spirit. We are called to indulge of the presence of God! Prayer flows out from the life of the Spirit! Discuss the differences between life-giving prayers and prayers of condemnation.

11. Read 1 Thes. 5:16-25 and discuss the following: Rejoice always; Pray without ceasing; In everything give thanks; Don't quench the Spirit; Don't despise prophecies; Hold fast what is good; Always remain one with God in your spirit, soul, and body; Depend on His faithfulness; Pray for those in authority and pray for others.

Application In
A Spiritual House:

We have looked at each of the seven aspects of the Holy Spirit's perfecting power. God has given His sevenfold Spirit of Grace to perfect His Church. The Holy Spirit is the key to the spiritual house of God. God is not interested in the natural house we often call the church. He is building His true Church by the power of His amazing grace. He is interested in making manifest His spiritual house wherein He dwells by His Spirit. There is one Body and one Spirit with the hope of one calling (Eph. 4:4). We are the temple of the Holy Spirit (1 Cor. 3:16). We have come to Jesus to become His living house filled with His living presence.

1 Pet. 2:4 Coming to Him as to a living stone, rejected indeed by men, but chosen by God and precious, 5 you also, as living stones, are being built up a spiritual house, a holy priesthood, to offer up spiritual sacrifices acceptable to God through Jesus Christ.

God is not just interested giving us salvation. He doesn't just want us to be the people of God who are saved by His grace. He wants us to become empowered by His grace. He wants us to be the spiritual house of God that He lives in. The sevenfold Spirit of God is changing our lives so that we can be the fullness of God's house. He is transforming our lives to become like Christ in order to join us to the fullness of Him in all that He is.

1 Pet. 2:6 Therefore it is also contained in the Scripture, "Behold, I lay in Zion a chief cornerstone, elect, precious, and he who believes on Him will by no means be put to shame." 7 Therefore, to you who believe, He is precious; but to those who are disobedient, "The stone which the builders rejected has become the chief cornerstone," 8 and "A stone of stumbling and a rock of offense." They stumble, being disobedient to the word, to which they also were appointed.

Jesus is the cornerstone of the Church. The very substance of the foundation is the same as the substance of the house. The foundation stone of Christ is described in terms that quote the prophet Isaiah. We see that the

251

substance of Christ is revealed in the attributes of being a tried stone, a costly stone, and a sure foundation (Isa. 28:16).

We can find some principles and patterns in the construction of the temple by David's son Solomon that testify of these three elements of the cornerstone of Christ. It was king David's desire to build a house for God's habitation. His desire was for the manifestation of the presence of God upon the earth. He was a man after God's own heart, and he sought for the glory of God to be revealed. Truly this was an expression of a New Covenant truth that God desires to raise up in the heart of His Church. David was a man of war, however, and was therefore disqualified from the task of building God's house. God responded to David's heart by making a promise with him that David's son would build God a house. We know that God was testifying of the day when Jesus, the Son of David, would build the spiritual house of God. In David's day, Solomon represented the task. Solomon responded to that promise and sought to build God's house in Jerusalem. A pattern of the three characteristics found in the cornerstone of Christ was seen in the material Solomon used to build the temple.

1 Kin. 5:17 And the king commanded them to quarry large stones, costly stones, and hewn stones, to lay the foundation of the temple.

The stones that were quarried were large stones. Large stones speak of "stones that can pass the test". They are "faithful" stones. They are stones of "greatness" and not limited to the natural substance of humanity as fragile men. They represented the living stones of God's spiritual house that can endure in the day of testing. Jesus was a stone of "greatness", a stone of "faithfulness" and a stone that "passed the test". The sevenfold Spirit of God is perfecting stones that are "large stones" in this hour even as Jesus, the cornerstone, is a "large stone". Living stones are "large stones". Living stones are stones that are "faithful", stones that "pass the test". Without a "test" there is no "testimony". Stones that pass the test are stones that hear the voice of God. Stones that hear the voice of God are stones that are filled with faith, as faith comes by hearing the word of God. Faith filled stones will be living stones of the testimony of God. Faith only works through love. Stones that hear the voice of God are stones that have a revelation of God's love for them. We are becoming spiritual stones with a great "testimony" in this hour. It is a testimony of God's love for us and His love working in and through our lives!

The stones that were quarried for Solomon's temple were "costly stones".

Costly stones are "precious stones". They are stones with an extremely high value. Father God set the value of the stones of His house when He allowed His only begotten Son to die for our sins. Jesus was a "costly stone". Costly stones reflect the heart of the builder. Cheap stones come from a cheap builder. Costly stones come from the heart of an extravagant builder; one who is willing to pay a high price for a "passionate" building. "Costly stones" are "passionate" stones that reflect the builder's heart. They reflect the heart of the Father. Jesus was a "passionate" stone who reflected the values of His Father's heart. As a spiritual house for God, we must become "costly stones". We must become "passionate stones" that reflect the values within the heart of our Heavenly Father. These are stones that reflect God's glory. We must become stones that pay the price of our own lives for one another in order to see the glory of God manifested within His house.

The stones of Solomon's temple were "hewn stones". Hewn stones are "stones that fit with other stones". They are "relational" stones. Hewn stones are polished and finished. They are stones that find their place in relationship with other stones. Jesus was a "hewn stone". He was the firstborn of many that He might establish a house built upon relationship with one another. Even as He brought us back into relationship with God as our Father, He also brought us into relationship with one another to become a house where God can dwell. Living stones are "relational stones". They are stones that fit with other stones in order to see the full manifestation of God in His covenant love. Hewn stones are stones that provide a "sure foundation" and a "sure structure" that can be depended upon as a shelter and a house of provision. They reveal a house of relationship with God and one another in every room. These living stones will never act hastily, but will depend on God's presence to sustain the divine relationships of their lives.

God is causing us to become a spiritual house of His presence. How is this made manifest in our lives? God has given us His sevenfold Holy Spirit to empower us to become the large stones, costly stones, and relational stones of the Body of Christ. There is one Body, one Spirit, and one hope of our calling together as the spiritual habitation of God in the earth (Eph. 4:4). The hope of our calling in Him is fulfilled by the sevenfold grace of the Holy Spirit. There are seven attributes to the spiritual house of God. I believe each of these seven attributes correlates to the work of the Holy Spirit in perfecting the Church.

1 Pet. 2:9 But you are a chosen generation, a royal priesthood, a holy nation, His own special people, that you may proclaim the

253

> *praises of Him who called you out of darkness into His marvelous light; 10 who once were not a people but are now the people of God, who had not obtained mercy but now have obtained mercy.*

These verses reveal that the living members of the Body of Christ are: 1) A chosen generation; 2) A royal priesthood; 3) A holy nation; 4) His own special people; 5) Those who proclaim His praises; 6) The people of God; and 7) Those who have obtained mercy. These are the testimony of: 1) One Lord; 2) One Faith; 3) One Submersion (Baptism); 4) One God and Father of all; 5) One God Above all; 6) One God Through all; and 7) One God In all (Eph. 4:5, 6). It was the Spirit of the Lord that changed our hearts to become those who have returned to our first love. God has chosen us. We have been empowered by the Spirit of Wisdom to do works that speak of our faith. We do not live lives that are naturally focused and motivated. We are a royal priesthood. We serve God with the priestly sacrifices of works that speak of our faith. We are continually submerged in the presence of the Holy Spirit by His baptism of Understanding. We have the outward evidence of the fruit and charisma of the Spirit to reveal that we are the Holy people of God. The Spirit of Counsel has empowered us to be part of the sent light of Christ with a corporate testimony of being submitted one to another as God's own special people. Together we are the light of the Father of lights. The Spirit of Might empowers us to be a part of the fellowship of Christ in the power of His resurrection. We are a testimony of God's praise by His Resurrection Might. The Spirit of Knowing has joined us to the Body of Christ as the people of God. Our motivation in every aspect of our lives is to live to love God and to live to love others as we love ourselves. The Spirit of the Fear of the Lord has revealed to us the AWE of God because Christ's mercy has given us entrance to the throne of His ruling grace. Mercy has triumphed over judgment, and we have been granted a place of eternally reigning with Christ.

Let's put these things in some practical terms that we can all relate to in our daily lives. We often think of the church as the place to which we go, but the true Church is the place that we are. It involves and affects every area of our lives: Our church involvements, our family relationships, and our marketplace influences. We are the Church no matter where we are or go. We are empowered by the sevenfold Spirit of God to become the Church in every expression of our lives. The sevenfold Spirit of God could be seen as a pattern in the seven sacrifices of the Old Covenant expression of Israel as each tribe sought the place that God chose for His name to abide for them (Deut. 12:5, 6). The seven sacrifices of burnt offerings, sacrifices, tithes, heave offerings, vowed offerings, freewill offerings, and firstling offerings all relate to the seven relational aspects of the Holy Spirit at work in our lives. He is the Spirit of the Lord, the Spirit of Wisdom, the Spirit of Understanding, the Spirit of Counsel, the Spirit of Might, the Spirit of Knowing, and the Spirit of the Fear of the Lord. What are some terms that are perhaps more practical for us to understand? Let's use words like: commitment, faith, response, submission, contribution, love, and dedication. The Holy Spirit has come to make our lives those that are motivated for commitment, empowered to do works of faith, activated to respond to the overflowing presence of God in our lives, enlightened to the testimony of submission one to another, awakened to give the contribution of our lives to the testimony of Christ, drawn to the love of God and one another, and impassioned to dedicate our lives to God and His purposes in our lives. It is the Holy Spirit in His expression of the Spirit of the Lord that empowers us to make a commitment to God, to our spouses, our families, our churches, and everything that is in our lives. He is the motivator of our hearts. The Holy Spirit is the Spirit of Wisdom that empowers us to do works of faith in our homes, our churches, and our communities. He empowers us to give edifying words, acts of service, and practical expressions of our time, substance, and commitment. The overflowing power of the Spirit of Understanding activates us to manifest with the power of the Holy Spirit's charisma and fruit in every aspect of our daily lives. The testimony of God's favor upon us anoints us as fathers, mothers, sons, daughters, friends, neighbors, and active members of our communities. The Spirit of Counsel enlightens us to submit with the light of Christ in our homes, our congregations, and our everyday relationships. Together we express the light of Christ. The Spirit of Knowing causes us to know the love of God that draws us to love those we are relationally joined to in life. The Spirit of the Fear of the Lord gives us the passion to be dedicated to our families, our friends, and all of our divine connections. We live to see our children and our children's children living in the blessings of God. God guarantees the fullness of a future and a hope for all of our posterity. With the sevenfold Spirit of Grace at work in our lives we can become a spiritual house that knows God is our God, we are His people, and we live together with Him in all situations. We hear God and thus we know He is our God. The testimonies of our lives reflect His values, and we are thus revealed as His special people. We live for His divine relationships in every area of our lives. The testimony of His presence with us reveals that we are the spiritual house of God. The *Seven Eyes of Grace* are progressively at work in our lives to reveal all that we are in Christ. We are the New Covenant people of the living God!

Made in the USA
Middletown, DE
02 May 2023

29873010R10144